The Mitchell Beazley Pocket Guide to

German Wines

Ian Jamieson

SECOND EDITION

MITCHELL BEAZLEY

KEY TO SYMBOLS

w.	white wine
r.	red wine
(in parentheses)	relatively unimportant
★	everyday wine
★★	above average
★★★	excellent, highly reputed
★★★★	exceptional, prestigious, expensive
★★ → ★★★	for example, indicates
	above average to excellent

SMALL CAPS indicate a cross-reference within the A-Z section

ABBREVIATIONS

Hess. Berg.	Hessische Bergstrasse
Mrh.	Mittelrhein
M-S-R	Mosel-Saar-Ruwer
Rhg.	Rheingau
Rhh.	Rheinhessen
Rhpf.	Rheinpfalz
Würt.	Württemberg

g	grams	m.	million
g/l	grams per liter	med-dry	medium-dry
ha	hectares	mg/l	milligrams per liter
hl/ha	hectoliters per hectare	pop.	population
km	kilometers	v'yd	vineyard
m	meters		

See pages 6-7 for more information

The Pocket Guide to German Wines
Edited and designed by
Mitchell Beazley International Limited
Artists House, 14-15 Manette Street, London W1V 5LB
© Mitchell Beazley Publishers 1984, 1987, 1988
First edition 1984
Second edition 1987

British Library Cataloguing in Publication Data

Jamieson, Ian, 1934–
The Mitchell Beazley pocket guide to
German wines.—2nd ed.
1. Wine and wine making—Germany
I. Title
641.2'2'0943   TP559.G3
ISBN 0 85533 681 1

Maps by Eugene Fleury
Typeset by Hourds Typographica, Stafford.
Printed by Mandarin Offset in Malaysia

Editor	Alison Franks
Production	Androulla Wakefield
Senior Executive Editor	Chris Foulkes

Contents

Foreword

German wines, and all the sensuous subtleties of pleasure they offer, are rather like a story-book castle whose key is hidden in a tortuous labyrinth guarded by ravaging heraldic beasts. The generality of wine-drinkers take the autobahns labelled Liebfraumilch, Niersteiner or some such safe and familiar name. They skirt the problem, and never find the reward. Our hero, though, steadies his gaze at the menacing Gothic script, braves the barbed entanglements of nomenclature, and carries off the chalice of golden nectar. In other words, if German labels scare you, you will never discover how glorious German wine can be.

This book is the code-cracker. It can put the chalice in your hands. I won't pretend that all obscurities will dissolve as you turn the first page. But Ian Jamieson is a practical man, a wine-merchant whose knowledge of Germany and its wine has been sharpened on the steel of commerce. He knows the ways of grower and merchant. He knows the laws. And he knows and cares where the real treasures lie.

Ian has often been my guide through the more arcane complexities of his favourite subject. To me it has fascinations, and offers rewards, that are a match for any category of wine. Let Jamieson lead you to them.

Hugh Johnson

Introduction

A profile of the wine most consumers look for today shows it to be white and light in alcohol, and balanced in sweetness and acidity. German wine fits this description exactly and is appealing increasingly to the new generation of wine drinkers, especially in the English-speaking world. Much that is seen abroad is of the cheap and cheerful variety, but as soon as we expect more of a German wine than that it should simply be thirst-quenching and refreshing we are faced with the complications of the language of wine and what it tries to tell us.

Communication is the aim of this book. I have not set out to tell the story of wine from vineyard to consumer but to provide answers to direct questions. What does that word on the restaurant list or bottle mean? How much does the label tell about the wine in the bottle? How can one distinguish the varying qualities and styles of wine that are so comprehensively – and incomprehensibly – described on the label? How to spot the difference between a true German wine and a blend of wines from other countries bottled in Germany, when the labels of both are so essentially Germanic in design, down to the last flourish of the Gothic script on the brand name? These are the matters with which the book is concerned. German wine is more than capable of speaking for itself, provided one can understand its language. This book is here to help.

For those who enjoy individuality in wine, the estate bottlers have much to offer. The most famous names among the growers are found mainly in the northern regions, particularly in the Mosel-Saar-Ruwer and in the Rheingau. Here many estates, including some of the less well known, date from the 18th century or earlier. All of them have built their reputation on the Riesling grape, which supplies the fresh, firm, positive wine made unique by the German climate. Other vines tend to play a supporting role, offering the interested wine lover a diversion from Riesling but never a substitute for it.

Although the future of Riesling in the best vineyard sites seems certain, there is a gentle swing to the Spätburgunder (Pinot Noir) on many Rheinland estates to meet the growing demand for German red wine. Large and impressive cooperative cellars handle more than a third of the German wine harvest. Their wines, particularly those of the Mosel-Saar-Ruwer and the Rheinhessen, are widely available, usually under well-known Bereich (district) or Grosslage (collective site) names. Unfortunately, the law allows them to be offered as "estate-bottled", although the members of the cooperatives, who supply the grapes, have no direct control over the wine makers and vice versa.

From the large number of estate bottlers, some 290 have been chosen for a potted but detailed description in this guide.

The great and the famous selected themselves and account for about 80 of the estates in the A-Z section. The record of the remainder, particularly their achievements at the DLG (German Agricultural Society) national wine competitions, ensured their selection, but one of the exciting facets of German wine-making is the number of estates that remain to be "discovered". Every visit to the vineyard area can bring with it new and stimulating introductions, and the results of formal viticultural school training are obvious. Twenty years ago the outlook of many growers was parochial to say the least, but that has now changed and most are well aware of the developments in wine-making elsewhere in the world. Many have contributed towards the changes, and the skills of German wine producers are valued as highly in the Napa Valley as they are on the Mosel.

Of all the wine villages, over 200 are included in the pages that follow. Inevitably and deliberately, those in the regions best known outside Germany are well represented, for these are the names found in the wine stores of the world. But recognition has also been made of a number of relatively unfamiliar villages whose wines are seldom seen beyond the borders of their Bereich. They, in particular, have earned their inclusion because their wines deserve wider appreciation.

Finally, I should like to thank all those vineyard owners and wine makers who interrupted their day's work to supply the details about themselves that are recorded in this book. The always accurate technical and legal information so efficiently and pleasantly offered over the years by Manfred Völpel of Deinhard & Company has also been of great help to me. *Die Weinwirtschaft*, with its up-to-date reporting of the German wine-trade scene, and the many books produced under the auspices of Dr Hans Ambrosi have provided a valuable source of reference, as has the work of Dr Horst Dohm and also of Dr Karl Ludwig Bieser of the Weinabsatzzentrale Deutscher Winzergenossenschaften. Herr Riquet Hess of H. Sichel & Söhne read this book in proof form and his experienced advice has been most welcome. If order and precision have been maintained, it is thanks to the guidance of Christopher Foulkes and the eye for detail of Dian Taylor and Alison Franks of Mitchell Beazley, to all of whom I am very grateful. And last, but certainly not least, I am indebted to my wife Ulla, who has excused my absence from the family while I enjoyed the pleasure of writing this book.

IAN JAMIESON

How to Use this Book

This book is divided into four sections: introductory chapters, an A–Z section, a statistical section and a map section. The introductory chapters cover the background and structure of German wine, and ideally should be read first as scene-setters. In order to look up an estate, a vineyard or a wine term, etc., turn to the A–Z section which begins on page 26. The maps, starting on page 152, show the basic geography of the German wine regions and list some of the estates in these regions. For guidance to important growers of, say, Rheingau wines, turn to the map on pages 154–155. The names can then be looked up in the A–Z section.

In the A–Z section the top line of geographical entries – regions, rivers, towns, villages, vineyard sites and so forth – is printed in colour so that locations can be easily distinguished from entries for wine producers, grape varieties, general wine terms and other categories of information.

The top line of the geographical entries gives the following information, where applicable, in abbreviated form:

1. The wine region in which the entry is located. The 11 wine regions (and their abbreviations) are:

Ahr	Mosel-Saar-Ruwer (M-S-R)
Baden	Nahe
Franken	Rheingau (Rhg.)
Hessische Bergstrasse	Rheinhessen (Rhh.)
(Hess. Berg.)	Rheinpfalz (Rhpf.)
Mittelrhein (Mrh.)	Württemberg (Würt.)

   A map of all the wine regions is on page 10.

2. The type of wine produced: w. for white, r. for red, (w.) or (r.) if the quantity produced is relatively unimportant.

3. A general rating as to quality, a necessarily rough and ready guide based on the following ascending scale:

   ⋆ everyday wine
   ⋆⋆ above average
   ⋆⋆⋆ excellent, highly reputed
   ⋆⋆⋆⋆ exceptional, prestigious, expensive

The entries for wine producers, export houses and cooperative cellars include as much information as can be condensed into the necessarily limited space available. Approximate production figures are expressed in cases (e.g. annual production 20,000 cases) to indicate the output of wine so that comparisons can be made between entries. These are average figures as the yield in the German vineyards can vary greatly from year to year. A "case", for the purposes of this book, is taken as 12 × 750ml (0.75 litre) bottles, or 9 litres (in the wine trade, the term "case" is being replaced by "carton"). All liquid measurements are given in litres, the standard liquid measurement for German wine (1 litre equals 1.76 pints, UK). Alcohol is expressed as % by volume.

Cross-references in SMALL CAPS throughout the A–Z section help to expand the information given in individual entries. However, the wine regions (e.g. Ahr, Baden) and grape varieties (e.g. Riesling) are automatically included in the A–Z and are not cross-referred.

All figures are the most up to date available.

Germany, in all cases, means West Germany.

WINE TERMS

The following terms are described in the A–Z section:

Ansprechend	Flach	Meaty
Aromatisch	Flaschenreife	Mild
Ausdrucksvoll	Frisch	Muffig
Ausgeglichen	Frostgeschmack	Nervig
Blume	Fruchtig	Neutral
Bodengeschmack	Grasig	Oxidativ
Bodenton	Hagelgeschmack	Pappig
Bottle sick	Halbtrocken	Plump
Brandig	Harmonisch	Rassig
Breit	Herb	Reif
Bukett	Herzhaft	Reintonig
Duftig	Hochfarbig	Saftig
Durchgegoren	Holzgeschmack	Slaty
Eckig	Jung	Sortencharakter
Edelsüss	Kernig	Spritzig
Elegant	Korkgeschmack	Stahlig
Erdig	Kratzig	Stumpf
Fassgeschmack	Lebendig	Süffig
Feine, feinste	Leicht	Süss
Feurig	Lieblich	Ton
Firn	Markant	Trocken

German Wine Law

Wine production in Germany is as meticulously structured as the wording on a German wine label. This is the result of Germany's own wine laws and those of the European Common Market.

In 1970 the EEC produced regulations for the organization of wine within its borders. These came into immediate effect and took precedence over national laws, so that Germany was obliged to revise its own wine laws forthwith. In 1971 the fifth German Wine Law came into force, replacing the previous law of 1930. Since then there have been further amendments, including a major revision in 1982 that established Landwein as a new category of Deutscher Tafelwein, made Eiswein into a Prädikat of its own (quality distinction) and altered several other details of the earlier law.

Probably the best-known results of all this legislation – and the most significant to the consumer – are the division of wine into different quality categories and the organization of the wine regions (see following pages).

The Quality Categories

Wine in the EEC is separated into quality wine and table wine. In German terms this means Qualitätswein (QmP, the top quality, and QbA, a middle level); Tafelwein (Deutscher Tafelwein, or DTW, comes entirely from German vineyards; plain Tafelwein is wine from other EEC countries blended in Germany); and Landwein, a superior Deutscher Tafelwein, from one of 15 specified districts.

The chart shows the relationship of the 11 quality-wine

Quality Wine (QbA, QmP)	
Region	**Bereich**
Ahr	Walporzheim/Ahrtal
Hessische Bergstrasse	Starkenburg, Umstadt
Mittelrhein	Bacharach, Rheinburgengau, Siebengebirge
Nahe	Kreuznach, Schloss Böckelheim
Rheingau	Johannisberg
Rheinhessen	Bingen, Nierstein, Wonnegau
Rheinpfalz	Südliche Weinstrasse, Mittelhaardt/Deutsche Weinstrasse
Mosel-Saar-Ruwer	Zell/Mosel, Bernkastel, Obermosel, Saar-Ruwer, Moseltor
Franken	Steigerwald, Maindreieck, Mainviereck, Bayerischer Bodensee
Württemberg	Remstal-Stuttgart, Württembergisch Unterland, Kocher-Jagst-Tauber, Württembergischer Bodensee
Baden	Bodensee, Markgräflerland, Kaiserstuhl-Tuniberg, Breisgau, Ortenau
	Badische Bergstrasse/Kraichgau, Badisches Frankenland

regions to the table-wine and Landwein districts. Unlike France, where the grading of quality wines is largely geographical, in Germany exactly the same vineyards that produce quality wine can also produce table wine and Landwein. The source remains the same; only the category of the wine changes, depending on the quality.

Do not expect to meet all the Bereich, district and subdistrict names on wine labels – some of them exist more for administrative purposes than for the benefit of the consumer trying to unravel the intricacies of German laws and labelling (see Learning from the Label, pages 12-13).

Table Wine (DTW)		Landwein
District	Sub-District	District
		Ahrtaler Landwein
Rhein-Mosel	Rhein	Starkenburger Landwein
		Rheinburgen-Landwein
		Nahegauer Landwein
		Altrheingauer Landwein
		Rheinischer Landwein
		Pfälzer Landwein
	Mosel	Landwein der Mosel
	Saar	Landwein der Saar
Bayern	Main	Fränkischer Landwein
	Donau	Regensburger Landwein
	Lindau	Bayerischer Bodensee-Landwein
Neckar		Schwäbischer Landwein
Oberrhein	Römertor	Südbadischer Landwein
	Burgengau	Unterbadischer Landwein

The Wine Regions

Germany lies at the northern edge of that part of Europe in which grapes will ripen. The climate is cool in comparison with that of other European wine-producing countries – a fact recognized by the EEC which divides member states, for administrative purposes, into wine-producing zones that correspond very approximately to the different climatic condi-

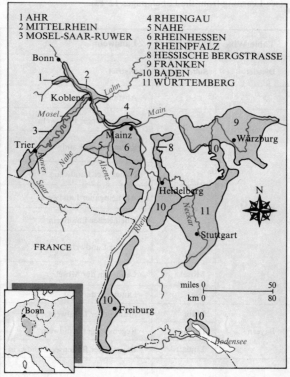

1 AHR
2 MITTELRHEIN
3 MOSEL-SAAR-RUWER
4 RHEINGAU
5 NAHE
6 RHEINHESSEN
7 RHEINPFALZ
8 HESSISCHE BERGSTRASSE
9 FRANKEN
10 BADEN
11 WÜRTTEMBERG

tions. All the German vine-growing regions, with the exception of Baden in the south, are placed in Zone A (with the UK and Luxembourg). Baden shares the warmer Zone B with Alsace, Lorraine, Champagne, Jura, Savoie and the Loire valley.

There are 11 specified regions for quality wine production (Anbaugebiete) in Germany. They are described in the A–Z section and are shown in more detail in the maps that begin on page 152.

In the most northerly regions – the Ahr, Mittelrhein and Mosel-Saar-Ruwer – usually only those sites facing SSE–SW can usefully bear vines, with the very best vineyards facing from S–SSW. An additional rule of thumb is that the average temperature will drop some 0.5°C for every 100m (330ft) above sea level. As a result, while 300m (990ft) above sea level is regarded as the maximum height for vineyards on the Mosel near Koblenz, in the sunnier south of Baden, on the Bodensee, vines are grown successfully at 530m (1,739ft).

Of the 99,806ha (246,631 acre) under vine in Germany, the Rheinhessen and Rheinpfalz between them account for almost half, with 25.2% and 23% respectively, followed by Baden with 15%, the Mosel-Saar-Ruwer 12.7%, Württemberg 9.7%, Franken 5.2%, Nahe 4.6%, Rheingau 3%, Mittelrhein 0.8%, Ahr 0.4%, Hessische Bergstrasse 0.4%.

Each of the wine regions is organized into districts (Bereiche), collections of sites (Grosslagen) and individual sites (Einzellagen). This is where the style and quality of wine begin to be more narrowly defined.

A Bereich is a combination of collective or individual sites. It is usually the largest wine-producing unit within a region and allows a well-known name – Bernkastel in the Mittelmosel, for example – to be applied to wine from anywhere within the Bereich boundaries. Wine marketed solely under a Bereich name is unlikely to be more than a pleasant everyday blend, and this will be reflected in its price.

A Grosslage is a grouping of sites centred on one or more villages or towns (Gemeinden). In the Bereich Bernkastel, for example, the Grosslage Badstube covers six (since 1986) Einzellagen at Bernkastel. Generally Grosslagen include a number of wine villages within their boundaries, all of which will lie within the same region. As from 1st September 1987 the village names that can be used with those of Grosslagen have been curtailed. However, a Grosslage, or an Einzellage, must always be accompanied by the name of a village or community e.g. BERNKASTELER Badstube, not just Badstube, must appear on the label.

These Grosslagen enable the bottler or wine merchant to offer large quantities of wine of similar quality and style under one name familiar to the customer. Use of a Grosslage name does not mean that the wine will automatically be inferior, but the best quality wines in any grower's or bottler's range will normally be offered under the Einzellage name.

An Einzellage is an individual site, the smallest vine-growing unit recognized by the law. There are currently some 2,600 Einzellagen, varying in size from half a hectare up to about 250ha (618 acres). They are officially registered and in most cases their boundaries are precisely defined. Only quality (QbA and QmP) wines may carry an Einzellage name – not table wine (DTW) or Landwein.

The unifying factor within an Einzellage is the flavour and style of wine it can produce. Some sites, because of their inherent qualities combined with the wine-making ability of the growers concerned, have a reputation for producing top-quality wine (e.g. Bernkasteler Doctor). In larger sites, where many growers will have holdings, the quality will be more variable. In these circumstances, for the consumer the grower's name is more important than that of the Einzellage.

Where all this organization of the wine regions is less than helpful to the consumer is that it is impossible, without memorizing all the 2,600-plus Einzellagen and the 150 or so Grosslagen names, to tell from the information on the label whether a wine comes from an individual site or from a collective site. The entries in the A–Z section of the book, however, will help.

Learning from the Label

All bottled wines sold to the consumer in the European Common Market must be labelled and all labels must carry certain information.

Most German wines have a main (body) label and a neck label that shows the vintage, if applicable. Some estate bottlers abandon the neck label and include the vintage on the main label. (The famous Karthäuserhof estate on the Ruwer, however, takes the opposite course and uses only a neck label.)

As well as being a legal requirement, labels are considered to be a most important part of the marketing and selling of wine. The use of back labels carrying extra information is increasing and can be very helpful to the consumer. When a wine has won an official award (DLG, etc.), it is usually shown by a strip or circular label.

Labelling regulations are unavoidably complicated for they must provide for all the possibilities of nomenclature and description legally open to wine.

German quality-wine labels bear most of the type of information (where applicable) shown on the sample label that follows. That which is obligatory (specified region of origin, liquid content of the bottle, etc.) must be easily read. The size of the lettering used for the specified region is important, for to it must be related that of the Prädikat (Kabinett, Spätlese, Auslese, etc.), where there is one, and the name of the village or town in which the wine was bottled. For a 700 ml or 750 ml bottle, the liquid content must be indicated in characters at least 4 mm high.

MOSEL-SAAR-RUWER

Bernkasteler Bratenhöfchen   3

1983er

RIESLING KABINETT   6

Qualitätswein mit Prädikat

Halbtrocken

A.P. Nr. 1 23 456 789 84

Erzeugerabfüllung

J. M. SCHMIDT

Bernkastel-Kues

750 ml e   Produce of Germany   14

1. Specified region (Anbaugebiet)
2. Village (Gemeinde)
3. Individual site (Einzellage)
4. Vintage. The "er" is an adjectival ending. See Recent Vintages pages 19–21.
5. Grape variety. If a wine is not made from Riesling, the vine variety will often not be mentioned on the label.
6. Quality distinction. See the entry for Qualitätswein mit Prädikat in the A-Z section.
7. Quality category. See also the entry for Qualitätswein eines bestimmten Anbaugebietes in the A-Z section.
8. Medium-dry, as defined by German law.
9. Control number (Amtliche Prüfungsnummer). The first figure is the number of the control centre where the wine was tested. The next two figures are the number of the location in which the wine was bottled. The third set of figures is the registered number of the bottler. The fourth set is the sequential number in the year of application from the bottler, unique to this bottling. The last two figures are the year of application for the A.P. number.
10. Estate-bottled
11. The name of the bottler
12. The address of the bottler
13. The liquid content, which might also be shown as 0,75 l. The "e" indicates that the wine was bottled according to EEC regulations.
14. Country of origin. It is important to read the small print on labels of wines bottled in Germany to ensure that they are of German origin and not blends of wines from other EEC member states.

Vine Varieties

Of the area under vine, 87% is planted with varieties that produce white wine – although in some cases (the Ruländer, for example) the grape may be "blue" but the wine it produces remains white. At the last official survey in 1979/80 14% of the vines in Germany were 20 years old or more, 36% were 10–20 years old, 41% 3–10 years old and 9% were under 3 years old. (Vines do not become productive until they are 3 years old.) The high proportion of vines under 10 years old was partly the result of the reconstruction and subsequent replanting of the vineyards (Flurbereinigung) over the last 40 years to make vine-growing more efficient.

Vine	Area under vine in hectares				% Variation 1985 to 1964
	1964	% of Total	1985	% of Total	
Müller-Thurgau	14,115	21.2	25,292	25.3	+ 74.2
Riesling	17,083	25.6	19,615	19.6	+ 14.8
Silvaner	18,781	28.2	8,050	8.1	− 57.1
Sub-total	(49,979)	(75)	(52,957)	(53)	(+ 6.0)
Kerner	5	–	6,960	7.0	
Spätburgunder (r.)	1,839	2.8	4,486	4.5	
Scheurebe	342	0.5	4,385	4.4	
Bacchus	2	–	3,573	3.6	
Portugieser (r.)	5,323	8.0	3,183	3.2	
Ruländer	1,283	1.9	3,123	3.1	
Morio-Muskat	1,052	1.6	2,641	2.6	
Faber	–		2.280	2.3	
Trollinger (r.)	1,662	2.5	2,196	2.2	
Huxelrebe	56	–	1,758	1.8	
Müllerrebe (r.)	323	0.5	1,473	1.5	
Gutedel	1,192	1.8	1,258	1.2	
Ortega	–		1,208	1.2	
Elbling	1,234	1.9	1,178	1.2	
Others	2,393	3.5	7,147	7.2	
Sub-total	(16,706)	(25)	(46,849)	(47)	+ 180.4
GRAND TOTAL	66,685	100	99,806	100	+ 49.7

Other white-wine varieties

Auxerrois	Muskat	Rieslaner
Ehrenfelser	Nobling	Schönburger
Freisamer	Optima	Septimer
Huxelrebe	Perle	Siegerrebe
Kanzler	Regner	Traminer
Klingelberger	Reichensteiner	Weissburgunder

Other red-wine varieties

Dornfelder	Helfensteiner	Limberger
Frühburgunder	Heroldrebe	Urban

The chart on page 14 shows the extent to which the distribution of the main vine varieties altered between 1964 and 1985. It is followed by a list of other vine varieties, which are also described in the A–Z section of the book.

To grow grapes at all in Germany is a triumph of science, planning and dedication over less than ideal conditions. At these latitudes, local environmental factors take on an importance unknown in places with a more equable climate, and the choice of which variety to plant is crucial. German wine-growing regulations offer a long list of varieties to choose from – varieties that vary considerably in their needs, and yield widely differing types and amounts of wine.

In making his decision, the grower must consider the climate, the site and the soil of his vineyard, and the present and future state of the wine market. The climate is, at best, predictably uncertain: unseasonable rain, hail and frost are constant hazards at different times of the year. Each grower must decide whether to aim for quality or quantity, but often the vineyard site will make the decision for him – a high yield cannot be expected from a 45° slope, and only the return that comes from quality wine production can justify viticulture in the long term at such a bizarre angle. Most vines adapt to a wide variety of soils but some have individual preferences. Silvaner, for example, dislikes a dry soil on a sloping site that Riesling will tolerate quite happily.

These being the facts of viticultural life in Germany, there remains the choice of vine. Although the area planted in Müller-Thurgau was enlarged by 79.2% between 1964 and 1985, in the last five years of the period, the increase amounted to under 2%. In the first half of the 1980s, Riesling plantation went up by 4.2% and that of Silvaner dropped by 12%. Müller-Thurgau's susceptibility to frost in winter and drought in summer has been noticeable of late, while Riesling and Spätburgunder are both benefiting from the wish of the German consumer to return to dry, firm, well-structured wines from traditional vine varieties. The delight in scented, medium-sweet, soft wines from new crossings of the 1960s and 1970s has considerably diminished.

In fact Riesling most consistently provides what we look for in German wine: freshness and fruitiness of flavour and a clean bouquet. In 1979/80, in spite of Flurbereinigung (see facing page), 21% of Germany's Riesling vines were more than 20 years old. A mature vine produces the best wine but yields a small crop. However, the Germans have greatly improved their vines through work at their viticultural institutes and the point at which increasing yield results in decreasing quality has been steadily raised.

For a greater yield still, or for more exotic flavours, the grower can turn to the crossings, which now account for more than half the total area under vine. The object of their development over the last 100 years has been to achieve improved resistance to disease and adverse weather conditions, greater suitability for a variety of sites and soils, and a higher must weight and increased yield. 15

Wines from new crossings, with their sometimes rather outré smell and style, have their place as an addition to the traditional, more neutral flavours. A disadvantage of some crossings is that they can often achieve sufficient must weight to be called Spätlese or Auslese without having the quality found in a Riesling or Silvaner in these categories. The established crossings, however, are steadily being improved, and Müller-Thurgau, once regarded solely as a mass producer of rather ordinary wines, can now occasionally add elegance and style to its other qualities. The most important crossings are Bacchus, Faber, Huxelrebe, Kerner, Morio-Muskat, Müller-Thurgau, Ortega and Scheurebe.

In some cases these names are unfamiliar to consumers as they seldom appear on labels. It is easy for the estate bottler to introduce new crossings by name to his private customers, as the lines of communication are short and explanations can be given. To launch them into the general wine trade is more difficult and therefore, in many cases, the crossings lose their identity but provide useful constituents of commercial blends.

Anatomy of the German Wine Market

Over the last decade the trend has been for the number of growers to decline and the viticultural area to increase. The cooperative movement has become stronger, and the number of growers bottling their own wine has risen. More and more sales are being made directly to the consumer, with the grower benefiting from the additional profit they offer – and, let it be said, from a less exacting buyer. The fragmentation of German wine producers is very slowly disappearing.

At the last national census in 1979/80, each of the 89,471 growers worked on average 1.05 hectares (2.6 acres) of vineyard divided into 6.1 different parcels of land. Since then the average size of holding has increased as the wine industry moves toward a more economic way of growing vines.

Undoubtedly the next census will show that many more grape growers have linked themselves not only to Winzergenossenschaften (cooperative cellars) but also to Erzeugergemeinschaften (producers' associations). In Rheinland-Pfalz, with 66,521 hectares (164,380 acres) of planted vineyard making it the largest wine-producing state in Germany, the average size holding increased from 1.87 hectares (4.6 acres) in 1979 to 2.5 hectares (6.2 acres) in 1985. Approximately half the Rheinland-Pfalz wine harvest is now sold by cooperative cellars or producers associations, but there is still much to be done. In 1985/86, none of the eleven wine-growing regions in Germany achieved such a low price for its wine through the cooperative cellars as did the Rheinland-Pfalz regions of Mosel-Saar-Ruwer, Rheinhessen and Rheinpfalz.

From the figures quoted so far, it is obvious that taking the country as a whole, vine-growing operates on a part-time basis, in which women do much of the donkey work. 240,661 women and 140,495 men worked less than 100 hours per year in the vineyards or cellars in 1979/80, and only 70,298 worked for longer than that.

25% of the German vineyards are so steep or so inaccessible that they can be cultivated by hand only and, of course, many of the best vineyards are also the steepest. Vine growing in these conditions will always be time-consuming and expensive, and only viable if fine wine is produced.

Some 290 estate-bottlers have kindly cooperated in the revision of this guide. Although a few own a substantial amount of land by European vine-growing standards, others gather their grapes from a mere two or three hectares. Of the 16% German vine-growers with formal viticultural and wine-making training, a high proportion will be found amongst the private estate-bottlers. Given the current economic difficulties and the small size of many estates, it is not surprising that half of the vineyard and cellar workers are also members of the owning family. Without unpaid or low-paid help from grandparents and children many of the small estates could not continue to function.

In 1985 Germany exported 2,727,028 hectolitres of wine – of which the UK took 49.9%. If we deduct the possible amount of 470,000 hectolitres for wines that were not made in, but merely exported, from Germany (blends of EEC table

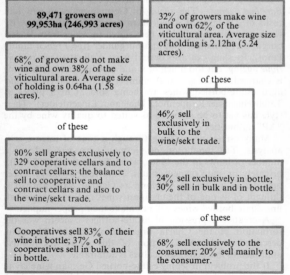

89,471 growers own 99,953ha (246,993 acres)

68% of growers do not make wine and own 38% of the viticultural area. Average size of holding is 0.64ha (1.58 acres).

of these

80% sell grapes exclusively to 329 cooperative cellars and to contract cellars; the balance sell to cooperative and contract cellars and also to the wine/sekt trade.

Cooperatives sell 83% of their wine in bottle; 37% of cooperatives sell in bulk and in bottle.

32% of growers make wine and own 62% of the viticultural area. Average size of holding is 2.12ha (5.24 acres).

of these

46% sell exclusively in bulk to the wine/sekt trade.

24% sell exclusively in bottle; 30% sell in bulk and in bottle.

of these

68% sell exclusively to the consumer; 20% sell mainly to the consumer.

Source: Statistisches Bundesamt Wiesbaden

wines), we see that the 1985 German wine exports amounted to 25% of the average 1980–85 wine harvest.

Although the export market is important for the German wine industry as a whole, for the estate-bottlers it is still statistically insignificant. One of the best known estate-bottlers outside Germany exports only 4.5% of its production, and on most estates the percentage will be even smaller.

The result is that changes in the style of wine are almost exclusively influenced by the changing taste of the German home market, and here there has been much activity in the 1980s which can be summarized as follows:

The move to drier wine – The swing away from medium-sweet wines that gained pace in the 1970s has continued into the 1980s. At first it seemed that dry wine might be a matter of fashion, but now it has become one of personal choice. Top-quality German restaurants sell estate-bottled dry wines in considerable quantities, not cheaply but at prices lower than that of fine white Burgundy. Many Rheinland estates now sell their dry Spätlesen much more quickly than the previously regarded as "normal", medium-sweet versions.

The move back to traditional vine varieties – Where technically possible, many estates are increasing the area planted in Riesling, Weissburgunder and Spätburgunder – the first two for dry white wine production and the Spätburgunder to meet the demand in Germany for red wine. The newly consummated marriage of wine and food is gaining strength steadily. New crossings such as Morio-Muskat, used mainly as a part of medium-sweet blends, are losing favour.

Barrique ageing – The ageing of German wines in new oak casks of 225 litres or so is still in its experimental stage. By some it is considered to be best suited to wines from Weissburgunder, Ruländer and Spätburgunder (the French family Pinot). Riesling can also benefit from a slight touch of *barrique* ageing, but too much of it and the character of the wine is changed, if not spoilt. A number of top-quality *barrique* aged estate-bottled wines are being sold at high prices as Tafelweine (see Rappenhof, Diel and Lingenfelder). Their style has yet to be accepted as suited to quality wine by the "AP" authorities.

Many estates are passing through a time of intense self-analysis. The reputation of German wine has suffered a number of blows in the 1980s, which has nothing to do with privately or state owned estates. Nevertheless, no producer operates in a vacuum. As long as German wine abroad is thought of as one of the cheapest wines in the supermarket, fine estate-bottled wines will not make their proper impact.

A creative expression of estate-bottlers concern was the formation of the Charta organization in the Rheingau, described in the A–Z section of this guide. Its positive approach to marketing difficulties is admirable.

If the problem in selling estate-bottled German wine lay in its quality the future for many growers would be grim indeed.

Fortunately, it is much less serious than that and really only a matter of communication and, therefore, of marketing. It is difficult to see that in a world where wines of character are never too numerous, why fine estate-bottled German wine should not take up a much more prominent position in the wine-shelves of the world by 1990.

Recent Vintages

A perfect German vintage seldom happens more than twice in a decade. It will usually be the result of an early flowering, allowing the grapes as long as possible to ripen. Adequate rain in summer will prevent the inhibiting effect of drought on the formation of sugar, and in a warm and sunny autumn noble rot (Edelfäule) may well appear.

More usually, by harvest time, while some grapes are very ripe others are still distinctly sour. To judge the true potential quality of the crop, care is taken to see that the samples of grapes gathered before the main picking starts are truly representative. Except in great years, such as 1971 and 1976, it is only when the pressing has started and the must weight and acidity have been measured that the real value of the harvest can be accurately assessed.

The quality of cheap German wine maintains a steady level, almost regardless of vintage, as blending and skilful vinification smooth away the bumps. Most everyday wine is made to be drunk within two years of the harvest, so there is little point in storing it longer.

On the other hand, Riesling QbA and the better, usually estate-bottled QmP wines improve with bottle age (see page 38 in the A–Z section of the book).

Because of the predictability of much QbA wine, vintage assessments refer more to the QmPs – Kabinett, Spätlese, Auslese, Eiswein and, in great years, Beerenauslese and Trockenbeerenauslese. A poor year for a grower is one that produces little or no Spätlese wine. In a good vintage the sugar and acid contents are high, but this is a theme with many variations. Nevertheless, the following are generally accepted as the top-quality vintages since 1970: the 1971, '73, '75, '76 and '83. The Mosel also did well in 1979, '81 and '85.

In almost every vintage it is possible for the effect of a good microclimate to produce wines of above the average quality, but it is only in the really great years that fine wine is made throughout Germany. Often the wines of any one year will have a particular style or flavour, be it good or otherwise, that makes them easily identifiable. This was the case in 1972 (high malic acid content from unripe grapes) and in 1976 (musts with high sugar content). The differences often fade with bottle age. It is not obligatory for a wine of one year to bear a vintage, but if it does, 85% of the grapes used for the wine must have been grown in the year stated and the wine must show the characteristics of the vintage.

The qualities that can be expected from the various grades of German wine in poor, average and great years are set out on the following page. Of course, within any region there can be many exceptions to the general standard of the harvest, brought about by site, microclimate and the wine-making. Paradoxically, a great year can be too good for Riesling QbA: the wines can lack acidity and show a certain coarseness, although these deficiencies are less common than they once were. In mediocre years interesting and enjoyable German wines can still be produced, as their attraction does not depend on a high alcohol content.

Eiswein can be made in small amounts in most years when it is sufficiently cold, usually from mid-November onwards.

Poor Year	
QbA Riesling	Good, sound wine
Kabinett	Light, agreeable. Lacks real quality
Spätlese	None, except for small quantities of non-Riesling wines
Auslese	None
Average Year	
QbA Riesling	Good, balanced wine
Kabinett	Light, stylish, typical of vine variety and site
Spätlese	Sound, reflecting regional character well, but limited in quantity
Auslese	Rare except from non-Riesling
Great Year	
QbA Riesling	Many good wines, but also some that are coarse and lack acidity
Kabinett	Good quality, but some can miss the charm of those in an average year
Spätlese	Splendid wines of great depth of flavour
Auslese	Superb, unique wines
Beerenauslese and Trockenbeerenauslese	Rarities. Only possible in significant quantities in great years

1985 was a small but good quality vintage with Riesling Kabinett and Spätlese wines that will need more ageing than those of 1983. 1984 was mainly a vintage of attractive QbA. The percentage of Spätlese and Auslese in the Mosel-Saar-Ruwer and Nahe in 1983 was less than in 1979, but the quality of the Riesling wines made them the best since 1971 or 1976. For the Rheingau, 1983 was the most successful year since 1979.

1981 produced attractive fruity wines in all the regions.

The table that follows shows the percentage of wine in the most common quality categories produced by the five main exporting regions. These are the official figures declared after the harvest during the five years to 1985. It should be noted that each year some wine will be downgraded from one category to another, either because it fails to meet the standards expected by the producer or simply to fulfil a commercial need for more wine of a lower (and cheaper) category.

SUMMARY OF RECENT VINTAGES
IN THE FIVE MAIN EXPORTING REGIONS

Total quantity of wine declared at harvest, in hectolitres
(approximate yield in hl per ha in brackets)

	Mosel-Saar-Ruwer hl	Nahe hl	Rhein-gau hl	Rhein-hessen hl	Rhein-pfalz hl
1985	1,195,000 (103)	263,000 (61)	180,000 (66)	1,082,000 (47)	1,388,000 (67)
1984	1,106,000 (94)	312,000 (73)	163,000 (59)	1,855,000 (83)	2,311,000 (113)
1983	1,829,000 (155)	612,000 (146)	298,825 (111)	3,400,000 (156)	3,252,000 (162)
1982	2,365,000 (205)	716,700 (173)	485,000 (182)	3,773,000 (177)	3,847,000 (192)
1981	1,113,500 (97)	249,900 (61)	171,500 (65)	1,724,500 (83)	2,166,700 (109)

Percentage of quality wine, by category
of total harvest

		Mosel-Saar-Ruwer %	Nahe %	Rhein-gau %	Rhein-hessen %	Rhein-pfalz %
1985	QbA	63	57	40	38	47
	Kabinett	27	27	53	28	32
	Spätlese	8	13	6	29	17
	Auslese	2	3	1	5	4
1984	QbA	79	82	73	78	75
	Kabinett	1	1	2	6	7
	Spätlese	0	0	0	2	2
	Auslese	0	0	0	0	0
1983	QbA	43	48	30	46	52
	Kabinett	12	15	50	19	23
	Spätlese	31	25	19	25	16
	Auslese	9	8	0	2	3
1982	QbA	61	67	74	73	72
	Kabinett	30	24	25	18	12
	Spätlese	4	5	0	7	4
	Auslese	2	1	0	0	0
1981	QbA	63	54	71	54	54
	Kabinett	28	35	25	35	33
	Spätlese	9	10	2	10	11
	Auslese	0	1	0	1	2

Visiting the Vineyards

The ideal way to discover German wines is, of course, to visit the wine regions. Indeed, the only way to enjoy many German wines is in the setting of the vineyards that produce them, because they may seldom be seen beyond their place of origin.

By happy circumstance the vineyards encompass some of the most picturesque countryside in Germany, even without the attraction of the wines to be tasted in the restaurants and wine bars. "Wine roads" (Weinstrassen) are marked by appropriate signs with such symbols as a bunch of grapes or a wine glass. For the more energetic there are also well-marked footpaths (Weinlehrpfade) in many of the vineyards, punctuated at timely intervals by rest stops where the local wines can be sampled.

Visiting wine cellars is not quite as simple as it is in France, and the equivalent sign to *"Visitez nos caves"* is absent. Nevertheless, most estate and cooperative cellars are happy to welcome interested visitors during business hours – usually between 9 a.m. and 5 p.m. on weekdays – although they do expect advance warning, either by letter or by telephone. Some cellars set a firm maximum and minimum to the number of persons they will receive in any one party. If a tasting is provided free of charge, it is courteous to buy a few bottles when leaving. The Germans are, by nature, very hospitable, but the visitor to a small estate should remember that although tasting in a producer's cellar is one of the most enjoyable aspects of visiting a wine region, it may be occupying a large part of the estate owner's working day and the welcome should not be overstayed.

Many estates sell almost all their wines directly to the consumer and have a wine bar or tasting room set aside for this purpose. While customers sit around tables the wines are served to them. Facilities for spitting at "sitting" tastings are not normally offered. General comment on the wines is made, after each has been introduced by the cellar master (Kellermeister) or by the estate owner (Weingutsbesitzer). Such tastings quickly become a social occasion, although the wines still receive proper attention. Their relatively low alcohol content makes it possible to taste many wines in this way and remain clear-headed. (In the course of his duties the professional taster will willingly tackle 70 or more German white wines in one session. For wines with a higher alcohol content this would hardly be possible.)

Each region has a number of wine festivals of varying sizes, especially in the months of August and September – in the Mosel-Saar-Ruwer alone there are some 45 local festivals in August. There are also a number of wine museums, among the best known being that housed in the Historisches Museum der Pfalz in Speyer, which traces vine-growing in Germany back to its origins, and the important Deutsches Weinbaumuseum in Oppenheim. Small local wine museums also have much to tell about the history of wine-making in Germany.

More information can be obtained from the regional wine information offices (see Useful Addresses, page 25) or from the central wine information office, the Deutsches Weininstitut, Gutenbergplatz 3–5, Postfach 1705, 6500 Mainz, telephone 06131 28 29 0.

GERMAN PRONUNCIATION

The German language is often more daunting in appearance than in practice, thanks largely to the German fondness for combining into one eye-numbing word what might be an entire sentence in English (a Gebietswinzergenossenschaft, for example, is simply the cooperative cellar of a district). Fortunately, in spoken German every word is clearly articulated and never runs into the following word, as happens in French officially and in English colloquially, so at least it is usually possible to distinguish where words begin and end.

A few ground rules are worth bearing in mind, to which of course there are always exceptions.

The main variations in pronunciation between German and English arise from the following differences:

"j"	as in Juffer	pronounced as in English "y"
"v"	as in Vollrads	,, ,, ,, ,, "f"
"w"	as in Winkel	,, ,, ,, ,, "v"
"z"	as in Zwierlein	,, ,, ,, ,, "ts"
"ch"	as in Enkirch	prounced as in "loch" by a Scot (i.e. not "lock")
"d"	as in Boppard, at the end of a word, is pronounced as a "t"; elsewhere as in English
"eu"	as in Neumagen	is pronounced "oi" as in "rejoice"
"g"	as in muffig, following an "i" at the end of a word, is soft, almost like "ch"; elsewhere as in English
"Sch"	as in Schönhell	pronounced as the English "sh"
"sp"	as in Spiegelberg	,, ,, ,, ,, "shp"
"st"	as in Stuttgart	,, ,, ,, ,, "sht"
"s"	as in Siegerrebe	,, ,, ,, ,, "z" before a vowel

In addition, the pronunciation of German vowels is altered by an Umlaut:

"ä"	as in Spätlese	"Spät" rhymes, more or less, with the English "ate"
"ö"	as in Östrich	"Ö" rhymes with the English "fur"
"ü"	as in Mühlheim	no equivalent English sound; similar to the French "u" as in "*tu*"

The general rule on "ei" and "ie" is:

"ei"	as in Wein	pronounced as "i" as in "vine"
"ie"	as in Riesling	,, ,, "e" as in "geese"

Consonants are always pronounced, and so is the "e" at the end of a word, e.g. in Auslese the "Aus" is pronounced as the English "house" without the "h", "lese" is pronounced as in "laser".

Food and Wine
in Germany

With food, as with wine, in Germany, the best policy is usually to ask for the local speciality. And while the food, in general, may lack the light touch that characterizes much of the wine, there is ample compensation in the form of diversity, quality and quantity.

The main meal of the day is Mittagessen, served from about 12.30–2.00 p.m. A Gaststätte, or restaurant, will provide a full menu, usually fairly international in style. A Gasthof or Gasthaus is an inn where sound but more modest meals of the Wiener Schnitzel and salad variety can be enjoyed. In large towns, the Ratskeller or Rathauskeller – a restaurant in the cellar or basement of the town hall – often serves traditional and local specialities of very good quality at reasonable prices well worth trying. Throughout the vine-growing regions there are Weinstuben, or wine bars, where simple food is available and wine is served by the glass (Pokal) and bottle.

In the wine regions, in any but the smartest restaurants, local wines will dominate the list, and these are certainly the ones to drink.

The Speisekarte is the regular printed menu; the Tageskarte lists the dishes of the day. Key menu words include Vorspeisen: hors d'oeuvre; Suppen: soups (Tagesuppe is the soup of the day); Eierspeisen: egg dishes; Fisch: fish; Fleisch: meat; Geflügel: poultry; Wild: game; Kartoffeln: potatoes; Gemüse: vegetables; Salate: salads; Nachtisch: dessert. Nudeln and Spätzle are noodles; Knödeln are dumplings.

The undoubted heaviness of some German food can be offset by a light white wine. Some wine producers like to be very specific in their suggestions for partners in the marriage of food and wine, but the choice of happy matches is considerable. The modern dry and medium-dry white estate-bottled German wines have won the position previously held by Chablis and other white French wines in a number of leading restaurants. In general, wine of Kabinett quality, light and delicate, accompanies most first courses well, except those which have a very sharp flavour, from which no wine would benefit. Riesling Spätlese marries with white meats or fish dishes. With roast game or red meat, a good-quality red wine (probably a Spätburgunder) would drink splendidly. In contrast, a full, powerful Ruländer or Traminer tastes excellent when served with game in a rich sauce. The finest German wine, of Auslese quality or better, is best enjoyed on its own, away from the table, with its possible conflict of flavours.

These, of course, are only guidelines. Enjoyment is what eating and drinking in Germany is about, and nobody need worry too much if a choice of wine is gastronomically correct or not.

Guten Appetit!

Useful Addresses

More information about visiting the wine regions, including details of wine festivals, wine museums, etc., may be obtained from the Wine Information Office in each region:

Ahr
Gebietsweinwerbung Ahr
Marktplatz 11
5483 Bad Neuenahr-Ahrweiler
West Germany

Baden
Weinwerbezentrale Badischer
Winzergenossenschaften e.G.
Kesslerstrasse 5
7500 Karlsruhe 1
West Germany

Franken
Frankenwein-Frankenland e.V.
Juliusspital-Weingut
Postfach 5848
8700 Würzburg
West Germany

Hessische Bergstrasse
Weinbauverband Bergstrasse
Königsbergerstrasse 4
6148 Heppenheim/Bergstrasse
West Germany

Mittelrhein
Mittelrhein-Burgen & Wein e.V.
Am Hafen 2
5407 St. Goar
West Germany

Mosel-Saar-Ruwer
Weinwerbung Mosel-Saar-Ruwer
e.V.
Gartenfeldstrasse 12a
5500 Trier
West Germany

Nahe
Weinland Nahe e.V.
Brückes 6
6550 Bad Kreuznach
West Germany

Rheingau
Der Rheingau-Der Weingau
Weinwerbung e.V.
Im Alten Rathaus
6225 Johannisberg
West Germany

Rheinhessen
Rheinhessenweine e.V.
An der Brunnenstube 33-35
6500 Mainz
West Germany

Rheinpfalz
Rheinpfalz-Weinpfalz e.V.
Robert-Stolz-Strasse 18
6730 Neustadt/Weinstrasse
West Germany

Württemberg
Werbegemeinschaft
Württembergischer
Weingärtnergenossenschaften
Postfach 94
Heilbronnerstrasse 41
7000 Stuttgart 1
West Germany

A-Z of German Wine

Abfüllung

Bottling. Top-quality (QmP) wine is bottled as soon as it is micro-biologically and chemically stable, normally between March and June following the vintage. Cheaper wines are usually stored in bulk and bottled when an order has to be despatched. Many German wine retains residual sugar, so a necessary part of the bottling operation is the removal of all yeast and undesirable micro-organisms. To achieve this "wine sterility", approx. 70% of German wine is bottled by the cold sterile method, in which the bottling machinery and other equipment is sterilized with steam. The remaining 30% is either warm-bottled (the wine is heated before bottling to between 45° and 60°C) and/or bottled with the addition of the sterilizing agent sorbic acid.

"Abteihof", Weingut M-S-R

300-year-old family-owned estate with small holdings in top-quality steep sites: Bernkasteler BRATENHÖFCHEN and Graacher HIMMELREICH, Wehlener SONNENUHR, Brauneberger JUFFER. 100% Riesling. Fresh and fruity wines, made by careful vinification, some 20% bottled dry or med-dry. The average annual production is 2,500 cases. Address: Otto-Ulrich Pauly, Gestade 32, 5550 Graach/Mosel.

Abtsberg M-S-R w. ★★★

Einzellage on the upper slopes of the great hill of vines at GRAACH in the heart of the MITTELMOSEL. 100% steep, facing SSW and planted mainly with Riesling. The wine has good, firm acidity; usually less full than that of the HIMMELREICH lower down the hill. Grosslage: MÜNZLAY. Growers: incl. Schorlemer Selbach-Oster.

Achkarren Baden w. (r.) ★★

One of the warmest and driest villages in Germany, famous locally for its orchards and wine. High proportion of Ruländer. Grosslage: VULKANFELSEN.

Acidity

See Säure

Adelmann, Weingut Graf Würt.

Quality-conscious estate of 15ha (37 acre), 70% on steep slopes (third terraced), n.e. of Stuttgart. The v'yds are known to date from AD 950. Average annual production is 10,000 cases (90% dry) of red (Trollinger, etc) and white (Riesling, etc). Maturation in young oak casks for some wines. Address: Burg Schaubeck, 7141 Steinheim-Kleinbottwar.

Affaltrach, Schlosskellerei Würt.

Estate dating from the 13th century, owned since 1928 by the family of Dr Reinhold Baumann. 7.5ha (19 acre) in Affaltrach and Willsbach near HEILBRONN, planted with a wide range of red and white vine varieties, producing about 5,400 cases annually. The wines are mainly dry or med-dry, designed to accompany food and sold principally in the region. A 1973 EISWEIN from the Zeilberg site at Affaltrach reached 292° Oechsle (40% potential alcohol!). The estate also takes in grapes and makes wine for 250 local growers, who have formed an ERZEUGERGEMEINSCHAFT. Address: 7104 Obersulm 1.

Affental, Affentaler Spätburgunder Rotwein

Certain villages immediately s. of Baden-Baden have the right to produce "Affentaler Spätburgunder Rotwein", either as QbA or QmP. Affental, which translates as "monkey valley", is a corruption of Ave Maria Tal. Affentaler Spätburgunder ROTWEIN is sold in a normal slim German wine bottle, embossed with a monkey clinging to its sides.

Ahr r. (w.)

Second-smallest of the wine regions with 426ha (1,053 acre) of v'yds on both sides of the R. Ahr, which flows into the Rhein just s.

of Bonn. In spite of its northerly position 70% is planted with red-wine varieties, mainly Spätburgunder and Portugieser, which at this latitude produce wines that incline to the pale, light and pleasant. The white wines from Riesling and Müller-Thurgau are attractive but cannot compare in quality to the finest from regions further south. The best Rieslings, from slaty soil, recall the wines of the nearby Mittelrhein, with their somewhat earthy, occasionally steely flavour. For many vine-growing in the Ahr valley is a part-time occupation and more than half the crop is made into wine by cooperative cellars.

Ahr wine does not attempt to compete with the best that can be found on the international market and therefore the place to meet it is in the valley itself. The region is exceedingly pretty and the steep vineyards are easily accessible through the "Rotweinwanderweg", a well-signposted footpath some 30km (19 miles) in length, which can be joined at many different points. The valley is a great attraction for tourists, especially those from Köln and the Ruhr district. Its narrow roads are often crowded but there are many places to eat and to enjoy the local wines. The capital is BAD NEUENAHR.

Alcohol

Alcohol level is not so significant as a quality factor in wines from Germany as it is in those from elsewhere. Its importance lies mainly in its relationship to the acidity, to the sugar content and the extract content. See also ANREICHERUNG.

Alf M-S-R w. ★★

One of the better-known small wine villages in the Bereich ZELL, on the Lower Mosel near COCHEM. The steep vineyards are planted mainly with Riesling. Grosslage: Grafschaft.

Allendorf, Weingut Fritz Rhg.

Noted Winkel estate owned by a family established in the Rheingau since 1192, with 29.5ha (73 acre) in ASSMANNS-HAUSEN, RÜDESHEIM, JOHANNIS-BERG, GEISENHEIM, WINKEL, OESTRICH, HALLGARTEN, ELT-VILLE, etc. Vines are 77% Riesling, 16% Spätburgunder. The largest holding is in the Winkeler JESUITENGARTEN, of which Allendorf owns a quarter. The estate makes the full range of regional wines,

matured in wood. Annual prod: 29,200 cases, sold in Germany and abroad. Address: Georgshof, Kirchstr. 69, 6227 Oestrich-Winkel.

Alsenz Nahe w. ★★

Secluded wine village on a Nahe tributary of the same name. Grosslage: Paradiesgarten.

Alsheim Rhh. w. ★★★

Attractive village between WORMS and OPPENHEIM, making distinguished Riesling wines. The best-known Einzellage is the large FRÜHMESSE in the Grosslage RHEINBLICK, which is restricted to the sloping sites. Alsheim's flatter land is in the larger Grosslage KRÖTENBRUNNEN.

27

Altärchen M-S-R w. ★★→★★★
Large Einzellage of some 245ha (605 acre) lying on both sides of
the Mosel at TRITTENHEIM. 60% is on steep slopes facing SSE-W,
producing good-quality wines from Riesling and Müller-Thurgau.
Grosslage: MICHELSBERG. Growers: Bischöfliche Weingüter, Milz,
Reh (Josefinengrund), Ronde.

Alte Badstube am Doctorberg M-S-R w. ★★★
High quality Riesling Einzellage at BERNKASTEL, created in 1986
by the re-definition of the boundaries of the Bernkasteler Doctor
site. Grosslage: Badstube. Owners: Lauerburg, Pauly-Bergweiler,
Thanisch, Wegeler-Deinhard.

Altenahr Ahr r. (w.) ★★
Small town on the R. Ahr, near the upstream end of the vine-
growing region. It almost sinks under the weight of the well-
behaved tourists who arrive in coachloads from the Ruhr district.
Some 54ha (133 acre) of vineyard are planted with Riesling, Spätburgunder, Müller-Thurgau, etc., producing typical Ahr wines that
are drunk almost exclusively in the region. Grosslage: Klosterberg.

Altenbamberg Nahe w. ★★
Secluded village on the R. ALSENZ where excellent wine is made
from Riesling grown on porphyritic soil. Grosslage: BURGWEG.

Altenberg M-S-R w. ★★→★★★
Altenberg is a frequently used site name – there are at least 20 scattered across Germany. The Einzellage Altenberg at KANZEM is a
steep site typical of the best in the Saar, producing wines of quality
and charm, mainly from Riesling. Grosslage: SCHARZBERG.
Growers: Bischöfliche Weingüter, Schorlemer (Schlangengraben),
Vereinigte Hospitien.

Altenkirch, Weingut Friedrich Rhg.
Family-owned estate dating from 1826 with 11.2ha (28 acre) of
vineyards, mainly in LORCH but also in RÜDESHEIM. Vines are 76%
Riesling, 7% Spätburgunder. The present energetic owner, Peter
Breuer, is proud of the fruity acidity of his wines from steep sites,
matured in the 300m (984 ft) long cellars that lie deep beneath his
vineyards. Annual production is some 10,000 cases, of which 40%
is sold on the export market. Address: Binger Weg 2, 6223
Lorch/Rheingau.

Alzey Rhh. w. ★★
Town first mentioned in AD 223, set in rolling country deep in the
Rheinhessen. Very much a centre for the local wine trade, it is best
known for its Landesanstalt für Rebzüchtung – the viticultural
institute whose first director, in 1909, was Georg Scheu, who bred
the Scheurebe and other well-known vines. The town also has its
own wine estate, the Weingut der Stadt Alzey (see next entry). It is
the home of the wine exporting house SICHEL. Grosslagen: Petersberg, Sybillenstein.

Alzey, Weingut der Stadt Rhh.
Estate of 15ha (37 acre) owned by the town of ALZEY, established in
1916 and producing some 8,300 cases only a year. 18 different vine
varieties are in commercial production, with Müller-Thurgau and
Riesling each occupying 17% of the area under vine. The administ-
rator, Herr U. Kaufmann, aims to make balanced, positive, wines,
15% are dry or med-dry. No exports. The estate is one of the few in
Germany to be owned by a town. Address: Schlossgasse 14, 6508
Alzey.

Ämälienhof, Weingut Würt.
24.8ha (61 acre) estate founded in 1954. Sole owners of 20ha (49
acre) Beilsteiner Steinberg Einzellage, with further holdings at
HEILBRONN. FLEIN and Talheim. 36% Riesling, 16% Trollinger, 12%
Müllerrebe, etc., 20,700 cases produced annually and sold exclusively in Germany. Address: Lukas-Cranach-Weg 5, 7100
Heilbronn.

Amtliche Prüfung
Official testing. Quality German wines (approx. 95% of the annual
harvest) of all categories must submit to an official "blind" tasting
and chemical analysis. If successful, a wine will be granted an
Amtliche Prüfungnummer (A.P. number) which must be dis-

played on the label. Usually 93-97% of applications for an A.P. number are successful. This countrywide system of quality control, operating through nine centres, is claimed to be unique to West Germany. It ensures that wines with apparent faults at the time of examination do not reach the market.

Anbaugebiet, bestimmtes

A designated wine region, of which there are 11 in Germany (shown on the map on page 10). It is the largest geographical unit for quality wine and the Anbaugebiet name must always appear on the label of a quality (QbA or QmP) wine. The differences between the wines of the various regions are clear, although they naturally tend to be less pronounced in the vineyards at the boundaries of adjoining regions.

Anheuser, Weingut Ökonomierat August E. Nahe

Large estate of some 52ha (129 acre) founded in 1869 by the Anheuser family, to whom the exporting house Anheuser & Fehrs also belongs. Sites incl. BRÜCKES, KRÖTENPFUHL and NARRENKAPPE at BAD KREUZNACH; DELLCHEN at NORHEIM; HERMANNSHÖHLE at NIEDERHAUSEN and KÖNIGSFELS at SCHLOSSBÖCKELHEIM. 74% of the vines are Riesling, the rest are mainly Müller-Thurgau, Silvaner, Ruländer and Scheurebe. 45% of production is dry/med-dry. High quality wine-making. Address: Brückes 53, 6550 Bad Kreuznach.

Anheuser, Weingut Paul Nahe

Estate est. in 1888 by the vine-growing Anheuser family, also responsible for the American brewery Anheuser-Busch, covering 76ha (188 acre). Vines are 70% Riesling in leading sites at ALTEN-BAMBERG, BAD KREUZNACH, NIEDERHAUSEN, NORHEIM, ROXHEIM and SCHLOSSBÖCKELHEIM. No Grosslage names are used. Cool fermentation and maturation in oak cask produces the full range of Nahe flavours. 50% of the wines are dry or med-dry. Annual production 41,500 cases. Address: Strombergerstr. 15-19, 6550 Bad Kreuznach.

Anheuser & Fehrs, Weinkellereien Nahe

Wine merchants established in 1869, under the same family ownership as Weingut Ökonomierat August E. Anheuser, selling quality wines on the home and export markets. Address: Brückes 41, 6550 Bad Kreuznach.

Annaberg Rhpf. W. ★★★→★★★★

Famous little 5ha (12 acre) Einzellage planted with 30% Riesling, 30% Scheurebe, 20% Weissburgunder, 10% Sylvaner and 10% Ruländer. Until 1971 the wine was sold simply under the site name Annaberg but now the label must include the village name KALL-STADT. Grosslage: FEUERBERG.

Annaberg Stumpf-Fitz'sches, Weingut Rhpf.

Small but important estate dating from the 16th century or earlier – the site itself was a Roman settlement. The grapes are harvested late and produce top-quality, powerful, concentrated wines that can last for years. At present the estate is virtually out of production, whilst a new owner is found. Address: 6702 Bad Dürkheim-Leistadt.

Anreicherung

Enrichment. The addition of sugar in various forms (saccharose, concentrated grape juice, etc.) to increase the actual alcohol content and thus produce a balanced wine has been practised for some 200 years in many countries. In Germany only QbA and DEUTSCHER TAFELWEIN, incl. LANDWEIN, may be enriched. This means that wines of KABINETT quality and upwards will never have sugar added, as their superior quality depends on freshness and elegance, not on enhanced alcohol content. See also ALCOHOL.

Ansprechend

Attractive. A somewhat imprecise but useful term for describing a wine, often used as in Ansprechende Süsse ("attractive sweetness") or Ansprechende Säure ("attractive acidity").

A.P.

See Amtliche Prüfung

A.P. Nr.

Abbreviation of Amtliche Prüfungsnummer (A.P. number).

Äpfelsäure

Malic acid. With tartaric acid (WEINSÄURE) it forms approx. 90% of the acidity in German grape MUST (it is also found in many other fruits). The process of malolactic fermentation, in which malic acid is converted into lactic acid and carbon dioxide, does not normally occur in the relatively acidic German white wines. If the malic acid content of a wine is excessive it may legally be chemically reduced. See also SÄURE.

Apfelwein

Wine made from apple juice by a process that is very similar to grape-wine vinification. Additions of sugar and water are normal. A popular drink in s. Germany.

Apotheke M-S-R w. ★★→★★★

Einzellage lying on both sides of the Mosel at TRITTENHEIM, prod. good-quality, elegant Rieslings. Grosslage: MICHELSBERG. Growers: Bischöfliche Weingüter, Friedrich-Wilhelm-Gymnasium, Dünweg, Kesselstatt, Milz, Reh (Josefinengrund), Ronde.

Arnet, Wilhelm Rhg.

Small 2.6ha (6.4 acre) estate est. in 1632, producing powerful, full cask-matured wines (100% Riesling) at ELTVILLE, MARTINSTHAL and WALLUF. Annual production 2,500 cases all sold to private customers. Address: Mühlstr. 96, 6229 Walluf.

Arnsteiner Gült, Weingut Rhh.

Ancient 15ha (37 acre) estate at OSTHOFEN and METTENHEIM, planted 20% Riesling plus a range of other vine varieties. 15-20% of the production is in red wine, 40% is dry or med-dry and 30% is sold in cask. Of the balance, the consumer takes 80%. Address: Friedrich-Ebert-Str. 36, 6522 Osthofen.

Aromatisch

Aromatic. Term used to describe wines with a pronounced bouquet, esp. the wines of the Rheinhessen and Rheinpfalz, from vine varieties such as Morio-Muskat, Traminer and Scheurebe. The strength of the aroma will be affected by the style of the vintage, the soil, vinification and length of maturation in bottle.

Aschrott'sche Erben, Geheimrat Rhg.

Estate dating from 1823 with 17ha (42 acre) of holdings in most of the best HOCHHEIM sites, incl. DOMDECHANEY, HÖLLE and

KIRCHENSTÜCK. The vines are 86% Riesling and the estate makes powerful, spicy wines which have won many awards. Annual production is 13,750 cases, sold in Germany and abroad. Address: Kirchstr. 38, 6203 Hochheim am Main.

Assmannshausen Rhg. r. (w.) ★★

Small town some 4km (2½ miles) downstream from RÜDESHEIM, where the river turns n. and the Wagnerian Rhein gorge begins. It is best known for its Spätburgunder and its fine old "Zur Krone" hotel and restaurant. Wine from this area is among the most distinguished red wine in Germany. It improves with bottle age and usually shows clear varietal characteristics. Grosslage: STEIL.

Auctions

See Versteigerungen

Auflangen Rhh. w. ★★
Grosslage of 159ha (393 acre) covering some of the best south-facing sites on the RHEINTERRASSE above NIERSTEIN, incl. ÖLBERG and ORBEL. Distinguished wines from Riesling and Silvaner, rounded but not flabby, with powerful flavour in good years.

Aus dem Lesegut
On a label this indicates that the wine has been made from grapes grown by the person stated (e.g. Aus dem Lesegut Herr Schmidt). Not a term that is used very often. See also LESE, LESEGUT.

Ausdrucksvoll
Characterful. Suggests that the positive qualities of a wine are strongly pronounced. It might be applied to a well-developed Riesling wine from the Rheingau or Rheinpfalz.

Ausgeglichen
Well balanced. Describes a wine in which the constituent parts, particularly alcohol, acids and residual sugar, are in harmony. Sometimes only achieved after several years' bottle age.

Auslese
Legally established term used in Germany to describe quality (QmP) wine made from selected – but not necessarily late-picked – grapes whose MUST weight reached certain minimum levels (e.g. for Rheingauer Riesling Auslese the minimum level is 95° Oechsle = 13% of potential alcohol). Riesling Auslese wines from the Rhein regions are made in great years from grapes with an increased sugar content caused by "noble rot" (EDELFÄULE). Such wines will also taste sweeter (through an enhanced fructose and glycerin content) and will be darker in colour than wines of lower quality. Auslese wines from most of the new vine varieties cannot compare in quality with a Riesling Auslese.

Ausschankwein
German equivalent of the French *vin ouvert* ("open wine"), usually bottled into litres and served in a large, 200ml (250ml in s. Germany) glass in cafés and wine bars. It is never the most expensive of wines although the quality is by no means always inferior. Many estates offer their better quality (QmP) wine by the glass in their own wine bar.

Auxerrois
Vine variety producing a low yield of white grapes with a MUST weight some 10° Oechsle higher than that of Müller-Thurgau. The wine is relatively soft, full-bodied and neutral in flavour. Planted in 73ha (180 acre), 78% in Baden. Varieties bearing a larger crop are likely to replace it in coming years.

Ayl M-S-R w. ★★★→★★★★
Rural village in the Saar devoted to viticulture, where great wines are made in the best years. The finest wines usually come from the Einzellage HERRENBERGER and the best parts of the KUPP. Grosslage: SCHARZBERG.

Bacchus
White grape variety, a crossing of (Silvaner × Riesling) × Müller-Thurgau, usually producing a larger crop than Müller-Thurgau with a greater MUST weight but less acidity. The wine has a slight Muskat bouquet and is at its best when young and fresh. It blends well with wines of pronounced acidity, to which it brings body and flavour. In 1976 Bacchus was planted in 1,447ha (3,576 acre), in 1985 in 3,573ha (8,829 acre), more than half in the Rheinhessen.

Bacharach Mrh. w. ★★
Attractive old village, once a marketplace for wine from the whole of the Rheinland, now respected for its own steely Rieslings grown exclusively on very steep slopes. The wines are similarly priced to those from the Nahe. Grosslage: Schloss Stahleck.

Bad Cannstadt Würt r. w ★★
Suburb of Stuttgart known for centuries for its mineral water from 18 springs as well as for its approx. 80ha (198 acre) of v'yds, planted mainly in Trollinger and Riesling. Grosslage: Weinsteige.

Bad Dürkheim Rhpf. Pop. 15,700 w. (r.) ★★★
Busy town and spa 25km (15 miles) w. of Mannheim at the foot of the Pfälzerwald (Pfalz Forest) overlooking the v'yds of the Bereich

MITTELHAARDT/DEUTSCHE WEINSTRASSE, and the site every September of the largest wine festival in the world, the Dürkheimer Wurstmarkt (Sausage Market). Excellent white wine is made from a range of vine varieties, although Dürkheim's wines are probably not quite as fine as the best from neighbouring FORST or DEIDESHEIM. Three Grosslagen: FEUERBERG, HOCHMESS and SCHENKENBÖHL.

Bad Kreuznach Nahe Pop. 41,500 w. (r.) ★★★

The largest town in the Nahe and a spa since the 17th century; the s. part of the town with its well laid out gardens reflects its pre-1914 heyday. Some of the finest wine of the Nahe is made within the boundaries of the Grosslage KRONENBERG, surrounding Bad Kreuznach.

Bad Kreuznach, Staatsweingut: Weinbaulehranstalt Nahe

Estate est. in 1900, with an educational and experimental role, owned by the government of RHEINLAND-PFALZ. It has 22ha (54 acre) of v'yds in BAD KREUZNACH and NORHEIM, 39% Riesling, 22% Müller-Thurgau, and many new crossings are on trial. The estate pioneered controlled fermentation under carbon-dioxide pressure and aims to produce individual, cask-matured wines with length and fine acidity. Annual production 16,700 cases. Sales are mainly on the home market. Address: Rüdesheimerstr. 68, 6550 Bad Kreuznach.

Bad Münster am Stein-Ebernburg Nahe Pop. 3,600 w.

Small and charming spa 5km (3 miles) s. of BAD KREUZNACH near the distinguished Traisen v'yds which back on to high, warmth-retaining rocks. Grosslage: BURGWEG.

Bad Neuenahr-Ahrweiler Ahr Pop. 26,000 r.

Principal town in the Ahr valley 30km (18 miles) s. of Bonn. Much damaged in World War II, now skilfully restored and again a centre of tourism. The wine is red, light in weight and flavour. The best comes from Spätburgunder. Grosslage: Klosterberg.

Baden w. (r.)

Most southerly grape-growing region in Germany, covering 14,999ha (37,064 acre) and producing some 15% of the total annual German wine production. The soil is varied, warm and fruitful. Most of the v'yds lie on level or gently sloping ground, although here and there they climb the hillsides, not so much to reach a better exposure to the sun as to avoid the cold air and frosts of the valleys. The EEC recognizes that the climate in Baden is warmer than that elsewhere in West Germany and places the region, for administrative purposes, in wine-producing Zone B, with French regions incl. Alsace and certain parts of the Loire valley. (All other wine-producing regions in Germany are placed in Zone A, together with the UK and Luxembourg.)

85% of the Baden crop is handled by cooperative cellars, incl. the largest wine-producing cellar in Europe, the ZENTRALKELLEREI BADISCHER WINZERGENOSSENSCHAFTEN eG (ZBW) at Breisach, and

BADEN
BEREICH
ORTENAU

QUALITÄTSWEIN
MIT
PRÄDIKAT

Durbacher Schloß Staufenberg
Klingelberger (Riesling) · trocken
KABINETT
A.P.Nr. 502-01-84
Erzeugerabfüllung   0,75 *l*
MAX MARKGRAF von BADEN
Markgräflich Badisches Weingut Schloß Staufenberg, Durbach

it is to the cooperatives that credit must be given for the success of Baden wines in Germany. There are also a number of private estates making top-quality, individual wines.

The range of vines grown is large with Müller-Thurgau, Ruländer and Gutedel heading the list. Perhaps because the region extends over 300km (187 miles) from the R. Main to the Swiss border, there is considerable variation in the style of wine from one Bereich to another. The modern international taste seems to be for lightness and crispness rather than for the heavier, broader flavours favoured in the past. Baden produces both types, and both have their merits. Some wines are allowed to retain sufficient natural carbon dioxide to make them slightly SPRITZIG and most attractive.

The region, which in many places backs on to the Black Forest, is exceptionally pretty and rural, with small v'yds mingling with orchards and meadows covered in wildflowers. Very definitely worth a detour.

Baden-Württemberg
Federal State in which lie the wine regions Baden and Württemberg. Area under vine is 24,655ha (60,925 acre). The capital is STUTTGART.

Badisch Rotgold
Quality rosé wine made in Baden exclusively from mixing Ruländer (Grauburgunder) and Spätburgunder grapes (not wine).

Badstube M-S-R w. ★★→★★★
Small Grosslage of about 51ha (126 acre) that incl. three of the most distinguished sites on the Mosel: DOCTOR, GRABEN and BRATENHÖFCHEN. The sites are sloping or very steep indeed and almost 100% Riesling. Often wines are sold for marketing reasons under the respected Grosslage name Badstube, rather than their individual site names.

Baiken Rhg. w. ★★★→★★★★
Einzellage on sloping ground at RAUENTHAL that makes splendid, balanced, elegant Riesling wines of outstanding quality in great years. Grosslage: STEINMÄCHER. Growers: Staatsweingut, Simmern'sches Rentamt.

Balbach Erben, Weingut Bürgermeister Anton Rhh.
Great NIERSTEIN estate. The Balbach family, engaged in vine-growing since 1650, cleared woods in the 19th century and laid out the top-quality PETTENTHAL v'yd. Today the estate has holdings in

18ha (44 acre) of prime sites incl. HIPPING, ÖLBERG, etc. Vines are 80% Riesling, the rest mainly Kerner (8%) and Müller-Thurgau (7%). Some 13,750 cases (4,250 from Pettenthal) of good-quality, fresh wines are made and stored in stainless steel and fibreglass before being sold in Germany and abroad. Address: Mainzerstr. 64, 6505 Nierstein.

Barrique
Wooden cask of approx. 210-225 litres. Maturation in aged casks of 500 litres or more is common in Germany. Since the early 1970s some estates have experimented with storage in smaller casks of new oak that give the wine a particular flavour and bouquet. Although many of these new casks are French and of the exact size found in their region of origin, the term "barrique aged" seems to

be used loosely to describe any wine that has spent a period in a new cask of less than 500 litres. German leaders in barrique ageing are ADELMANN, DIEL, "SCHWARZER ADLER", RAPPENHOF, etc.

Bart, Weingut Gebr. Rhpf.

18th century, family-owned 11.8ha (29 acre) estate, with holdings at BAD DÜRKHEIM (SPIELBERG, FUCHSMANTEL, etc), UNGSTEIN and WACHENHEIM. Many vine varieties are grown incl. 28% Riesling, 13% Müller-Thurgau and 10% Gewürztraminer. Only cask-matured QmP are sold in bottle (80% to the consumer). The Kabinett Kerner and Scheurebe and the red and rosé wines are particularly appreciated. Annual production is 6,500 cases. Address: Kaiserslauterer Str. 42, 6702 Bad Dürkheim.

Base wine

See Grundwein

Bassermann-Jordan, Weingut Geheimer Rat Dr. v. Rhpf.

Estate known to have been in existence in 1250, came into the hands of the Jordan family in 1816. The 40ha (99 acre) are divided among the best sites in the Bereich MITTELHAARDT/DEUTSCHE WEINSTRASSE, incl. GRAINHÜBEL, HOHENMORGEN and LEINHÖHLE in DEIDESHEIM, JESUITENGARTEN and UNGEHEUER in FORST, etc. Vines are 99% Riesling. Wines are matured in oak and the estate aims for fine Riesling acidity and fruit. 20% are dry. Annual production is 33,300 cases. Sales are worldwide. Address: 6705 Deidesheim.

Bastei Nahe w. ★★★ → ★★★★

Mainly steep 2ha (5 acre) Einzellage at the foot of the 200m (656 feet) high rock face near TRAISEN called the Rotenfels, planted entirely with Riesling. The wine has great character and a positive, spicy flavour that comes from the soil. Grosslage: BURGWEG. Growers: Crusius, Niederhausen-Schlossböckelheim Staatl. Weinbaudomäne.

Basting-Gimbel, Weingut Rhg.

Family-owned estate of 10ha (25 acre) dating from the early 17th century. 86% Riesling. Elegant, mainly dry/med-dry wines from WINKEL (HASENSPRUNG), GEISENHEIM and JOHANISBERG. Sold in Germany and abroad. Many old vintages, going back to 1950, can be tasted in the estate's own wine bar. Address: Hauptstr. 70-72, 6227 Winkel.

Baumann, Weingut Friedrich Rhh.

Estate founded in 1909, with 8.6ha (21 acre) in leading sites in OPPENHEIM (e.g. SACKTRÄGER) and NIERSTEIN (FINDLING, PETTENTHAL), producing a large choice of wines (incl. dry and med-dry) from Riesling (40%), Silvaner, Kerner, Müller-Thurgau, etc. They are fresh and lively, matured in wood, and have won many awards. Annual prod. is 9,000 cases. Sales are in Germany and abroad. Address: Friedrich-Ebert-Strasse 55, 6504 Oppenheim.

Bechtheim Rhh. w. ★

Village with 290ha (717 acre) of mainly sloping v'yds. Most widely known in connection with its Grosslage: PILGERPFAD.

Becker, J. B., Weingut Weinkellerei Rhg.

Estate dating from 1893 with 10.6ha (26 acre) of Riesling (80%), Spätburgunder (15%) and Müller-Thurgau in WALLUF, MARTINSTHAL, RAUENTHAL and ELTVILLE, producing approx. 8,000 cases annually. The Spätburgunder is traditionally made, and about 60% of the white wines are dry or med-dry. Sales are to the home and export markets. Address: Rheinstrasse 5-6, 6229 Walluf/Rheingau.

Beeren

Grapes. The structure of the grape has a bearing on wine-making. Many substances that contribute to the aroma are concentrated in the skin, as is the colour in red grapes. The content of the outer and inner areas of the flesh is not the same, with more sugar and less acid being found near the skin. As a result, the first and second pressings of the same grapes do not share the same chemical make-up and produce noticeably different wines.

Wine grapes vary in size, but small grapes, with their greater proportion of skin to flesh, will have a powerful bouquet if white (e.g. Scheurebe), and a good colour if red – all things being equal.

The tightness with which grapes are packed on the bunch has a direct effect on the rate at which fungus diseases may spread.

Beerenauslese

PRÄDIKAT awarded by the control (AMTLICHE PRÜFUNG) authorities to wines made from individually selected overripe grapes, probably attacked by EDELFÄULE, and always intensely sweet. The legal minimum MUST weights vary from 110–128° Oechsle, depending on where the grapes are grown. Although 128° Oechsle is the equivalent of 18.1% alcohol by volume, most Beerenauslesen will contain relatively little alcohol (the legal minimum is 5.5%), the rest of the sugar remaining unfermented.

Usually Riesling produces the finest Beerenauslesen, with a high acid content and pronounced yellow-gold colour when young, that can turn to deepest amber in old age. The concentrated flavour of a Beerenauslese tends to mask the obtrusive characteristics of some new grape crossings, replacing them with the honey flavour of the Edelfäule.

Beilstein M-S-R w. ★→★★

Picturesque old wine hamlet a few km. upstream from COCHEM, overlooked by the castle Burg Metternich. A good centre from which to visit the Bereich ZELL. Grosslage: Rosenhang.

Bensheim Hess.Berg. Pop. 33,000 w. ★★

Ancient town s. of Darmstadt. Steep sites produce Riesling wines with good acidity, drunk mainly in the region. The style of Bensheimer wines is similar to that of Rheingau Rieslings but the quality is less exalted. Grosslage: Wolfsmagen.

Bensheim, Weingut der Stadt Hess.Berg.

One of a few town-owned estates in Germany covering 12.5ha (31 acre). 65% is planted with Riesling and 10% with Rotberger for rosé production. Much of the v'yd has been recently re-built and most of the annual production of 9,700 cases is sold locally. Address: Am Ritterplatz, 6140 Bensheim 1.

Bentzel-Sturmfeder'sches Weingut, Graf Würt.

17.6ha (43 acre) estate occupying practically all of the sloping Schozacher Roter Berg Einzellage, planted 28% Riesling, 22% Spätburgunder, 18% Samtrot, etc. The wines from heavy soil are cask matured and long lived. Annual production of 13,000 cases is sold exclusively in Germany. Address: Sturmfederstr. 4, 7129 Ilsfeld-Schozach.

Bercher OHG, Weingut Baden

The Bercher family has made wine in Burkheim for over 300 years. In a district dominated by cooperative cellars, this estate, planted 30% Spätburgunder, 20% Müller-Thurgau, 12% Riesling, etc., produces 14,000 cases annually of individually made, dry or med-dry, wines (including Auslesen). The great interest for the future is in red wine from restricted yields. Sales mainly in Germany. Address: Mittelstadt 13, 7818 Vogtsburg-Burkheim.

Bereich

District. Combination of v'yd sites (GROSSLAGEN or EINZELLAGEN) within one region (ANBAUGEBIET) with more or less similar growing conditions and style of wine. In some instances the reason for a Bereich being created has been to help administration rather than to identify a particular style of wine. Generally, a wine bearing a Bereich name must be a quality wine, although in certain areas a Bereich name can still be used to describe a table wine. The quality of a Bereich wine should be good within its category (QbA, QmP) but is unlikely to be outstanding.

Berg Roseneck Rhg. w. ★★★→★★★★

Sloping Einzellage on the hill at RÜDESHEIM making top-quality Riesling wines with a slightly earthy background flavour. Grosslage: BURGWEG. Growers: Breuer, Staatsweingut, Frankensteiner Hof, Groenesteyn, Hessisches Weingut, Holschier, Mumm'sches Weingut, Nägler, Schlotter, Wegeler-Deinhard.

Berg Rottland Rhg. w. ★★★→★★★★

Einzellage on the outskirts of RÜDESHEIM producing stylish, fruity, top-quality Riesling wines. Grosslage: BURGWEG. Growers: Altenkirch, Breuer, Staatsweingut, Frankensteiner Hof, Groenesteyn,

Hessisches Weingut, Mumm'sches Weingut, Nägler, Ress, Schlotter, Wegeler-Deinhard.

Berg Schlossberg Rhg. w. ★★★

Steep, slaty Einzellage directly overlooking the confluence of the Nahe and Rhein at RÜDESHEIM. Excellent Riesling wines with good acidity. Grosslage: BURGWEG. Growers: Breuer, Staatsweingut, Frankensteiner Hof, Groenesteyn, Mumm'sches Weingut, Nägler, Ress, Schloss Schönborn, Schlotter, Wegeler-Deinhard.

Bergdolt, F.u.G. Rhpf.

15ha (37 acre) estate s.e. of NEUSTADT, founded in 1290 and acquired by the Bergdolt family in 1754. Riesling (30%), Müller-Thurgau (12%) and Kerner (15%) are the main vine varieties, plus other white varieties, producing 12,500 cases of fresh, flowery wines, nearly 50% are dry. The most successful are the dry Riesling wines. Sales are 95% directly to the consumer in Germany. Address: Klostergut St Lamprecht, 6730 Neustadt-Duttweiler.

Bergstrasse, Staatsweingut Hess.Berg.

Top-quality HESSEN estate of 36ha (89 acre) under the control of the large ELTVILLE STAATSWEINGUT and dating from the early part of the century. Vines are 70% Riesling, 10% Müller-Thurgau, 6% Ruländer, etc., and many new crossings are on trial. The estate is sole owner of the 17.5ha (43 acre) Centgericht site at HEPPENHEIM. Some 25,000 cases are produced annually of fruity, lively wines, 63% dry or med-dry, sold mainly in Germany. Sales direct to the public are to be increased. EISWEIN is a speciality. Address: Grieselstr. 34-36, 6140 Bensheim.

Bergsträsser Gebiets Winzergenossenschaft eG Hess.Berg.

Cooperative cellar in the smallest wine-producing region. 634 members have holdings in 295ha (729 acre). Vines are 52% Riesling, 18% Müller-Thurgau, 10% Ruländer, 9% Silvaner. Approx. annual production is the equivalent of 255,500 cases, sold almost entirely in Germany. Address: Darmstädterstr. 56, 6148 Heppenheim.

Bergweiler-Prüm Erben, Zach.

See Pauly-Bergweiler, Weingut Dr.

Bernkastel, Bereich M-S-R w.

One of five Bereiche in the M-S-R. Downstream a few km. from TRIER at SCHWEICH the steep slopes begin to rise from the n. bank of the Mosel. Here the Bereich Bernkastel begins and continues on both sides of the river until a little short of ZELL. The top-quality wines from these v'yds are offered under their own village and Einzellage names. The cheaper wines are often sold under the Grosslage names – Bernkasteler KURFÜRSTLAY, Klüsserather ST MICHAEL, Piesporter MICHELSBERG. Generally speaking, any wine called simply Bereich Bernkastel is likely to be of similar quality to these Grosslagen wines. Today, such wines will probably contain a high proportion of Müller-Thurgau, but when drunk young they should still be fresh and crisp in the proper Mosel manner. Bereich Bernkastel Riesling is likely to be distinctly better.

Bernkastel-Kues M-S-R Pop. 6,800 w. ★★→★★★★

Important wine-producing town on the Mosel. Many of the finest v'yds of the MITTELMOSEL, incl. the Bernkasteler DOCTOR and Wehlener SONNENUHR, are concentrated around Bernkastel on the right-hand river bank. Ancient half-timbered houses, narrow fairy-tale streets and the pleasure of drinking wine at source attract many tourists. In Kues (on the left bank and over the bridge from Bernkastel) several enormous cellars draw their wine from the whole of the Mosel and beyond. Grosslagen: BADSTUBE and KURFÜRSTLAY.

Besenwirtschaft

Name used particularly in Württemberg but also elsewhere for STRAUSSWIRTSCHAFT.

Bestes Fass

Best cask. Term used by some growers before 1971 to identify wines from the best of two or more casks of the same description, e.g. 1953 Oppenheimer Sackträger Riesling Auslese "Bestes Fass". No longer permitted.

Bestimmtes Anbaugebiet
See Anbaugebiet, bestimmtes

Beulwitz, Weingut Erben von M-S-R
250-year-old 4.5ha (11 acre) 100% Riesling estate taken over in 1983 by Herbert Weis. All the holdings, incl. parts of NIES'CHEN, HITZLAY and KEHRNAGEL are at KASEL. Some of the annual production equalling 4,400 cases is made into bottle-fermented sparkling wine. Sales are in Germany and abroad. Address: Hauptstr. 1, 5501 Kasel.

Bezner Fischer
See Sonnenhof, Weingut

Bickensohl Baden w. (r.) **
Part of Vogtsburg in the Bereich KAISERSTUHL-TUNIBERG producing powerful, intensely flavoured Ruländer wines in particular. Grosslage: VULKANFELSEN.

Biffar, Weingut Josef Rhpf.
Estate with 12ha (30 acre) in the best sites at DEIDESHEIM and RUPPERTSBERG, 80% Riesling, 10% Müller-Thurgau, producing some 10,000 cases annually. A full range of long-lasting cask matured wines is offered, with the swing to dry wines continuing. Address: Niederkirchenerstr. 13, 6705 Deidesheim.

Bildstock Rhh. w. **→***
Large Einzellage behind the town of NIERSTEIN, that separates it from the Rhein. Most of the site is flat, producing good-quality, fruity wines. Grosslage: SPIEGELBERG. Growers: Balbach Erben, Gessert, Heyl zu Herrnsheim, Kurfürstenhof, Georg Schneider, Strub, Wehrheim.

Bingen Rhh. Pop. 24,000 w. **→***
Town at the confluence of the R. Nahe and Rhein, severely damaged in World War II but some of the old provincial terraced town houses remain. Several large brandy- and wine-producing companies (Racke, St Ursula, Scharlachberg, Texier) face the Rheingauer RÜDESHEIM v'yds across the Rhein. The best-known individual v'yd site is the Binger SCHARLACHBERG. Grosslage: ST ROCHUSKAPELLE.

Bischöflichen Weingüter, Verwaltung der M-S-R
A combination of four estates of ecclesiastical origin, totalling 105ha (259 acre), their v'yds a roll-call of some of the finest of the M-S-R incl. Erdener TREPPCHEN, Ürziger WÜRZGARTEN, Trittenheimer APOTHEKE, Kaseler NIES'CHEN and KEHRNAGEL, Ayler KUPP, SCHARZHOFBERG, Piesporter GOLDTRÖPFCHEN. The v'yds are mainly steep, 98% Riesling, and produce approx. 72,000 cases annually. The grapes are pressed near the v'yds and the wine is vinified in the central cellar in TRIER (part of the cellar is 400 years old), maturing in wood. 55% are dry or med-dry. Top-quality, elegant and characterful wines, sold all over the world. Address: Gervasiusstr. 1, 5500 Trier.

Black Forest
See Schwarzwald

Blankenhorn K.G., Weingut Fritz Baden
16.5ha (41 acre) estate in the Bereich MARKGRÄFLERLAND, producing true-to-type mainly dry and med-dry wines from Gutedel, Spätburgunder, Müller-Thurgau, Riesling, etc. Sold principally in Germany. Address: 7846 Schliengen.

Blankenhornsberg
See Freiburg, Staatliches Weinbauinstitut, "Blankenhornsberg"

Blauer Frühburgunder
See Frühburgunder

Blauer Limberger
See Limberger

Blauer Portugieser
See Portugieser

Blauer Spätburgunder
See Spätburgunder

Blend
See Verschnitt

Blume
Translated literally means "flower". As a description of German wine it is positive and refers to the smell of a fresh, balanced and stylish white wine, without any unpleasant overtones or excesses in its make-up. Such a wine is said to have a "schöne (lovely) Blume". A Riesling Kabinett from the Mosel, a year after the vintage, might be so described.

Bockenheim an der Weinstrasse Rhpf. w. (r.) ★★
Small town nr. the Rheinpfalz-Rheinhessen border, where Silvaner still predominates. Sound, quality wines. Grosslage: Grafenstück.

Bocksbeutel
A flagon-shaped bottle of ancient design used exclusively in West Germany for the white and red quality wines of Franken and certain areas of n. Baden.

Bockstein M-S-R w. ★★★
One of the best-known Einzellagen of the Bereich Saar-Ruwer at OCKFEN, planted mainly with Riesling. Stylish wines with a lovely fruity acidity. Grosslage: SCHARZBERG. Growers: Fischer, Geltz, Reverchon, Rheinart, Schorlemer, Trier Staatl. Weinbaudomäne.

Bodengeschmack
"Taste of the soil". Certain v'yds and their soils transmit a flavour to the grapes that are grown in them and the flavour is retained when the MUST becomes wine. Exactly how this happens is not fully understood. Among the wines with a sometimes pronounced Bodengeschmack are Mosels (slate taste), Nahe wines from TRAISEN and NORHEIM (rhyolite rock) and Franken wines from various soils. In all three, the taste of the soil is regarded as a virtue. Bodengeschmack is also known as Bodenton.

Bodenheim Rhh. w. ★★
Small town of the RHEINTERRASSE producing excellent wine from red soil. Some attractive old buildings, incl. the town hall and old wine cellars. Grosslage: ST ALBAN.

Bodensee w. r.
Alias Lake Constance. The v'yds lie within three regions: Baden, Franken and Württemberg. The steep, high-lying sites are planted with a number of vine varieties incl. Spätburgunder (frequently made into WEISSHERBST) and Müller-Thurgau. The reflected light and additional warmth from the lake help to compensate for a climate of modest warmth in summer.

Bodenton
See Bodengeschmack

Böhlig Rhpf. w. ★★★
Einzellage of 9ha (22 acre) on mainly level land at WACHENHEIM making splendid, meaty wines, full of strong regional flavour. Grosslage: MARIENGARTEN. Growers incl. Bürklin-Wolf.

Bonnet, Weingut Alfred Rhpf.
24.5ha (61 acre) family estate of Huguenot descent now in its 10th generation. The holdings are at KALLSTADT (STEINACKER), BAD DÜRKHEIM, FORST, WACHENHEIM, etc. Vine varieties incl. Riesling (53%), plus a wide range of others. The aim is fresh white wines, stored in stainless steel and matured in bottle, and red wines matured in cask. 22,500 cases are sold annually in Germany and abroad. Address: 6701 Friedelsheim.

Boppard Mrh. w. ★→★★
Riverside town on the Rhein, a major anchorage for pleasure boats and the site of a fine sweep of v'yds – the Bopparder Hamm. Its steep Einzellagen, more than 90% Riesling, produce racy wines with a good earthy flavour, drunk mainly in the region. Grosslage: Gedeonseck.

Botrytis cinerea
See Edelfäule

Bottle
Flasche. The typical German wine bottle – ignoring the BOCKSBEUTEL of Franken – is tall, slim and elegant and contains 700 or 750ml. Since the 18th century, amber-coloured bottles have been used for Rhein wine. Mosel wine has been sold in green

bottles for rather longer. Today, clear glass is used increasingly for dry wines, although in the past clear glass in Germany was filled mainly with WEISSHERBST and Ruländer.

Bottle age

Wines with high acidity (e.g. Riesling) require more time in bottle to reach their peak of quality than do softer wines (e.g. Müller-Thurgau). In general, the better the quality the more bottle age is needed, as these very approx. figures for Riesling's development in bottle show. The first column represents the number of years after the vintage before the wine has reached its peak, the second column shows for how many years thereafter the wine will remain at its best.

QbA, Kabinett	1½ 1½	Beerenauslese	7 7+
Spätlese	2 2	Eiswein	7 7+
Auslese	5 5	Trockenbeerenauslese	7 7+

These approx. timings can vary widely with different vintages and the conditions under which the wine is stored. Dry Rieslings up to and incl. SPÄTLESE take longer to reach their peak than those with usual amounts of residual sugar, but the sweetness in some wines will often hide the signs of incipient senility. In spite of these general comments, well-made, estate-bottled Rieslings of all qualities may give pleasure, and surprise by remaining fresh and attractive, for many more years than those suggested above.

Bottle sick

Immediately after bottling a wine will sometimes taste "tired" and not show at its best. This is said to be the result of the physical disturbance caused by the bottling operation. The malady normally disappears after a few weeks.

Bottling

See Abfüllung

Bowlen

Wine cups. Those sold commercially must be based at least 50% on wine. If the word "wine" appears in their description the proportion must reach a minimum of 70%. More interesting are the homemade Bowlen spiced with woodruff (Waldmeister) or those with fruits such as strawberries or peaches. Other ingredients used are sugar, sometimes brandy, and usually sparkling wine added just before serving, well chilled. There are many variations on this theme.

Branded wine

See Markenwein

Brandig

"Burnt". Describes a wine with a high alcohol and a low acid content, and little sweetness. This characteristic was very common in wines of the 1959 vintage – a year of excessive heat and drought.

Bratenhöfchen M-S-R w. ★★★

Einzellage at BERNKASTEL producing excellent Riesling. Sometimes a little overshadowed by the more luscious wine of the adjacent GRABEN but nevertheless a top-quality site. Grosslage: BADSTUBE. Growers: "Abteihof" Pauly-Bergweiler, Kesselstatt, Lauerburg, J. J. Prüm, Selbach-Oster, Vereinigte Hospitien, Wegeler-Deinhard.

Braubach Mrh. w. ★→★★

Riverside town, claiming to date from the Stone Age and overlooked by one of Germany's most spectacular castles, the Marksburg. Sound Rieslings from the steepest of sites, not generally as distinguished as those from BACHARACH upstream. Grosslage: Marksburg.

Brauneberg M-S-R w. ★★★

Small village upstream from BERNKASTEL. High percentage of Riesling and top-quality wines. Grosslage: KURFÜRSTLAY.

Braune Kupp M-S-R w. ★★★→★★★★

Highly rated, small, steep Einzellage at Wiltingen, considered on a par with Scharzhofberg. Famous for Rieslings of great finesse. Grosslage: SCHARZBERG. Growers: le Gallais, Vereinigte Hospitien.

Braunfels M-S-R w. **★★→★★★**
Steep Einzellage on the Saar. Riesling and Müller-Thurgau produce good-quality wines. Grosslage: SCHARZBERG. Growers: Kesselstatt, Koch, Müller-Scharzhof, Vereinigte Hospitien, Bernd van Volxem.

Breisach am Rhein Baden Pop. 9,300
Small town in s. Germany near the Bereich KAISERSTUHL-TUNIBERG, known as the home of Europe's largest winery belonging to the ZENTRALKELLEREI BADISCHER WINZERGENOSSENSCHAFTEN eG (ZBW).

Breit
Broad. Describes a full-flavoured wine that is low in acidity. Most often applicable to wines from the south of Germany.

Bremm M-S-R w. **★★**
Village of the Bereich ZELL. Its Calmont Einzellage is the steepest v'yd (65% inclination) in Germany, planted, almost inevitably, in Riesling. Elegant wines are produced. Grosslagen: Grafschaft and Rosenhang.

Brentano'sche Gutsverwaltung, Baron von Rhg.
Estate of 9.3ha (23 acre), family-owned since 1804. Holdings incl. part of Winkeler HASENSPRUNG. Vines are 96% Riesling, 4% Spätburgunder. The estate has romantic associations: its wines were

enjoyed by Goethe, Beethoven, von Arnim and his circle, and the attractive estate buildings incl. a Goethe museum. The wines are typical of the region: fruity, fresh and elegant. Annual production is 5,800 cases, sold in Germany and abroad. Address: Am Lindenplatz 2, 6227 Oestrich-Winkel.

Bretzenheim Nahe w. (r.) **★★**
Village with approx. 100ha (247 acre) of v'yd, the home of the Nahe Zentralkellerei since 1977, well known locally for its Portugieser red wine, although the majority of the wines are white. Grosslage: KRONENBERG.

Breuer, Weingut G. Rhg.
7.5ha (19 acre) estate dating from 1880 mainly on steep slopes planted 80% Riesling, all on RÜDESHEIM sites of which BERG SCHLOSSBERG is claimed to be the best. Founder member of CHARTA. Annual production is 5,000 cases of steely, firm wines with good fruit, sold in Germany and abroad. Address: Grabenstrasse 8, 6220 Rüdesheim am Rhein.

Broker
There are over 400 wine brokers (Kommissionäre) who act as links between grower and buyer handling over 60% of German wine. Many broking firms are generations old and have a formidable knowledge of the v'yd area in which they operate. They know what the growers have to offer, and their experience of the needs of their customers is the source of their success. At wine auctions in Germany only brokers are allowed to bid and all sales at auctions must, by law, be through them.

Brückes Nahe w. **★★★**
Einzellage on mainly sloping land close to BAD KREUZNACH. Its Riesling can produce top-quality, stylish wines in good years.

Grosslage: KRONENBERG. Growers: August E. Anheuser, Paul Anheuser, Finkenauer, Plettenberg, Schlink-Herf-Gutleuthof.

Bruderschaft

A brotherhood. There are a number of wine brotherhoods and similar organizations in Germany, organized by wine enthusiasts both in and outside the wine trade, to promote a love and understanding of wine and its culture.

Bruderschaft M-S-R w. ★★

Steep Einzellage of some 250ha (618 acre) at KLÜSSERATH, not far from TRIER, with a high proportion of Riesling. Much good wine is made but little that compares with the finest from villages such as PIESPORT or BERNKASTEL. Grosslage: ST MICHAEL. Growers: Friedrich-Wilhelm-Gymnasium, Reh (Marienhof).

Brut

The French word is also used in Germany to describe a sparkling wine with less than 15 g/l sugar, which will therefore taste dry or very dry depending on the balance of its other constituents. About 2% of German sparkling wine is "Brut".

Brutsekt

Written as one word, Brutsekt is the term given to sparkling wine when it has passed through its second fermentation and has not yet had a final sweetening of beet sugar and wine.

Buhl, Weingut Reichsrat von Rhpf.

Great estate with exciting wines and a young, dynamic management team. The property was christened Weingut F. P. Buhl in 1849 but its origins, with family connections to the BASSERMANN-JORDAN estate, reach back into the 15th century. 97ha (240 acre) of v'yds cover parts of most of the best sites in FORST, DEIDESHEIM and RUPPERTSBERG, etc. Vines are 81% Riesling, 17% Müller-Thurgau, etc. Annual prod. is 78,000 cases of the full range of top-quality Rheinpfalz wines, sold throughout the world. Address: Weinstrasse 16, 6705 Deidesheim.

Bukett

The "smell" (or literally bouquet) of a wine.

Bukettsorten

Collective noun covering vines that produce wine with a powerful bouquet (BUKETT), e.g. Scheurebe, Morio-Muskat. The attraction for the consumer of a strongly scented wine is often as a brief change from the more neutral Riesling or Silvaner. Wines with an overpronounced smell can quickly cloy, and their popularity in Germany is somewhat in decline.

Bullay M-S-R w. ★★

Typical Lower Mosel village near ZELL with a high proportion of Riesling on steep sites. Grosslage: Grafschaft.

Bundesweinprämierung

National wine competition run by the DEUTSCHE LANDWIRTSCHAFT GESELLSCHAFT (DLG), open to QbA and QmP estate bottlings that have passed the regional wine competitions successfully. In 1986 the Bundesweinprämierung was open to wines of the 1982, '83 and '84 vintages. 4,690 wines were entered, representing more than 1.4m. cases. 1,598 received a Grosser Preis (First Prize), 1,834 a Silberner Preis (Second Prize) and 838 a Bronzener Preis (Third Prize). The winning of an award may be shown on the bottle by means of a strip label running between the neck and body labels, or by a small circular coin-sized label.

Burg

Castle or fortress. EEC law allows the word Burg to be used as part of a wine name if the wine is made solely from grapes grown and vinified by the Burg's estate. In practice, Burg usually appears on a label as part of a community name, e.g. BURG LAYEN.

Burg Layen Nahe w. ★→★★

Small wine village near DORSHEIM, just s. of BINGEN,. Grosslage: SCHLOSSVAPELLE.

Burgberg Nahe w. ★★★

Small, steep Einzellage at DORSHEIM nr. BINGEN, producing well-balanced Rieslings. Grosslage: SCHLOSSKAPELLE. Grower: Niederhausen-Schlossböckelheim Staatl. Weinbaudomne.

Burgeff & Co. GmbH Rhg.

One of the oldest sparking-wine producing companies in Germany, founded in 1836, now owned by Seagram. Leading brands: Burgeff Grün and Schloss Hochheim. Address: 6203 Hochheim.

Bürgermeister

Mayor. In Rheinland-Pfalz the mayor of a community heads the committee that decides when the various stages of the harvest may start. Found in the titles of some estates, e.g. Weingut Bürgermeister Anton Balbach Erben.

Bürgerspital zum Heiligen Geist Franken

Great Würzburg estate, 4th largest in Germany, with 140ha (346 acre) planted with 25% Riesling, and Silvaner and Müller-Thurgau (20% each) plus other varieties incl. Spätburgunder produce an average 89,000 cases annually. The estate is a charitable institution dating from 1319, supporting an old people's home. There is a wine bar with places for 500 guests. Most of the wines are "FRÄNKISCH TROCKEN", very dry with less than 4 g/l residual sugar. Top-quality wine-making. Big wines, sold 95% to the wine trade and to private customers in Germany and 5% abroad. Address: Theaterstr. 19, 8700 Würzburg.

Burgunder

See Frühburgunder, Grauburgunder, Spätburgunder, Weissburgunder

Burgweg Franken w. ★★

Small Grosslage in s. Franken that incls. the v'yds of IPHOFEN.

Burgweg Nahe w. ★→★★

Grosslage of about 900ha (2,224 acre) incl. top-quality sites such as Schlossböckelheimer KUPFERGRUBE and the 2ha (5 acre) Traisener BASTEI. as well as some rather ordinary v'yds. The best sites are 100% Riesling but much Silvaner is also still found. The wine often has a strong flavour given to it by volcanic soil.

Burgweg Rhg. w. (r.) ★★

Grosslage of a little under 700ha (1,730 acre), split in two at the w. end of the Rheingau by the smaller STEIL Grosslage at ASSMANNS-HAUSEN. Wines sold under the name Burgweg are not the cheapest – no Rheingau wine is or should be. When made from Riesling they will be, in German terms, full-flavoured, and benefit from a year's bottle age or more, depending on the quality category (QbA, Kabinett, etc.)

Bürklin-Wolf, Weingut Dr Rhpf.

Great family estate, dating back in part to the 16th century. 110ha (272 acre) of top-quality sites at WACHENHEIM, FORST, DEIDESHEIM and RUP-PERTSBERG, 70% Riesling, 15% Müller-Thurgau, etc., plus some Spätburgunder. Annual production is approx. 75,000 cases. Maturation is in wood. 50% of the wines are dry or med-dry. Many trainee wine makers, from Germany and abroad, have studied on this estate, and its wines are found all over the world. Address: Weinstr. 65, 6706 Wachenheim.

Buscher, Weingut Jean Rhh.

Enterprising 14.5ha (36 acre) estate, now in its fourth generation. Holdings are all at BECHTHEIM, 17% Riesling, 14% Spätburgunder, 12% Kerner. White wines are typical of the grape variety and the reds deliberately have little tannin. 55% of the total production of 10,400 cases is dry or med-dry, and sales are 70% to the consumer. Address: Wormser Str. 4, 6521 Bechtheim.

Cabinet

See Kabinett

Capsule
A tight-fitting cap enclosing the mouth and part of the neck of a bottle, originally intended to protect the cork. The main job of a capsule today is to complete the "dressing" of a bottle but some estates, notably SCHLOSS JOHANNISBERG and SCHLOSS VOLLRADS, use different coloured capsules to denote different qualities of wine. See also LACK.

Carstens KG, Sektkellerei Rhpf.
Sparkling-wine manufacturers, est. in 1959 and wholly owned by HENKELL AND CO. of Wiesbaden. The brand "Carstens SC" is well known on the German market. Price (1987) about DM 5.79. Address. Maximilianstr. 18, 6730 Neustadt/Weinstrasse.

Case
Until the early 1960s German bottled wine was exported in wooden cases, each holding 12 bottles horizontally packed in straw. Today the most usual form of packing is the vertically loaded 6-bottle or 12-bottle carton, in which the contents should be stored neck downwards. In this book, the term "case" when used as a measure of quantity means 12 × 0.750ml bottles, or 9 litres.

Castell Franken w. (r.) ★★★
Village in the middle of the v'yds below the Steigerwald, producing excellent dry wine from Silvaner and Müller-Thurgau. Most of the holdings are owned by the CASTELL'SCHES DOMÄNENAMT.

Castell'sches Domänenamt, Fürstlich Franken
Great estate dating back to the 13th century, on the edge of the Steigerwald. The family of the owner, Fürst zu Castell-Castell, are bankers, farmers and foresters as well as vine growers. 58.2ha (144 acre) of v'yds: 33% Müller-Thurgau, 26% Silvaner, 8% Kerner, 7% Rieslaner – the last is a speciality. The wines can be described as earthy and spicy, with good acidity. Annual prod. is approx. 46,550 cases, sold in Germany and, increasingly, abroad. The estate is also senior partner in an ERZEUGERGEMEINSCHAFT, making wine from its members' 70ha (173 acre), greatly increasing the throughput of its own impressive cellar. Address: Schlossplatz 5, 8711 Castell.

Chaptalization
The addition of sugar to MUST or wine (see ANREICHERUNG). A practice developed by Jean Antoine Chaptal (1756-1852) in France.

Chardonnay
The famous white grape of Burgundy is being grown on a number of estates, officially on an experimental basis, and usually for the production of dry wines, or sometimes sekt.

Charmat-Verfahren
A technique for producing sparkling wine, developed in the 19th century by the French scientist Eugene Charmat. The secondary, sparkle-producing fermentation takes place in bulk instead of in bottle. Today more than 90% of German-made sparkling wine is tank fermented. (See also FLASCHENGÄRUNG.)

Charta
An association of Rheingau growers, founded in October 1984, with rules for the production of its wine, stricter than those of the 1971 Wine Law. It must be 100% Riesling, estate-bottled in a special, tall, embossed bottle, of enhanced must weight depending on the quality category, contain between 12 and 20 g/l residual sugar for all wines up to and incl. Spätlesen, and 35 to 45 g/l for Auslesen, have a total acid content between 7 and 10 g/l, and be accepted by the association's tasting panel, etc.

Christmann, Weingut Arnold Rhpf.
8ha (20 acre) estate with holdings at GIMMELDINGEN AN DER WEINSTRASSE, planted 54% in Riesling. Although the majority of the wines are full-bodied, dry or med-dry the 1983 Riesling Trockenbeerenauslese is claimed to have had the heaviest Riesling must weight ever recorded (243 degrees Oechsle). Annual production: 6,700 cases sold mainly to the consumer. Address: Peter Koch Str. 43, Gimmeldingen, 6730 Neustadt.

Christoffel Jr, Jos. M-S-R
Small family estate that makes award-winning wines from top-quality sites at Erden (TREPPCHEN), Ürzig (WÜRZGARTEN), Wehlen (SONNENUHR) and Graach (DOMPROBST, HIMMELREICH). 100% Riesling. Christoffels have been vine-growing for more than 300 years. Total annual production is 3,300 cases, sold in Germany and abroad. Address: Moselufer 1-3, 5564 Ürzig/Mosel.

Christus in der Kelter
Christ in the wine press. The representation of Christ in the wine press has been given many different symbolic and allegoric meanings in German since the 12th century, apart from the obvious eucharistic connection. There is a fine example in the Heiligkreuzkapelle above the v'yds of EDIGER-ELLER.

Clevner
See Frühburgunder, Traminer

Coblenz
See Koblenz

Cochem M-S-R Pop. 6,000 w. ★★
Strikingly pretty town and tourist centre on the Mosel, in the Bereich ZELL, overlooked by a dramatically situated castle. Stylish, racy Rieslings. Grosslagen: GOLDBÄUMCHEN and Rosenhang.

Constance
See Bodensee

Cooperative cellar
See Winzergenossenschaft

Crusius, Weingut Hans & Peter Nahe
Family-run estate with 11.5ha (28 acre) of prime sites incl. Traiser BASTEI and ROTENFELS, Norheimer Klosterberg, Schlossböckelheimer FELSENBERG. 72% Riesling, 13% Müller-Thurgau, 8%

Weissburgunder, etc. Stylish wines, traditionally matured in cask, made under personal family supervision to a high standard. 35% are dry or med-dry. Peter Crusius is a recognized expert on the relationship of quantity to quality in vine-growing. Production is 8,700 cases, sold in Germany and abroad. Address: Hauptstr. 2, 6551 Traisen.

Cuvée
EEC law defines a cuvée as the MUST or wine, or a blend of different musts or wines, destined to be converted into sparkling wine. The making of a cuvée requires organized tasting ability of a very high order. It is exacting work from which the palate can gain little pleasure. The satisfaction lies in the consistency of the end result.

Dachsberg Rhg. w. ★★
52ha (128 acre) Einzellage above the v'yds of SCHLOSS VOLLRADS, producing light wines, with fine acidity. Grosslage: ERNTEBRINGER. Growers: Allendorf, Basting-Gimbel, von Brentano, Engelmann, Mumm'sches Weingut, Schumann-Nägler.

Dahlem Erben, K.G., Weingutsverwaltung Sanitätsrat Dr. Rhh.
Estate with origins going back to 1702 and holdings in 25.3ha (63 acre) at OPPENHEIM (incl. SACKTRÄGER), DIENHEIM and GUNTERSBLUM. 25% Riesling, 20% Silvaner, 20% Müller-Thurgau. Many

award winning wines. Address: Rathofstrasse 21–25, 6504 Oppenheim.

Daubhaus Rhg. w. ★★

Grosslage covering more than 300ha (741 acre) at the e. end of the Rheingau on the R. Main, often clearly visible when flying into Frankfurt Airport. Its best-known wine-producing village is HOCHHEIM. A Rheingau Grosslage wine will be a paler reflection of the best wines produced from individual sites within the Grosslage. Nevertheless, the quality of wine from the Daubhaus is high, although it will be more earthy than wine from the central part of the region.

Dautenpflänzer Nahe w. ★★★

6ha (15 acre) Einzellage of the Lower Nahe at Münster-Sarmsheim. The wines are full-bodied, meaty and mainly Riesling. Grosslage: SCHLOSSKAPELLE. Grower: Niederhausen-Schlossböckelheim Staatl. Weinbaudomäne.

Deacidification

A relatively high acid content is expected and appreciated in German wine. However, in some years when the grapes are not fully ripe the acidity is too high and has to be lowered artificially. When this happens the natural reduction in acidity that occurs in wine-making is complemented by a chemical deacidification with calcium carbonate, or in years of feeble sunshine when the malic acid is particularly high with a double-salt called Acidex. The last nationwide poor vintage was 1972, and even in this year many enjoyable wines were produced with the aid of Acidex. In the state of RHEINLAND-PFALZ and in the Rheingau, tartaric acid may be added to Riesling and Elbling to reduce acidity by what is known as the Malitex process.

Deckrotwein

To darken the colour of red DEUTSCHER TAFELWEIN and QbA an addition of red wine from elsewhere in the EEC is permitted up to 5% until 1989. Attempts are being made to develop new vine varieties in Germany that will produce the necessary colour to darken such traditional wines as Trollinger and Portugieser. (See also FÄRBERTRAUBEN.)

Deidesheim Rhpf. w. ★★→★★★★

Attractive small town, recognized for centuries both in Germany and abroad as a source of distinguished wine and the home of a number of fine estates. A high proportion of Riesling in top-quality sites: GRAINHÜBEL, LEINHÖHLE, HERRGOTTSACKER, KIESELBERG, LANGENMORGEN. Two Grosslagen: MARIENGARTEN and SCHNEPFENFLUG AN DER WEINSTRASSE.

Deidesheim eG, Winzerverein Rhpf.

Cooperative with 473 members in the well-known wine villages DEIDESHEIM, FORST, RUPPERTSBERG, WACHENHEIM, etc., with 183.5ha (453 acre). Vines are 68% Riesling, 17% Müller-Thurgau. Approx. annual prod. is 218,800 cases. The wines are sold in Germany and abroad. Address: Prinz-Rupprecht-Str. 8, 6705 Deidesheim/Weinstrasse.

Deinhard & Co. KGaA

Important firm of wine merchants and exporters, founded in the 18th century. Deinhard was one of the earliest producers of sparkling wine in Germany, and at the end of the 19th century acquired its first v'yds. Today the holdings in OESTRICH, DEIDESHEIM and BERNKASTEL make it one of the largest privately owned producers of fine estate-bottled wines (see Wegeler-Deinhard). Best-known brands are the sparkling wines Lila Imperial, and Deinhard Cabinet and the Mosel still wine, Green Label. Address: Deinhard Platz 3, 5400 Koblenz.

Deinhard, Weingut Dr Rhpf.

Estate dating from the mid-18th century, separate from but occupying the same premises as the Gutsverwaltung DEINHARD DEIDESHEIM. 21.9ha (54 acre) in DEIDESHEIM (LEINHÖHLE, GRAINHÜBEL, KIESELBERG, etc.), FORST, RUPPERTSBERG (REITERPFAD, etc.). Vines are 71% Riesling, with small amounts of Müller-Thurgau, Scheurebe, Kerner, Ehrenfelser and others. The wines reflect clearly the variations brought about by site, soil and vine variety and are predominantly dry or med-dry. 18,750 cases, sold mainly in Germany. Address: Weinstrasse 10, 6705 Deidesheim.

Deinhard Bernkastel, Gutsverwaltung
See Wegeler-Deinhard, Gutsverwaltung.

Deinhard Deidesheim, Gutsverwaltung
See Wegeler-Deinhard, Gutsverwaltung.

Dellchen Nahe w. ★★★
Steep, 7.3ha (18 acre) Einzellage at NORHEIM that can produce absolutely top-quality Riesling wines of character with an attractive flavour that comes from the soil. Grosslage: BURGWEG. Growers: August Anheuser, Paul Anheuser, Bad Kreuznach Staatsweingut.

Dernau Ahr w. (r.) ★→★★
Small village of half-timbered houses, making Riesling, Müller-Thurgau and light Spätburgunder from steep v'yds. Grosslage: Klosterberg.

Deutelsberg Rhg. w. ★★
Grosslage of some 500ha (1,236 acre) in the neighbourhood of HATTENHEIM, incl. Mariannenau Island (see RHEINHELL) and the famous v'yds of ERBACH. The name Deutelsberg is normally used for the lesser wines, but Rieslings from competent producers will still be well-balanced, stylish, good-quality wines.

Deutsche Landwirtschaft Gesellschaft (DLG)
Society founded in 1885, along the lines of the Royal Agricultural Society of Great Britain, to promote good farming practices. Today the society awards three types of Deutsches Weinsiegel (wine seal): a yellow seal for dry wines, a green for med-dry, and a red for others that meet with its approval. (The standards set by the DLG tasting panels are higher than those of the AMTLICHE PRÜFUNG authorities.) The DLG also holds an annual national wine competition, open to quality (QbA and QmP) wines that have obtained their A.P. number and have succeeded in an official regional competition. DLG awards are familiar to German consumers and valued by many bottlers. See BUNDESWEINPRÄMIERUNG.

Deutscher Tafelwein (DTW)
German table wine. Quality category of German wine, below QbA, with an upper section called LANDWEIN. The v'yd area from which a DTW may originate is exactly the same as that which can produce quality wine. There are no areas that can produce table wine only. Whereas a high proportion of French and Italian wine is classified as "table wine", only approx. 5% of the total German wine harvest falls into this category. A DTW does not undergo an examination by the A.P. authorities and therefore does not show an A.P. number on the label. It must be made 100% from German-grown grapes.

Deutsche Weinstrasse
See Weinstrasse

Deutscher Sekt
Quality sparkling wine made from wine produced from grapes grown in Germany.

Deutsches Weinsiegel
See Deutsche Landwirtschaft Gesellschaft (DLG)

Deutsches Weintor eG, Gebiets-Winzergenossenschaft Rhpf.
Huge, expanding cooperative cellar nr. the French border, with some 1,300 members delivering grapes from a wide area of the Bereich SÜDLICHE WEINSTRASSE. Storage capacity is 38m. litres and the cellar is well equipped to produce vast quantities of well-made, agreeable, inexpensive wines from 50 different grape varieties, of which 35% is exported. Good dry wines. Address: 6741 Ilbesheim.

Deutz & Geldermann Sektkellerei, Breisach GmbH Baden
Founded in 1838 as producers of Champagne, started sparkling-wine production in Alsace in 1904 and in BREISACH in 1925. The technique used is FLASCHENGÄRUNG. Annual sekt sales are 208,000 cases (made from Pinot grapes). Address: Muggens-Turm-Str. 26, 7814 Breisach.

Dexheim Rhh. w. ★
Village which probably benefits from having one large Einzellage called "Doktor", a name (but not the spelling) it shares with the

famous DOCTOR at Bernkastel on the Mosel. Grosslage: GUTES DOMTAL.

Dhron M-S-R w. ★★★

Village linked with NEUMAGEN to form one community of some 2,500 inhabitants nr. PIESPORT, with whom it shares some of its sites. The steep v'yds are planted mainly with Riesling, producing full-flavoured, stylish wines. Grosslage: MICHELSBERG.

Diabetikerwein

Diabetes is such a common complaint in Germany that it has proved profitable to produce diabetic wines on a wide scale. They should be drunk by genuine diabetics, only after medical approval is given. German diabetic wine is subject to a number of restrictions and may contain a maximum of 4 g/l residual sugar, 40 mg/l free sulphur dioxide and 12% alcohol. Since 1970 the DLG has awarded a yellow seal to diabetic wines that meet its standards.

Diedesfeld Rhpf. w. r. ★★

Village just s. of Neustadt, with numerous, half-timbered vine growers' houses. Müller-Thurgau and Portugieser produce the good quality wines expected of a Mittelhaardt village, a small amount of Riesling does even better. Grosslagen: Rebstöckel, Pfaffengrund.

Diefenhardt Weingut Rhg.

Estate dating from 1917, but with a 300-year-old cask cellar. 11.7ha (29 acre) in ELTVILLE, MARTINSTHAL and RAUENTHAL, 85% Riesling, 10% Spätburgunder, all on sloping ground. Typical, firm Rheingauer wine. 60% dry/med-dry. Annual production is 8,300 cases, sold mainly in Germany but also abroad. Address: Hauptstr. 9-11, 6228 Eltville.

Diel, Schlossgut Nahe

Estate owned by the Diel family since 1802 with 9.7ha (24 acre) in BURG LAYEN and DORSHEIM. 65% Riesling. As a policy for the future all wines up to and incl. Auslesen will be dry. No Kabinett wines will be made as they are considered too light in weight. The estate therefore has its own view of wine-making and is particularly well represented in top German restaurants. Address: 6531 Auf Burg Layen.

Dienheim Rhh. w. ★★→★★★

RHEINTERRASSE village, possibly a little overshadowed by its neighbour, OPPENHEIM, producing good, full Riesling and Silvaner wines grapy characteristics, powerfully developed. Grosslagen: GÜLDENMORGEN, KRÖTENBRUNNEN.

Dirmstein Rhpf. w. (r.) ★

Attractive old town with approx. 250ha (618 acre) of v'yds, planted some 50% in Silvaner and Riesling. Best known in connection with the name of the local Grosslage: SCHWARZERDE.

DLG

See Deutsche Landwirtschaft Gesellschaft

Doctor M-S-R w. ★★★★

Small but outstanding Einzellage above BERNKASTEL. Site, soil and Riesling vine complement each other perfectly. The MUST weights are usually the heaviest in Bernkastel; the wine is positive, slaty, needing time to show its true quality. One of the best-known Einzellagen in Germany. Grosslage: BADSTUBE. Growers: Lauerburg, Thanisch, Wegeler-Deinhard.

Doktor Rhh. w. ★

Einzellage at DEXHEIM in the Grosslage GUTES DOMTAL.

Domäne

Domain. Name given to estates (Weingüter) owned by old noble families (e.g. Domänenweingut Schloss Schönborn) or by the Federal States (e.g. Staatliche Weinbaudomäne Niederhausen-Schlossböckelheim). Many of the state-owned Domäne have a training and experimental role as well as operating commercially as wine makers. The word "Domäne" may only appear on a label if the wine was made by the domain exclusively from grapes grown on its own estate..

Domänenamt

Estate office. Found in the title of Fürstlich Castell'sches Domänenamt.

Domblick Rhh. w. ★

Grosslage of more than 800ha (1,977 acre) in s. Rheinhessen, bordering on the Rheinpfalz. V'yds vary from level to steep and face all points of the compass except e. The wines can have a rather strong flavour that comes from the mainly clay soil. On a clear day, from the upper parts of the area, one has a view (Blick) of the cathedral (Dom) of Worms in the distance – hence Domblick.

Domdechaney Rhg. w. ★★★

Einzellage at HOCHHEIM on the R. Main producing full-bodied Riesling wines with a big flavour. Grosslage: DAUBHAUS. Growers: Aschrott'sche Erben, Frankfurt am Main Stadt Weingut, Schloss Schönborn, Staatsweingut, Werner'sches Weingut.

Domherr Rhh. w. ★

Grosslage in central Rheinhessen covering more than 1,700ha (4,201 acre). The terrain is mostly sloping or steep, producing good-quality but usually not the finest wine, displaying the traditional Rheinhessen characteristics: soft, agreeable, pleasant fruity flavour. The cathedral (Dom) at nearby MAINZ used to own much land in the area, hence the origin of the name Domherr (Canon of the Cathedral).

Domprobst M-S-R w. ★★★

Distinguished Einzellage at GRAACH, 100% steep and exclusively Riesling. The wine is usually crisper than that from the neighbouring Graacher HIMMELREICH and less full-bodied, sometimes spelt "Dompropst". Grosslage: MÜNZLAY. Growers: Christoffel, Friedrich-Wilhelm-Gymnasium, Kees-Kieren, Licht-Bergweiler, Pauly, Pauly-Bergweiler, J. J. Prüm, Richter, Schwab, S. A. Prüm, Schorlemer, Selbach-Oster, Studert-Prüm, Wegeler-Deinhard, Weins-Prüm, Vereinigte Hospitien.

Domtal Rhh.

Once a GATTUNGSLAGENAME, discarded in 1971. See also GUTES DOMTAL.

Doosberg Rhg. w. ★★★

Large Einzellage of 153ha (378 acre) on mainly level land at OESTRICH that makes top-quality, classic Riesling wines. Grosslage: GOTTESTHAL. Growers: Altenkirch, Eser, Ress, Schloss Schönborn, Vereinigte Weingutsbesitzer Hallgarten, Wegeler-Deinhard.

Dörflinger, Weingut Hermann Baden

12ha (30 acre) estate traditionally producing fully fermented dry wines from the Markgräflerland favourite Gutedel (50%), Spätburgunder (14%), Müller-Thurgau (12%), etc. Annual sales of some 8,300 cases are exclusively in Germany. Address: Mühlenstr. 7, 7840 Müllheim.

Dornfelder

Red grape variety, HELFENSTEINER (Frühburgunder × Trollinger) × HEROLDREBE (Portugieser × Limberger); a new crossing from the Württemberg state viticultural institute at Weinsberg. It ripens earlier than Trollinger and produces a large yield per vine of deep-coloured wine. From an experimental 12ha (27 acre) in 1976, Dornfelder now covers 620ha (1,532 acre), 79% in the Rheinpfalz and Rheinhessen.

Dorsheim Nahe w. ★★→★★★

One of the best wine-producing villages of the Lower Nahe, nr. BINGEN in the Bereich KREUZNACH. Outstanding meaty Rieslings from steep sites, usually cheaper than the top-quality wines of the Bereich SCHLOSS BÖCKELHEIM further south. Grosslage: SCHLOSS-KAPELLE.

Drathen & Co. KB., Ewald Theod. M-S-R

Small estate of 7ha (17 acre). Also internationally known as wine merchants exporting considerable quantities of inexpensive German wine and EEC table wines. Founded in 1860, the estate holdings are at NEEF, ALF and BULLAY, producing approx. 6,300 cases annually for sale in Germany and abroad. Address: 5584 Alf.

Dreikönigswein

Three Kings Wine. A description that until 1971 could be given to EISWEIN gathered on 6 January following the main October/

November harvest. The word Dreikönigswein may no longer appear on the bottle label, although reference to it may be made in advertising material. In practice, it is a rather charming description that now belongs to the past.

Dry

See Trocken

DTW

See Deutscher Tafelwein

Duftig

Finely scented.

Duhr Nachf., Weingut Franz M-S-R

Estate owned by Hermann Freiherr v. SCHORLEMER GmbH.

Dünweg, Weingut Otto M-S-R

Family-owned, 6.5ha (16 acre) estate established in 1837, in what claims to be Germany's oldest wine producing village. Holdings, 99.5% Riesling, are at NEUMAGEN, DHRON, TRITTENHEIM (APOTHEKE), and PIESPORT incl. GOLDTRÖPFCHEN, TREPPCHEN, and sole ownership of Kreuzwingert, probably the smallest Einzellage in Germany (0.3ha/0.74 acre). Wines are matured in FUDER and made to last. Annual production: 5,000 cases. Address: Moselstr. 5–7, 5559 Neumagen-Dhron.

Durbach Baden w. ★★→★★★

Attractive village nr. Offenburg, overlooked by steep v'yds. Claims the highest proportion of Traminer (Clevner) of any wine village in Germany and well known for its Riesling (Klingelberger). Produces powerful QbA incl. very successful Halbtrocken (med-dry) wines. Grosslage: Fürsteneck.

Durchgegoren

Fermented through. A term used to describe wines in which no fermentable sugar remains. Today many German wines up to and sometimes incl. Auslesen are stored in bulk "durchgegoren", thus avoiding the risk of further fermentation and making it possible to keep the sulphur dioxide content low. Such wines will usually be sweetened with SÜSSRESERVE shortly before bottling.

Eberle, Helmut Rhpf.

Estate of 7.5ha (19 acre) in n. Rheinpfalz, at Laumersheim and Gerolsheim, with a wide range of red and white vine varieties. The wines are stored exclusively in vat and in many awards. Sales are in Germany only. Address: Dirmsteinerstr. 15, 6711 Laumersheim.

Eckig

Angular. Describes an unbalanced wine with over-accentuated constituents, particularly acidity.

Edelfäule

"Noble rot": a fungus that in moist and mild conditions sometimes attacks grapes. If the grapes are already ripe the result is beneficial. The grapes shrivel and the water, sugar and acid content is reduced, but the loss of acids is proportionately greater than that of sugar. The result is highly concentrated juice.

Wine made from such grapes will normally have an enhanced MUST weight. In white wine the colour will be deeper and more golden than usual; in red wine there is a browning and loss of colour. The bouquet of the grape variety is to a greater or lesser extent replaced by an aroma reminiscent of honey. The impression of sweetness of flavour is increased, the wine tastes smoother and sometimes also a little honeyed. A Riesling BEERENAUSLESE will nearly always be made from Edelfäule grapes. 1953, '67 and '75 were years in which a considerable amount of Edelfäule occurred. In hot, dry years such as 1959 the high general level of ripeness partly compensates for a limited amount of Edelfäule.

Edelsüss

Noble sweetness. Term for the sweetness left in a wine of high quality as a result of incomplete fermentation, as is the case with Auslesen, Beerenauslesen or Trockenbeerenauslesen. It is often the result of grapes being attacked by EDELFÄULE ("noble rot") and will contain enhanced amounts of fructose and glycerin. Auslesen to which SÜSSRESERVE has been added should not be described as Edelsüss.

Edenkoben Rhpf. Pop. 5,500 w. ★→★★

Small but locally important wine town in the Bereich SÜDLICHE WEINSTRASSE. More than 500ha (1,236 acre) of v'yds, sprinkled with fig and almond trees, are planted with a wide range of varieties incl. Riesling, Müller-Thurgau and Silvaner. Good, sound, inexpensive wines. Interesting WEINLEHRPFAD. Grosslage: Ludwigshöhe.

Ediger-Eller M-S-R w. ★★

Two ancient and attractive villages linked in the Bereich ZELL, making elegant, fruity wines. Grosslagen: Rosenhang and Grafschaft.

eG

Eingetragene Genossenschaft. Registered Cooperative Society, eg. Winzergenossenschaft Wachtenburg-Luginsland eG.

Ehrenfelser

White grape variety, a crossing of Riesling × Silvaner, from the viticultural institute at Geisenheim. Dating from 1929, it is today planted in 554ha (1,369 acre). Recommended for good sites that do not quite reach the standards required by Riesling. The yield is greater, the MUST weight 5-10° Oechsle heavier than that of Riesling and the acidity slightly lower. The grapes can be harvested late in the season to produce SPÄTLESE and even higher qualities of elegant, fruity wine that will improve in bottle but develop more quickly than Riesling.

Ehrentrudis Spätburgunder Weissherbst

A WEISSHERBST QbA or QmP produced in the Bereich KAISERSTUHL-TUNIBERG in s. Baden, made exclusively from Spätburgunder.

Eigeneswachstum

Own growth. Term used before 1971 to describe wines to which no sugar had been added and which were bottled by the grower. Synonyms were Eigenbau, Eigengewächs and Originalabfüllung.

Eitelsbach M-S-R w. ★★★

Small village, overlooked by its v'yds, nr. the point where the little R. Ruwer decants into the Mosel. Forms part of the city of TRIER. Exceptionally racy and stylish wines in good years, great wines in the best years, mainly Riesling. Grosslage: RÖMERLAY.

Einzellage

An individual site, the smallest geographical unit in which vines are planted. Only quality (QbA and QmP) wines may carry an Einzellage name, which must always be accompanied by that of a village or community.

Eisheiligen

Ice Saints. The commemoration days of the "Ice Saints" fall between 11-14 May. The saints incl. St Pancras, the patron saint of children, and St Boniface, an English missionary who worked in Germany and founded the Abbey of Fulda that later (in 1775) was said to have been connected with the discovery in the Rheingau of the benefits of late-harvesting grapes. After 15 May, known as the Kalte Sophie, there is virtually no further risk of frost in the v'yds.

Eiswein

Ice Wine. Quality category for wines made from grapes naturally frozen at the time of pressing. The water in the grapes remains in the press in the form of ice crystals, concentrating the grape acids and sugar wonderfully. The MUST weight, measured in degrees Oechsle, has to reach BEERENAUSLESE level. As the necessary cold weather (approx. −8°C) seldom occurs before the third week in November, the risk of failure is serious (in the 1985 vintage, some estates did not gather the Eiswein crop until 8th February 1986!). Although Eiswein must be made from ripe grapes, it can be produced in less good years when Beeren- and Trockenbeerenauslesen are out of the question, hence its commercial interest for the grower. An Eiswein lacks the honeyed tones of a Beerenauslese, but its remarkable acidity and great residual sweetness gives it a "zip" and nervosity quite different to the more solid flavour of normally harvested top-quality sweet wines.

Elbling

One of the oldest white grape varieties growing in Germany, now restricted almost entirely to the M-S-R where it occupies 1,178ha

(2,911 acre). Until World War II it was still found in Franken and as a mixed plantation with other vine varieties on the Rhein. On the Mosel above TRIER it produces a high yield (sometimes in excess of 200 hl/ha) of acidic wine, light in body and with a neutral flavour, often converted into sparkling wine.

Elegant

A rather subjective wine description which must be the result of personal judgement rather than of chemical analysis. It may usually be correctly applied to a wine in which the bouquet and flavour are perfectly balanced and no one characteristic is too predominant. Normally, light wines with good acidity around which the other constituents are mustered achieve elegance more easily than heavy, alcoholic wines. In German wine, it is found particularly in Rieslings from the M-S-R, Nahe and Rheingau, esp. those of KABINETT quality. Bigger SPÄTLESE wines can also have tremendous style but their power and weight seem to make the description elegant less appropriate.

Ellenz-Poltersdorf M-S-R w. ★→★★

Two villages, linked by a ferry across the Mosel, next to the ancient hamlet of BEILSTEIN. High percentage of Riesling in most of the v'yds, some Müller-Thurgau, and unusually, a little Elbling. Grosslagen: GOLDBÄUMCHEN and Rosenhang.

Eltville Rhg. Pop. 15,800 w. ★★★

Important wine town, home of the Staatsweingut, Eltville (see next entry) and the Sekt producers Matheus MÜLLER. Good-quality Rieslings, similarly priced to those from other leading Rheingau communities. Grosslagen: HEILIGENSTOCK and STEINMÄCHER.

Eltville, Verwaltung der Staatsweingüter Rhg.

Collection of fine, state-owned holdings covering 160ha (395 acre) in the Rheingau and 36ha (89 acre) in the Hessische Bergstrasse (see Bergstrasse, Staatsweingut). V'yds in many famous sites incl. Rüdesheimer BERG ROSENECK, BERG ROTTLAND, BERG SCHLOSSBERG; Erbacher MARCOBRUNN; Rauenthaler BAIKEN; Hochheimer DOMDECHANEY and KIRCHENSTÜCK. Sole owners of the STEINBERG v'yd. 85% Riesling, 10% Spätburgunder. The variety of holdings indicates a wide range of styles but the goal is to produce wines with backbone, elegance and body. The estate is a founder member of CHARTA, and a great producer of Eiswein. Experiments are being made in ecological vine growing and wine-making. Total annual prod. is 125,000 cases. Address: Schwalbacherstr. 56-62, 6228 Eltville.

Emrich-Schönleber, Weingut Nahe

8.5ha (21 acre) estate. 60% Riesling, 13% Müller-Thurgau, 8% Kerner and 8% Bacchus, achieving much success at the national (DLG) competitions. Sales, from a list incl. a 1978 Trockenbeerenauslese-Eiswein, are mainly to the consumer. Annual prod: 7,100 cases. Address: Naheweinstr. 10, 6557 Monzingen.

Engelmann, Weingut Karl Fr. Rhg.

6.5ha (16 acre) family-owned estate dating from 1742 with v'yds in HALLGARTEN, HATTENHEIM, OESTRICH and WINKEL. 90% Riesling. The wines are spicy, fruity, elegant, matured in wood in the old vaulted cellar. 6,800 cases a year, ·sold in Germany and abroad. Address: Hallgartener Platz 2, 6227 Hallgarten.

"Engländer"

See Vereinigte Weingutsbesitzer Hallgarten eG

Enkirch M-S-R w. ★★

Village of half-timbered houses and old cellars and, unusually, two parish churches (Protestant and Roman Catholic). The reputation of Enkircher Riesling stands high in Germany but it is not often found abroad. Grosslage: SCHWARZLAY.

Enrichment

See Anreicherung

Erbach Rhg. w. ★★★→★★★★

Small village, home of the SCHLOSS REINHARTSHAUSEN estate, with its gaily painted hotel, and the Einzellage MARCOBRUNN, whose Riesling is among the most full-bodied – and expensive – in the region. Grosslage: DEUTELSBERG.

Erben
> Successors. Placed after the name of a company and forming part of the title, e.g. Weingut Bürgermeister Carl Koch Erben. It is similar to the English "& Sons".

Erden M-S-R w. ★★→★★★★
> Small MITTELMOSEL village, whose PRÄLAT Einzellage is considered one of the best on the river. A high standard of Riesling wine is maintained on other sites. Grosslage: SCHWARZLAY.

Erdig
> Earthy. See BODENGESCHMACK.

Ernte
> See Harvest

Erntebringer Rhg. w. ★★
> Most widely known Grosslage in the Rheingau, covering more than 300ha (741 acre) in the neighbourhood of JOHANNISBERG, GEISENHEIM and WINKEL. Wines sold as Erntebringer are often slightly lighter in flavour than the most positive wines from individual sites. They have charm and are easy to enjoy, but possibly lack the distinction of the finest Rheingaus.

Erzeugerabfüllung
> Estate or producer bottled. A term that appears on labels and in wine lists to indicate that a wine was made and bottled by the grower of the grapes. Cooperative cellars and ERZEUGERGEMEINSCHAFTEN that buy their grapes from their members but have no direct control over the viticulture are also legally entitled to sell their wine as estate bottled. This they do, even for the cheapest QbA, under the names of some of the biggest Bereiche and Grosslagen in Germany. A top-quality producer will usually sell only his QmP and better QbA with the description Erzeugerabfüllung.

Erzeugergemeinschaft
> Producers' Association. The formation of such associations became possible for farmers and vine growers when the German Market Structure Law came into force in 1969. As far as viticulture is concerned, they are associations of vine growers who have combined to link their production to the needs of the market. A further aim is to act as marketing groups capable of doing business with large buying organizations on equal terms. Even an estate as famous as the Fürstlich Castell'sches Domänenamt in Franken heads a local Erzeugergemeinschaft. More are constantly being formed, and the names of Erzeugergemeinschaften are beginning to appear on wine labels as estate bottlers.

Escherndorf Franken w. ★★→★★★
> Charming rustic village lying at the foot of its steep, modernized v'yds, planted mainly with Silvaner and Müller-Thurgau. Powerful wines with lasting flavour. Grosslage: Kirchberg.

Eser, Weingut August Rhg.
> Family-owned estate with 4.5ha (11 acre) in OESTRICH, HATTENHEIM, WINKEL, etc. Vines are 95% Riesling, 5% Ehrenfelser. 60% are dry or med-dry. Each QmP is sold with an analysis and a detailed history. No exports. Address: Friedensplatz 19, 6227 Oestrich-Winkel.

Espenscheid, Weingut
> See Frankensteiner Hof

Essigsäure
> Acetic acid. Acceptable at a level of 0.2 to 0.3 g/l in young white wine, and 0.3 to 0.5 g/l in red wine, depending on the method of vinification. An excessive amount of acetic acid, with its sharp taste, is very rare in German wine.

Estate bottled
> See Erzeugerabfüllung, Erzeugergemeinschaft and Winzergenossenschaft

Etikett
> Label. The first German wine labels were developed at the end of the 18th century. Since then they have become a legal necessity as well as an important aid to the marketing of wine.

Ewig Leben Franken w. ★★
> Grosslage at RANDERSACKER, nr. WÜRZBURG, covering four sites incl. TEUFELSKELLER. Mainly Silvaner and Müller-Thurgau.

Extract

Term used to describe the non-volatile substances in wine, incl. sugar, glycerin, acids, minerals and tannin. A wine with low extract will usually be described as hollow and/or short, but a wine high in extract will be full and its flavour will last in the mouth. In theory it might seem that to obtain a scientific, objective judgment of a wine it would only be necessary to determine the extract content. In practice this is not so, and there are many exceptions to the rule that top-quality wines contain more extract than those of lesser quality.

Faberrebe

White grape variety, a crossing of Weissburgunder × Müller-Thurgau from the viticultural institute at ALZEY in the Rhein-hessen, created by Dr Georg Scheu (best known for the Scheu-rebe). It produces a higher MUST weight than Müller-Thurgau with more acidity. Although the grapes ripen very early they can be left on the vine to produce stylish SPÄTLESE wine, before the Silvaner harvest has started. 2,280ha (5,634 acre), 76% in the Rheinhessen, with smaller plantings in the Nahe and Rheinpfalz.

Faber Sektkellerei KG

Founded in 1950, Faber produces approx. 47m. bottles of sparkling wine per year. The best-known brand, Faber Krönung, at about DM 4, is one of the cheapest sparkling wines on the German market. Annual sales 4.1m. cases, 99% in Germany. Address: Niederkircherstr. 27, 5500 Trier.

Falkenstein M-S-R w. ★★→★★★

Part of the Saar town of Konz. In the 18ha (44 acre) Hofberg Ein-zellage, the Friedrich-Wilhelm-Gymnasium makes very attractive, spritzig, relatively inexpensive wine. Grosslage: SCHARZBERG.

Färbertrauben

Literally, colouring grapes: grapes for improving the colour of red wine. As dark wine from outside the EEC may no longer be blended with red German wine (see DECKROTWEIN), interest is being shown in Färbertrauben in which the juice as well as the skin of the grapes is coloured. The MUST from these grapes can be made into SÜSSRESERVE to help both darken and sweeten otherwise pale, rosé-like "red" wine to the German taste. The most promising of such new vines is probably the Geisenheim-bred, early-ripening Dunkelfelder, planted in 59ha (146 acre), mainly in the Rheinpfalz and Rheinhessen.

Fass

Wooden cask. In Germany, in many large cellars, wooden storage casks have been replaced by vats of stainless steel or other man-made materials. These are more easily maintained and function rather like large bottles, keeping the wine fresh and free from oxidation. Traditionally, Rhein wine used to be sold in Halbstücke (casks) of approx. 610 litres and Mosel wine in the slightly smaller but longer Halbfuder. Today bulk wine is transported in large con-tainers, similar to those used for milk. Sales of Fassweine are de-clining but remain considerable within Germany. Of the 29,001 growers who make wine, 76% sell in Fass to the wine trade, which relies on such producers for their commercial blends. Few wines sold in this way, however, have ever known the feel of wood, and the term "Fasswein Geschäft" (cask trade) is, strictly speaking, obsolete. See also BARRIQUE.

Fassgeschmack

Cask taste, of which there are two entirely different sorts: the flavour that wine can pick up from tannin in the wood of a new cask (much sought-after in Bordeaux but until recently regarded as detrimental in German wine), and the dirty flavour that can appear in wine that has been stored in a poorly maintained cask where mould has developed. A wine from the latter sort of cask can easily be incorrectly thought to be "corked".

Fasswein, Fasswein Geschäft

See Fass

Federweisser

Partially fermented, still very sweet, cloudy young wine, served in wine bars during the harvest and in large helpings to the grape gatherers. It should be treated with caution as its pleasant sweetness and bubbly nature conceal volatile acids, esters, aldehydes and nasty things from the v'yd that can lead to interrupted sleep, heart problems, diarrhoea and skin complaints – according to the medical profession.

Feine, Feinste

Comparative terms meaning fine and finest, used before 1971 to describe superior qualities of SPÄTLESE, AUSLESE and BEERENAUSLESE wines, e.g. feinste Spätlese.

Felsenberg Nahe w. ★★★

Mainly steep Einzellage at SCHLOSSBÖCKELHEIM in the Nahe valley. Its Rieslings are attractive, a little earthy, and can be of top quality in a good year. Grosslage: BURGWEG. Growers: Paul Anheuser, Crusius, Niederhausen-Schlossböckelheim Staatl. Weinbaudomäne, Plettenberg.

Feuerberg Rhpf. w. (r.) ★★

Grosslage of just under 1,000ha (2,471 acre) nr. the town of BAD DÜRKHEIM. Its best-known v'yd is the Kallstadter ANNABERG, but the whole district has a high reputation for its white wine. Red wine is also produced from Portugieser and much is sold under the Grosslage name.

Feurig

Firey. Describes a red wine, rich in alcohol,that is thought to warm the blood rapidly, a notion helped by its sanguine colour. Might apply to a red wine from Baden.

Filzen-Hamm M-S-R- w. ★★→★★★

First wine village travelling up the Saar. Its sloping Riesling v'yds produce racy, spritzig wines. Grosslage: SCHARZBERG.

Findling

Mutation of Müller-Thurgau grown in 47ha (116 acre) mainly in the Mosel-Saar-Ruwer, producing a lower yield and heavier must weight than the source vine.

Findling Rhh. w. ★★★

Top-quality Einzellage at NIERSTEIN producing a fine range of wines with considerable elegance. Grosslage: SPIEGELBERG. Growers: Baumann, Gessert, Guntrum, Heyl zu Herrnsheim, Kurfürstenhof, Georg Schneider, Schuch, Sittmann, Strub, Wehrheim.

Finkenauer, Weingut Carl Nahe

Family-owned estate dating from 1828 with 33ha (82 acre), mainly in BAD KREUZNACH (incl. holdings in BRÜCKES and NARRENKAPPE). Also in ROXHEIM, Winzenheim, etc. 50% Riesling, 15% Müller-Thurgau, 11% Silvaner, plus other varieties incl. 6% Spätburgunder. Wines show clearly the characteristics of the grape variety. 75% of the wines, incl. Auslesen, are dry/med-dry. Annual production is approx. 20,000 cases. Address: Salinenstr. 60, 6550 Bad Kreuznach.

Firn

Term used to describe the effect of considerable age on wine, incl. a darkening of colour in white wine, and oxidation noticeable on nose and palate. A somewhat negative description.

Fischer, Weingüter Dr M-S-R

Saar estate of 24.6ha (61 acre) with holdings at OCKFEN (incl. BOCKSTEIN), SAARBURG and the solely owned 10.4ha (26 acre) Herrenberg site at Wawern. 92% Riesling. Approx. annual prod. 20,800 cases, The lively, fresh Saar wines with their forceful bouquet are sold in Germany and abroad. Address: Bocksteinhof, 5511 Ockfen.

Fitz-Ritter, Weingut K. Rhpf.

Old family estate of 23.3ha (58 acre), dating from 1785. The grounds around the elegant estate house are noted for their fine trees. The v'yd holdings are mainly in BAD DÜRKHEIM (the estate is sole owner of Dürkheimer Abtsfronhof). Vines are 65% Riesling. Annual production approx. 16,600 cases, almost entirely QmP, sold mainly in Germany. The Fitz-Ritter family (of Scottish descent) also own the Ritterhof-Sektkellerei KG, believed to have been producing sparkling wine since 1828. Address: Weinstrasse Nord 51, 6702 Bad Dürkheim.

Flach

Flat. A wine with insufficient acidity will taste flat. Not a common fault in German wine but can derive from low acid vine varieties (Bacchus, Auxerrois, etc.) if they are allowed to overproduce.

Flasche

See Bottle

Flaschengärung

Fermentation in bottle, as opposed to the more common fermentation in vat. Flaschengärung is very suitable for the production of small parcels (say 270 cases) of sparkling wine. For this reason it is the method usually chosen by sparkling-wine producers when making LAGENSEKT (quality sparkling wine from a particular site) for growers. However, almost all the large branded sparkling wines gain their sparkle in vat. In blind tastings at A.P. control centres, no difference in quality has been noted between wines fermented in bottle and those fermented in vat, that can be related to the method of second fermentation. (See also CHARMAT-VERFAHREN.)

Flaschenreife

Bottle ripeness. This term has two meanings. It can refer to the moment when a wine has stabilized and the acidity is at the appropriate level, which makes it ready or "ripe" for bottling, or to maturation in bottle.

Flaschenweinverkauf

Sale of wine in bottle. This is the message that is hung outside many cellars in Germany, advertising that wine is sold in bottle to the consumer. It is an increasingly popular form of trading: of the 15,314 growers who bottle their own wine, 88% sell directly to the public.

Flein Würt w. r. ******

Substantial village s. of Heilbronn with a high proportion of Riesling in sloping v'yds from which excellent dry wines are made. Grosslage: Kirchenweinberg.

Flurbereinigung

The reconstruction and reallocation of v'yds among the growers. It is supported by federal and local government and the aim is to improve the competitiveness of German wine by reducing labour costs, improving wine quality, making wine with strong regional and varietal characteristics. The work of reconstruction, incl. rebuilding hillsides and abolishing old terracing, offers the chance for the best possible vines to be planted. By 1982, 52% of the total area under vine had been "flurbereinigt".

Forst an der Weinstrasse Rhpf. w. *****→******

Small but important wine village, a few km. s. of BAD DÜRKHEIM, surrounded by top-quality Riesling v'yds and the base of a number of well-known estates with holdings in the famous JESUITENGARTEN and UNGEHEUER sites. Two Grosslagen: MARIENGARTEN (for the best sites) and SCHNEPFENFLUG.

Forster Winzerverein eG Rhpf.

Cooperative cellar, est. in 1918, owned by 114 members with 64ha (158 acre) of v'yds in top-quality sites (Forster JESUITENGARTEN, UNGEHEUER, etc.). Vines are 68% Riesling, 11% Müller-Thurgau, etc. Distinguished wines with a considerable reputation, sold in Germany and abroad. Address: Weinstrasse 57, 6701 Forst.

Forstmeister

Head forester, as in Weingut Forstmeister Geltz Zilliken.

Franckenstein Rentamt Weingut, Freiherr von und zu Baden

14ha (35 acre) estate planted 30% Riesling, 25% Spätburgunder, 15% Grauburgunder, 15% Müller-Thurgau, etc., producing some 10,000 cases annually of white, red and rosé wine. 80% is dry with well differentiated grape characteristics. Sales are in Germany and abroad. Address: Weingartenstr. 66, 7600 Offenburg.

Franconia

See Franken

Franken w. (r.)

The only wine region belonging to the beer-producing state of Bavaria covering nearly 5,000ha (12,356 acre) n. and s. of the R. Main are centred on the university city of WÜRZBURG. More than half the v'yd have been reconstructed and replanted since 1954. The most widely grown grape is the Müller-Thurgau, followed by Silvaner and the rapidly increasing Bacchus. The winters in Franken are often severe with temperatures sometimes dropping to −25°C. As a result the yield can vary greatly from year to year (in 1982 it was about 170hl/ha and in 1985 approx. 13hl/ha). Half the harvest is processed by cooperative cellars. Among the private growers some have high reputations for wines of outstanding flavour and style. Quality wine is bottled in the flagon-shaped BOCKSBEUTEL.

Wine from Franken is not cheap, and is far more expensive than a wine from the s. Rheinpfalz (Bereich SÜDLICHE WEINSTRASSE). It is however, good value for money when compared to the price obtained for a simple Mâcon Blanc, for example. It has character in abundance and is never boring. In EEC terms it is often dry, with a maximum 9 g/l of sugar. When it contains less than 4 g/l of sugar it warrants the

1982er
Würzburger Stein
Riesling Kabinett
Qualitätswein mit Prädikat
A.P.Nr. 3001 070 83
0,7 ℓ ℮
FRANKEN

description "FRÄNKISCH TROCKEN" (Franken Dry). The regional slightly earthy flavour is almost always present, no matter from what grape variety the wine is made.

In spite of the damage caused over the centuries by wars, medieval buildings in many of the old towns and villages still stand. In the countryside, inns and cellars provide opportunities to taste and buy wines in seductively rustic surroundings.

Franken eG, Gebietswinzergenossenschaft Franken

Seven cooperative cellars combined in 1959 and now produce the equivalent of 1.6m. cases a year. Vines are 57% Müller-Thurgau, 24% Silvaner, etc. Most of the wines are dry, sold mainly in Germany. Address: 8710 Kitzingen-Repperndorf.

Frankensteiner Hof Rhg.

Estate with origins going back to the 18th century. The holdings covering 4.5ha (11 acre), are at RÜDESHEIM (BERG ROSENECK, BERG ROTTLAND, BERG SCHLOSSBERG), WALLUF, MARTINSTHAL and RAUENTHAL. Vines are 85% Riesling, 6% Ehrenfelser, 5% Spätburgunder, 4% Kerner. The wines are clean, crisp and fruity, typical of the Rheingau, and have been very successful in regional and national competitions. Sales are mainly in Germany but also in East Africa. Address: Weingut Espenscheid, 6229 Walluf 2.

Frankfurt am Main, Weingut der Stadt Rhg.

The original owners of this 25ha (62 acre) estate were Carmelites and Dominicans. The estate was taken over by the city of Frankfurt in 1803. Holdings are in important sites at HOCHHEIM (DOMDECHANEY, KIRCHENSTÜCK, etc.) and the small 1ha (2.5 acre) residue of once-extensive v'yds in the suburbs of Frankfurt, the Lohrberger Hang, producing lively Riesling wines. The v'yds are 80% Riesling. Approx. annual production is 21,000 cases, much of which is sold in the estate's two attractive and well-situated wine bars. Address: Aichgasse 11, 6203 Hochheim.

Fränkisch trocken

Term used to describe Franken wine with less than 4 g/l residual sugar. In 1985, 25% of wines that passed successfully through the Franken A.P. control centre in Würzburg was Fränkisch trocken.

Freiburg Baden Pop. 175,000 w. (r.) ★★

University city, severely damaged in World War II but carefully rebuilt. V'yds are in the three Bereiche of Breisgau, KAISERSTUHL-TUNIBERG and MARKGRÄFLERLAND. The Grosslage name LORETTO-BERG is probably more widely known than any other name associated with Freiburg wine.

Freiburg, Staatliches Weinbauinstitut Baden

Founded in 1920, the Freiburg holdings of the state viticultural institute amount to 9.8ha (24 acre) planted with a range of varieties incl. Riesling, Traminer, Spätburgunder. The aim is powerful, balanced wines. Approx. 9,500 cases a year are sold in Germany and abroad. The Baden-Württemberg State owns four separate estates, with an investigative viticultural role: Blankenhornsberg at Ihringen, the largest (see next entry), Hecklingen and Durbach, each 3ha (7.4 acre) and Freiburg itself. Address: Merzhauserstr. 119, 7800 Freiburg.

Freiburg, Staatliches Weinbauinstitut, "Blankenhornsberg" Baden

One of four estates owned by the state of Baden-Württemberg. Founded as a private estate in 1842, it was sold to the state in 1919. Its 25ha (62 acre) of v'yds lie on steep volcanic slopes in splendid country in the extreme s.w. of the Bereich KAISERSTUHL-TUNIBERG. The wines (18% Müller-Thurgau, 17.8% Spätburgunder, plus many others) are sold under the village name Blankenhornsberg without mention of the Einzellage. They are full in weight and flavour and have pronounced acidity. Annual production is approx. 17,000 cases, sold in Germany, many to private customers. Address: Blankenhornsberg, 7817 Ihringen.

Freiherr

Baron. Found in some estate names, e.g. the Baden estate of Weingut Freiherr von Gleichenstein. A Freiherr would inherit the title from a REICHSFREIHERR, but the Reichs or "imperial" description could not be bequeathed.

Freisamer

White grape variety, a crossing of Silvaner × Ruländer from FREIBURG in Baden, with a small plantation of 64ha (158 acre) that has hardly varied in size for the last 10 years. Produces a crop of similar yield and MUST weight to the Ruländer and wine that is neutral in flavour, full-bodied and stylish. If the MUST weight is less than 80° Oechsle the wine tastes "woody", so overcropping must be avoided and ripeness is all.

Friedelsheim Rhpf. w. (r.) ★★

Situated a little e. of Wachenheim. The wines recall those of the best wine villages in the Pfalz. Good quality Rieslings. Grosslagen: SCHNEPFENFLUG and HOFSTÜCK.

Friedelsheim eG, Winzergenossenschaft Rhpf.

Cooperative cellar with 127 members and 150ha (371 acre) of holdings on the e. edge of the finest v'yds of the Bereich MITTELHAARDT/DEUTSCHE WEINSTRASSE, incl. Forster Bischofsgarten and Wachenheimer GERÜMPEL. Vines are 32% Riesling, 15% Müller-Thurgau, plus a host of other varieties. Annual production is claimed to be the equivalent of 238,000 cases, sold solely in Germany. Address: Hauptstr. 97-99, 6701 Friedelsheim.

Friedrich-Wilhelm-Gymnasium, Stiftung Staatliches M-S-R

Distinguished estate, founded in 1563 by Jesuits, with 45ha (111 acre) of holdings spread along the Mosel (DHRON, GRAACH, ZELTINGEN/RACHTIG, BERNKASTEL, etc.) and the Saar (OBEREMMEL, OCKFEN, etc.). Many of the sites are very steep, planted with 85%

Riesling, 13% Müller-Thurgau and new crossings. Maturation in wood is still valued, and the estate's cellars under TRIER produce racy wines with restrained sweetness. Sales mainly in Germany but also abroad. Address: Weberbachstr. 75, 5500 Trier.

Frisch

Fresh. As a result of a vinification that reduces oxydation to a minimum, gentle handling of the wine so as to retain the natural carbon dioxide, and good acid levels, most German wines taste fresh – even after some years in bottle. Applies particularly to Rieslings from the M-S-R, the Rheingau, and from the best v'yds of the Bereich Schloss Böckelheim in the Nahe.

Frostgeschmack

Frost taste. Flavour acquired by unripe grapes attacked by frost in autumn (e.g. in 1972). It can usually be removed with treatment but not always entirely successfully. The ripeness of grapes used in EISWEIN production, on the other hand, prevents them from developing a taste of frost in spite of the very low temperatures at which they are gathered.

Fruchtig

Fruity. Common description of wine that covers smell and flavour. As the word implies, it refers to pronounced grapey characteristics, often reinforced by high acidity. A Saar wine, made from ripe grapes but with good acidity, can well be described as fruity.

Fruchtwein

Fruit wine. Wine made from fruits, other than grapes, with the addition of water and sugar.

Fruchtzucker

Fruit sugar. Colloquial name for fructose, which tastes twice as sweet as dextrose. However, yeast ferments dextrose more easily than fructose, so the unfermented sugar in a fine sweet wine contains a high proportion of the sweet fructose.

Frühburgunder, Blauer

Red grape variety, an early-ripening mutation of Spätburgunder found mainly in Württemberg where it covers 19ha (47 acre), producing a small yield per vine. It is also known by the synonym "Clevner" – a name confusingly reserved in the Bereich ORTENAU in Baden for Traminer.

Frühmesse Rhh. w. ★★★

Large Einzellage on slopes at ALSHEIM, producing luscious, stylish Rieslings. Grosslage: RHEINBLICK. Growers: Rappenhof, Sittmann.

Fuchs, Weingut Reinhold M-S-R

Small 2ha (5 acre) estate, downstream from Cochem, planted with 95% Riesling. Vinification is traditional and the wines are expected to develop in bottle. Annual production is 2,200 cases, sold in Germany. Address: Bahnhofstr. 37, 5593 Pommern.

Fuchsmantel Rhpf. w. ★★→★★★

Mainly level Einzellage, on the outskirts of BAD DÜRKHEIM but shared with WACHENHEIM, producing good wines typical of the region. Grosslage: SCHENKENBÖHL. Growers: Bart, Karst, Schaefer.

Fuder

Cask of approx. 1,000 litres, used for storage in the M-S-R. See FASS.

Fuhrmann, Karl

See Pfeffingen, Weingut

Fürst

Prince, as in Fürst von Metternich-Winneburg'sches Domäne Rentamt at Schloss Johannisberg.

Fürst Löwenstein, Weingut

See Schloss Vollrads

Fürst, Weingut Rudolf Franken

9ha (22 acre) estate with modernized vineyards planted with 50% red vine varieties (mainly Spätburgunder), 23% Müller-Thurgau, 12% Riesling, etc. Red wines are matured in cask and the whites (all dry or med-dry) are stored in stainless steel. Annual production of 7,200 cases of wine in BOCKSBEUTEL, is sold mainly in Germany. Address: Hohenlindenweg 46, 8768 Bürgstadt.

Gallais, Weingut le M-S-R

Small 2.5ha (6 acre) Saar estate with holdings in the 5.8ha (14 acre) BRAUNE KUPP at WILTINGEN. Only wines of QmP class are sold under the Einzellage name. Approx. annual production is 1,600 cases, all Riesling. The estate is administered by Weingut Egon MÜLLER. Address: Saarstr. 23, 5511 Kanzem.

Gattungslagename

Predecessor of the GROSSLAGE but much vaguer in geographical definition, abolished by the 1971 Wine Law. It was a site name that could be given to a wine that came, usually, from within 10km (6 miles) of the village name to which the site was attached. Johannisberger (village name) Erntebringer (Gattungslagename), for example, could originate in a village as far away as Hallgarten or even further. Today, as a Grosslage, ERNTEBRINGER is more narrowly and precisely defined.

Gau-Bickelheim Rhh. ★

Small town nr. BAD KREUZNACH (in the Nahe), best known as the home of the large central cooperative cellar that serves the Rheinhessen and Rheingau. Grosslage: Kurfürstenstück.

Gebhardt, Ernst, Weingut Weingrosskellerei Franken

Estate founded in 1723, taken over by Georg Jakob Gebhardt in 1761. 15ha (37 acre) of steep, modernized v'yds in SOMMERHAUSEN, RANDERSACKER, etc., 26% Silvaner, 26% Müller-Thurgau, 20% Scheurebe.The wines are sometimes rather sweeter than is usual in Franken but they – and the estate that makes them – have often won awards at state and national competitions. A high proportion of QmP. 10,800 cases, sold almost entirely in Germany. The estate also operates as a wine merchant. Address: Haupstr. 21-23, 8701 Sommerhausen.

Gebiet

District. Not an official EEC designation, for which the word is BEREICH. Appears in ANBAUGEBIET and WEINBAUGEBIET.

Gebietswinzergenossenschaft

District cooperative cellar (Gebiets: district, Winzer: vine grower, Genossenschaft: association). There are approx. 40 in Germany. Sometimes they are known as Bezirkswinzergenossenschaften (Bezirk is a synonym for Gebiet).

Geheimrat, Geheimer Rat

Privy councillor. Can appear in estate names as one word, e.g. Geheimrat Aschrott'sche Erben, or as two, e.g. Weingut Geheimer Rat Dr v. Bassermann-Jordan.

Geilweilerhof Rhpf.

Home of the viticultural institute Bundesforschungsanstalt für Rebenzüchtung, nr. the village of SIEBELDINGEN a few km. w. of Landau in der Pfalz, where the grape varieties Morio-Muskat, Bacchus and Optima were developed.

Geisenheim Rhg. w. ★★★
Famous for its viticultural institute, Geisenheim produces Riesling wines of distinction,but with a slight additional flavour that comes from the soil. Grosslagen: BURGWEG and ERNTEBRINGER.

Geisenheim, Weingut der Forschungsanstalt für Weinbau, Gartenbau, Getränketechnologie und Landespflege Rhg.
Part of a complex of world-renowned institutes dealing with all sides of vine-growing and wine-making. As a result of the research that is continuously in progress, many vine varieties are grown in 22ha (54 acre) in Geisenheim (KLÄUSERWEG, ROTHENBERG, MÄUERCHEN, etc.) and at Rüdesheim.
The wines are matured in wood and vat. Approx. annual production is 12,000 cases, sold mainly in Germany. Address: Blaubachstr. 19, 6222 Geisenheim.

Geltz Zilliken, Weingut Forstmeister M-S-R
Family estate of 8.6ha (21 acre) that dates back to 1742, but it was the one-time Master Forester of the King of Prussia, Ferdinand Geltz (1851-1925), who built up its reputation. Today it is very active, selling its wines via brokers at the various important German wine auctions. The holdings in steep sites at SAARBURG and OCKFEN are 90% Riesling and produce fine, cask matured wines in the deepest cellar on the Saar. Annual production is approx. 6,600 cases. 70% is exported. Address: Heckingstr. 20, 5510 Saarburg.

Gemeinde
Community or village.

Gemmingen-Hornberg'sches Weingut, Freiherrl. von Baden
The 14.5ha (36 acre) wine estate of the castle of Burg Hornberg in the n. of Baden. Vines are 30% Riesling, 10% Müller-Thurgau, 6% Silvaner. Red wines are made from Spätburgunder, Trollinger and Müllerrebe. The castle was the home of Götz von Berlichingen, the one-handed soldier of fortune immortalized by Goethe's play. Annual production is 10,800 cases. Address: Burg Hornberg, 6951 Neckarzimmern.

Gerbstoff
Tannin. Derives from the skins, pips and stalks of the grape. A low tannin content is characteristic of, and desirable in, German white wine. Many German red wines might find more international appeal with a higher tannin content, which would bring with it more "backbone".

German Wine Academy
Since 1973 this organization has run five-day seminars in English, based at KLOSTER EBERBACH in the Rheingau. The basic course covers all aspects of vine-growing and wine-making, incl. many tutored tastings and visits to six vine-growing regions. Address: PO Box 1705, 6500 Mainz.

Gerümpel Rhpf. w. ★★★
Einzellage at WACHENHEIM producing top-quality, full-bodied wines, mainly from Riesling. Grosslage: MARIENGARTEN. Growers: Bürklin-Wolf, Schaefer, Wachtenburg-Luginsland, J. L. Wolf.

Geschwister
Collective noun meaning brothers and sisters, as in Weingut Geschwister Schuch.

Gessert, Weingut Gustav Rhh.
10ha (25 acre) estate on the RHEINTERRASSE at Nierstein, with holdings in ÖLBERG, ORBEL, PETTENTHAL, FINDLING, BILDSTOCK, etc., producing a typical mix of top quality Rheinhessen wines. Silvaner plantations are to be increased, with Riesling being reserved for the best sites only. 9,200 cases are sold annually in Germany and abroad. Address: Wörrstädter Str. 84, 6505 Nierstein.

Gewürztraminer
Opinion is divided as to the exact relationship of this vine to Traminer, but both names are found in Germany.

Gimmeldingen an der Weinstrasse Rhpf. w. ★★
Small town just n. of NEUSTADT producing sound wines. Best known for its Grosslage MEERSPINNE.

Gleichenstein, Weingut Freiherr von Baden
Estate dating from the 17th century, with buildings going back to
the 15th century. 18ha (44 acre), 40% Spätburgunder, 30% Müller-
Thurgau. 80% of the wines are dry, and in the rest the sweetness is
restrained. The Spätburgunder is fermented on the skins and
matured in cask. Approx. 10,800 cases, sold only in Germany.
Address: Bahnhofstr. 12, 7818 Oberrotweil.

Glühwein
Mulled wine: a hot drink, welcome in winter, based on red wine,
water and sugar with lemon peel, cinnamon and cloves.

GmbH
Gesellschaft mit beschränkter Haftung. Describes a private limited
company, as in P.J. Valckenberg GmbH.

Goldbächel Rhpf. w. ***
4.3ha (10.6 acre) Einzellage on almost flat ground on the outskirts of
WACHENHEIM. Planted mainly with Riesling, it produces top-quality
wine typical of the Rheinpfalz. Grosslage: MARIENGARTEN.
Growers: Bürklin-Wolf, J. L. Wolf.

Goldbäumchen M-S-R w **
Grosslage usually linked to the village of (ELLENZ-POLTERSDORF,
approx. 670ha (1,656 acre) mainly steep slopes. Good Riesling
wine is made that is lighter on average, and slightly cheaper, than
most other Mosels. Well known in Germany.

Goldlay M-S-R w. **
Steep Einzellage at REIL, producing Rieslings of excellent quality
but usually without quite the distinction of the best from WEHLEN,
BERNKASTEL, etc. Grosslage: VOM HEISSEN STEIN.

Goldloch Nahe w. ***
Steep Einzellage at DORSHEIM in the Bereich KREUZNACH, adjacent
to the busy Koblenz-Ludwigshafen motorway. Planted mainly
with Riesling, it produces top-quality, meaty wine. Grosslage:
SCHLOSSKAPELLE. Growers: Diel, Niederhausen-Schlossböckelheim
Staatl. Weinbaudomäne.

Goldtröpfchen M-S-R w. ***
Einzellage of some 122ha (301 acre) at PIESPORT and DHRON, by far
the best known of all Mosel sites because its wines are the most
widely distributed. Facing SE-S-SW, it is 100% steep and 100%
Riesling. The wines can be of excellent quality and the best are
superb, with a fine powerful flavour and firm acidity. Cheap and
genuine Goldtröpfchen is not likely to be found. Grosslage:
MICHELSBERG. Growers: Bischöfliche Weingüter, Dünweg, Haag,
Haart, Hain, Kesselstatt, Matheus-Lehnert, Reh (Marienhof),
Vereinigte Hospitien.

Göler'sche Verwaltung, Freiherr von Baden
Estate w. of HEILBRONN prod. approx. the equivalent to 12,000
cases. 50% is Riesling. Red wines are made from Limberger and
Müllerrebe. The wines, many of them winners of state and national
awards, can be tasted at the estate's Burg Ravensburg restaurant.
Address: Hauptstr. 44, 7519 Sulzfeld.

Gondorf M-S-R w. **
Wine village not far from KOBLENZ. The v'yds are extremely steep
and almost entirely Riesling. Attractive old buildings and much
wine-village atmosphere. Grosslage: WEINHEX.

Gottesfuss M-S-R w. ***
4ha (10 acre) steep, slaty EINZELLAGE at WILTINGEN considered by
some to be the best Saar site, after SCHARZHOFBERG. Being much
smaller than Scharzhofberg the quality of Gottesfuss wine is more
consistent. Growers: Reverchon, van Volxem.

Gottesthal Rhg. w. **
Grosslage based on OESTRICH, with a high proportion of Riesling.
The finest wines will always be sold under the names of the Ein-
zellagen – LENCHEN, DOOSBERG, Klosterberg (shared with the
Grosslage MEHRHÖLZCHEN) – and the Ortsteil SCHLOSS REICHHART-
SHAUSEN, but many good (QbA) Gottesthal wines have the acidity
necessary for development in bottle.

Graach M-S-R w. ***
Hardly more than a hamlet in size, Graach lies amid its v'yds on

the steep SW-SSW facing slopes above the Mosel nr. BERNKASTEL.
All its Einzellagen (ABTSBERG, DOMPROBST, HIMMELREICH, JOSEPHS-
HÖFER) are capable of producing some of the finest Rieslings of the
Mosel. Grosslage: MÜNZLAY.

Graben M-S-R w. ✳✳✳→✳✳✳✳

Top-quality Einzellage on the steep, S-SW facing hill of vines
above the Mosel at BERNKASTEL. 100% Riesling. The wines are elegant, racy and very "classy", not the cheapest of Bernkasteler
wines but realistically priced. Grosslage: BADSTUBE. Growers:
Pauly-Bergweiler, J. J. Prüm, St Johannishof, St-Nikolaus-
Hospital, Studert-Prüm, Wegeler-Deinhard.

Graf

Title equivalent to a count or an earl. Often appears in the names
of wine estates, usually of noble origin, e.g. Weingut Graf von
Kanitz.

Gräfenberg Rhg. w. ✳✳✳

Einzellage in a side valley set back from the Rhein at Kiedrich, producing very elegant, spicy Riesling wines particularly in great
years. Grosslage: HEILIGENSTOCK. Growers: Groenesteyn, Sohlbach, Weil.

Grainhübel Rhpf. w. ✳✳✳

One of the best of the distinguished ring of Einzellagen around DEI-
DESHEIM, producing top-quality wine. Its 12ha (30 acre) of v'yds are
virtually in the town and (unusually for Deidesheim) 40% of the
site is steep. The main grape is Riesling. Grosslage: MARIENGARTEN.
Growers: Bassermann-Jordan, Biffar, Dr. Deinhard, Hahnhof,
Kern, Spindler.

Grasig

Literally "grassy". Used to describe wines that are very "green"
(presumably herein lies the connection with "grassy"). Such wines
will have a high malic acid content and will have been made from
unripe grapes, as happens in vintages such as 1972. They are not
necessarily unattractive and can benefit from bottle age.

Grauburgunder

An increasingly popular synonym for the Ruländer grape (see
BADISCH ROTGOLD).

Groenesteyn, Weingut des Reichsfreiherrn von Ritter zu Rhg.

See Schloss Groenesteyn

Grosser Herrgott M-S-R w. ✳✳

Einzellage at WINTRICH on the Mosel making stylish, lively Rieslings. Grosslage: KURFÜRSTLAY.

Grosser Ring

A "ring" in the English auction world has sinister implications.
Not so in Germany, where the Grosser Ring (the large ring)
consists of 34 fine Riesling-growing estates in the M-S-R. Each
autumn they hold an auction in TRIER to promote their own wine
and the reputation of M-S-R wines as a whole.

Grosskarlbach Rhpf. w. r. ✳✳

Attractive, rural village, devoted to v'yds and orchards. Excellent
source of good quality, meaty white wines, that almost rival the
best in the region from Deidesheim, Forst, Wachenheim, etc.
Grosslage: SCHWARZERDE.

Grosslage

A combination of individual sites (EINZELLAGEN) within one region
(ANBAUGEBIET) producing quality (QbA and QmP) wines of similar
style. The name of a grosslage must always be accompanied by that
of a village or community. See page 11.

Grosslagefrei

Free of a GROSSLAGE. In some small areas there are EINZELLAGEN
but no Grosslagen. Common in Franken.

Grün

Green. Similar to GRASIG but less strong in meaning.

Grundwein

Base wine. Still wine from which sparkling wine is made and all-
important in deciding the quality of the final product. The ideal
Grundwein will have 9-11° alcohol, a high acid content and no residual sugar. It must be fresh and youthful. As a wine it is austere to

the point of unpleasantness, but converted into sparkling wine it becomes balanced and refreshing.

Grüner Silvaner

See Silvaner, Grüner.

Güldenmorgen Rhh. w. ★★

Grosslage of some 430ha (1,063 acre) on the RHEINTERRASSE, upstream from OPPENHEIM. The name Güldenmorgen was once reserved for an individual v'yd site but now, as a Grosslage, it includes within its boundaries such distinguished Oppenheimer sites as SACKTRÄGER and KREUZ.

Gunderloch-Usinger, Weingut Rhh.

Estate dating from 1890 with 11ha (27 acre) around NACKENHEIM, incl. the ROTHENBERG site. Vines are 75% Riesling, 15% Silvaner, 10% Müller-Thurgau, etc. The wines are very elegant and well defined. Approx. annual production is 5,800 cases, sold in Germany and abroad. Address: Carl-Gunderloch Platz, 6506 Nackenheim.

Guntersblum Rhh. w. (r.) ★★★

Small town at the s. end of the RHEINTERRASSE, known for fine wines. It has a number of old cellars, patrician houses and the "Kellerwegfest", a wine festival, at the end of August. Two Grosslagen: KRÖTENBRUNNEN and Vogelsgärtchen.

Gunterslay M-S-R w. ★★

Steep Einzellage at PIESPORT producing good, fresh, fruity Rieslings, not quite in the class of Piesporter GOLDTRÖPFCHEN. Grosslage: MICHELSBERG. Growers: Haag, Haart, Reh (Marienhof).

Guntrum-Weinkellerei GmbH, Louis Rhh.

Company operating as estate owners and wine merchants. 67ha (166 acre) in top-quality sites at NIERSTEIN, NACKENHEIM, OPPENHEIM and DIENHEIM, 30% Riesling, 25% Müller-Thurgau, 14% Silvaner, etc., producing approx. 40,000 cases a year. Efficient, modern

wine-making with emphasis on retaining fruity acidity and varietal characteristics. 40% are dry or med-dry. The company dates from 1824, although Guntrums were active as coopers and brewers in the 14th century. As wine merchants Guntrum sell some 250,000 cases a year in Germany and abroad. Address: Rheinallee 62, 6505 Nierstein.

Gut

Pronounced "Goot". As a noun has several meanings, incl. that of an estate. Frequently found as part of the word Weingut – wine estate.

Gutedel, Weisser

An ancient vine variety (known in France as the Chasselas) producing white grapes for the table and the press house, covering 1,258ha (3,109 acre), mainly in the Bereich MARKGRÄFLERLAND in Baden. It is most respected in Switzerland where it is known as Fendant. The wine is light in weight and low in acidity – a pleasant SCHOPPENWEIN, best drunk young.

Gutes Domtal Rhh. w. ★

Grosslage of more than 1,300ha (3,212 acre) behind the RHEIN-

FRONT at NIERSTEIN. It covers the v'yds of 15 villages and 31 Einzel-lagen, the best known being the DOKTOR at Dexheim because of its similarity (in name only) to the famous DOCTOR at Bernkastel on the Mosel. After LIEBFRAUMILCH, Gutes Domtal has the widest distribution of any Rhein wine. It is frequently very cheap, and drunk within the year following the vintage it can be very pleasant. Unfortunately, with the accepted market price set so low, there seems little incentive to produce simple-quality wine with much character under the name Gutes Domtal.

Gütezeichen für Badischen Qualitätswein
Award given by the Baden Winegrowers Association to quality (QbA and QmP) wines in standard-size (no litre) bottles, that have already won their A.P. Nr. and achieved a sufficiently high level of marks to qualify for the Gütezeichen. A special yellow award can be won by dry wines of Spätlese quality and less. The Badisches Gütezeichen is officially recognized by the state of Baden-Württemberg.

Gütezeichen Franken
Award first given to Franken quality wines in 1981, under the auspices of the Bavarian government, based on a tasting and analytical examination. Since 1983 only available to wine in BOCKS-BEUTEL. To qualify, dry wines must be FRÄNKISCH TROCKEN.

Haag, Weingut Fritz M-S-R
Small, 4.5ha (11 acre) family-owned estate dating from 1605 with holdings at BRAUNEBERG and GRAACH. Vines are 97% Riesling, 3% Müller-Thurgau. Approx. annual production is 4,800 cases of typical, high-quality, crisp Mosel wine (no Süss-Reserve), sold in Germany and abroad Address: Dusemonder Hof, 5551 Brauneberg.

Haart, Weingut Johann M-S-R
6ha (15 acre) estate belonging to the Haart family, owners of v'yds in PIESPORT since the 14th century. Holdings are in GOLDTRÖPFCHEN, GÜNTERSLAY, etc. 48% Riesling. Annual production is the equivalent of 6,500 cases of good quality wine, sold to the wine trade. 85% is exported. Address: Trevererstr. 12, 5555 Piesport.

Hagel
Hail. Hailstorms can cause damage at almost any time – they have been known to strip vines of leaf and fruit in mid-summer, destroying the current harvest and severely reducing the following year's crop. If a hailstorm occurs shortly before the vintage, many of the grapes may be knocked to the ground. In these circumstances, an early gathering (VORLESE) is allowed.

Hagelgeschmack
"Taste of hail." Hailstones can damage grapes in such a way that they rot on the vine and later pass on to the wine an unpleasant flavour (Hagelgeschmack), and often excessive volatile acidity as well.

Haidle, Karl Würt.
Estate of 16ha (40 acre) of which the yield from 10.5ha (26 acre) is contracted to an ERZEUGERGEMEINSCHAFT. One of the first to grow Kerner, in 1959, in cooperation with the WEINSBERG viticultural institute. Today, the holdings at Stetten and Schnait are planted 15% in Kerner, 40% Riesling and 10% Trollinger. Both the estate and its wines (100% dry or med-dry) have received an astounding number of top awards. Sales are exclusively in Germany. Address: Hindenburgstr. 21, 7053 Kernen i.R.-Stetten.

Hail
See Hagel

Halbfuder
The Mosel equivalent of the Rhein HALBSTÜCK, with a capacity of approx. 500 litres. Its disappearance parallels that of the HALB-STÜCK and for the same reasons. See FASS.

Halbstück
Round-shaped (as opposed to oval) wooden cask with a capacity of some 610 litres, used until the mid-1960s for transporting and storing Rhein wine. Still found to a small extent in some cellars, but steadily disappearing because of high maintenance costs and

the possible loss of freshness in white wine of relatively low acidity (e.g. Müller-Thurgau) when stored in wood. See FASS.

Halbtrocken

Medium-dry. When describing still (i.e. non-sparkling) wine, "halbtrocken" indicates that the sugar content is not more than 10 g/l greater than that of the total acid content, with a maximum of 18 g/l. For those who feel that German dry ("trocken") wines too often lack body, and do not want a sweetish wine, Halbtrocken seems an excellent compromise. It allows the true flavour to be easily tasted and can produce most attractive, balanced results. A Halbtrocken sparkling wine in the EEC can contain between 33 and 50 g/l sugar.

Hallgarten Rhg. w. ★★★

Small rural village away from the bustle of the Rhein and protected by the TAUNUS hills that border its n. v'yds. Produces fine Riesling wines. Grosslage: MEHRHÖLZCHEN.

Hallgarten GmbH, Arthur Rhg.

Respected firm of wine exporters, formed in 1933, with an associated company in London. Well-established brands incl. Domgarten Niersteiner Gutes Domtal and Kellergeist Liebfraumilch. Hallgarten also export a full range of estate-bottled wines, bought for quality rather than name, incl. at the lower end an estate-bottled LANDWEIN. Address: 6530 Bingen.

Hallgarten/Rhg. eG, Winzergenossesnschaft Rhg.

Cooperative with 191 members supplying grapes from 63ha (156 acre), 85% Riesling, 13% Müller-Thurgau, etc., all in sites at HALLGARTEN. Annual production is equivalent to 83,000 cases. No exports. Address: Hattenheimerstr. 15, 6227 Oestrich-Winkel.

Halsschleife

Neck label. It is common for German wine bottles to be dressed with a neck label, showing vintage or other optional information. Some estates, however, feel that a neck label does not improve the appearance of their bottles and omit its use (e.g. Schloss Reinhartshausen).

Hambach an der Weinstrasse Rhpf. w. ★★

Small picturesque wine town nr. NEUSTADT, well known in the region, producing wines of good quality (Riesling, Silvaner, etc.) but not comparable to the best from a few km. further n. The Hambacher Schloss carried great historical significance as a centre of German liberalism. Grosslagen: Rebstöckel and Pfaffengrund.

Hammel & Cie Weingut Weinkellerei, Emil Rhpf.

Estate of 56ha (138 acre), dating from 1723, producing approx. 41,600 cases a year from its own v'yds. 35% exported. The Weinkellerei also sells Alsatian wines and those of Ch. Soutard in St.-Emilion. The estate's holdings, all in n. Rheinpfalz, are planted with a wide range of vine varieties. The aim is to produce pleasant "drinking" wines, i.e. with a gentle acidity and agreeable fruitiness. In recent years more than half the estate-bottled wines have

been dry or medium-dry. Address: 6719 Kirchheim/Weinstrasse.

Hammelburg Franken Pop. 12,700 w. ★★

On the R. Saale, one of the oldest wine towns of Franken, with a tradition of 1,200 years of viticulture. Some fine old buildings and one of the earliest cooperative cellars in the region. Produces wines of good acidity from Müller-Thurgau and Silvaner. Grosslage: Burg.

Hammelburg, Städt. Weingut

See Schloss Saaleck.

Harmonisch

Balanced. Describes wine in which the constituent parts are in harmony. Fine wines, by definition, must be balanced; lesser wines may be balanced.

Harvest

The German grape harvest (Ernte) usually takes place over a period of two months from mid-September onwards. It starts with grapes such as Ortega and Siegerrebe, continues with Müller-Thurgau, Bacchus and Morio-Muskat and finishes with Riesling, the very last of which may not be gathered until the following year if EISWEIN is being made. (See also HAUPTLESE.)

Growers have to consider many factors when organizing their harvest, incl. the rate at which the grapes can be picked and pressed and the risks involved in leaving them on the vine to increase their sugar content. Because of the varying pace at which different grapes ripen, the gathering of SPÄTLESE Müller-Thurgau, for example, will often be finished before the main picking of Riesling has begun.

The timing of the harvest is officially controlled and the v'yds are put out of bounds except during the hours when picking is permitted. In recent years in the Rheinpfalz and Rheinhessen, mechanical harvesters have appeared in some force but their use, even in these regions, is not nearly as widespread as in France.

Hasensprung Rhg. w. ★★★→★★★★

Large, 100ha (247 acre) Einzellage at WINKEL producing top-quality, refined Riesling wines that are among the best in the region. Grosslage: HONIGBERG. Growers: Basting-Gimbel, Brentano'sche Guts., Hessisches Weingut, Hupfeld, "Johannisberger Rosenhof", Johannishof, Mumm'sches Weingut, Ress, Schloss Schönborn, Wegeler-Deinhard.

Hattenheim Rhg. w. ★★★→★★★★

Village with fine old half-timbered houses; produces some of the best Riesling wines in the region. Grosslage: DEUTELSBERG.

Hatzenport M-S-R w. ★★

Small riverside village in the Bereich ZELL, overlooked by steep v'yds, which are planted almost entirely in Riesling. Grosslage: WEINHEX.

Hauptlese

Main harvest; takes place when the overall ripeness of the grapes has reached the desired maturity. The main harvest of any one wine will last about 7–10 days, after which it may be followed by a SPÄTLESE harvest. Theoretically, all qualities can be picked during the main harvest with the sole exception of Spätlesen. (From an early-ripening vine such as Optima, BEERENAUSLESE can be gathered even before the main Riesling harvest has begun.) Because the weather is not sufficiently cold during the main harvest, EISWEIN picking will also take place, in practice, after the start of the Spätlese harvest. (See also HARVEST.)

Haustrunk

"Drink of the house." Usually a low-quality wine provided by a producer from the "left-overs" of his vintage, free of charge, for the everyday consumption of his workers.

Heckenwirtschaft

Term used in parts of Franken for STRAUSSWIRTSCHAFT.

Hectare

2.471 acres. The standard unit of measurement of v'yds.

Heddesdorff, Weingut Freiherr von M-S-R

One of the most distinguished estates of the Bereich ZELL, with origins in the 15th century. 4ha (10 acre) of holdings, all at WINNINGEN, are 100% Riesling, producing 3,900 cases of carefully made, often steely wine, 25% are dry and 25% are med-dry. Since its formation in 1981 the estate has been a member of the ERZEUGERGEMEINSCHAFT Deutsches Eck. Heddesdorff wines are not cheap but are worth their price and less expensive than those from comparable estates in the Bereich BERNKASTEL. Sales are mainly directly to the consumer in Germany. Address: 5406 Winningen.

Hegemann & Co. GmbH M-S-R
Since 1969 a subsidiary exporting company of Franz REH & Sohn, concentrating on selling inexpensive wine in the UK. Address: 5559 Leiwen/Mosel.

Heidelberg Baden Pop. 129,000 w. ★★
Famous old university town astride the R. NECKAR, escaped damage in World War II. Has many old buildings and the vast Heidelberger Fass (cask), dating from 1751, with a capacity of 220,000 litres (314,286 bottles). Produces sound wines from a wide range of vine varieties incl. Müller-Thurgau, Riesling, Silvaner and Weissburgunder, grown on steep or sloping sites. Grosslagen: Rittersberg and Mannaberg.

Heilbronn a. Neckar Würt. Pop. 113,000 r. w. ★★
Severely damaged in World War II, the rebuilt town as a whole lacks charm but produces Trollinger and Riesling wines to a very good standard at the Heilbronn-Erlenbach-Weinsberg Cooperative. Grosslagen: Staufenberg, Kirchenweinberg and Heuchelberg.

Heilbronn-Erlenbach-Weinsberg eG, Genossenschaftskellerei Würt.
A particularly well run cooperative cellar of 600 members, receiving grapes from 600ha (1,483 acre), producing excellent wines of real character and style. Main vine varieties are Riesling (30%), Tröllinger (26%), etc. Sales are exclusively in Germany. Address: 7100 Heilbronn.

Heiligenhäuschen M-S-R w. ★★
100% steep Einzellage on the edge of the Ruwer vine-growing area, shared by three communities incl. WALDRACH. Produces lively, fruity Rieslings in good years. Grosslage: RÖMERLAY.

Heiligenstock Rhg. w. ★★
Small Grosslage covering the v'yds of KIEDRICH. Mainly Riesling.

Heinrich, Weingut G.A. Würt.
A mainly red wine 8.5ha (21 acre) estate, planted 30% Trollinger, 20% Schwarzriesling and 5% each Lemberger and Samtrot, in organically manured v'yds. Gentle wines, 90% dry or med-dry, incl. a red 1983 Heilbronner Stiftsberg Clevner (Frühburgunder) Trockenbeerenauslese QmP, and eight top prize winners in the national (DLG) competition. Sales mainly to the consumer, but unusually incl. export to France. Address: Riedstr. 29, 7100 Heilbronn.

Heissen Stein, vom M-S-R w. ★★
First Grosslage of the top-quality Middle Mosel, travelling upstream from KOBLENZ. 628ha (1,552 acre), much of it on steep slopes, incl. the GOLDLAY site at REIL. The main grape is Riesling.

Helfensteiner
Red grape variety, a Frühburgunder × Trollinger crossing from the viticultural institute at WEINSBERG. 52ha (129 acre), 98% in WÜRTTEMBERG. It dislikes lime in the soil, ripens early and produces pleasant but undistinguished wine.

Henkell & Co., Sektkellereien
Sekt producers, est. in 1856, with a large share of the export market, where "Henkell Trocken", which sells for about DM 8.00

a bottle in Germany, is particularly well distributed. Sales of Rüttgers Club, a Sekt at about DM 4.50 a bottle produced by a Henkell subsidiary company, amount to some 30m. bottles a year. (See also CARSTENS KG.) Address: Biebricher Allee 142, 6200 Wiesbaden.

Heppenheim Hess.Berg. Pop. 24,000 w. ★★

Town 28km (17 miles) n. of Heidelberg, with some attractive old half-timbered buildings. The wines are lively, mainly made from Riesling. Largest producer is the local cooperative cellar. Grosslage: Schlossberg.

Herb

Austere. Sometimes used in restaurants as a synonym for "trocken". Elsewhere generally describes the effect of tannin in red wine, without residual sugar.

Hermannsberg Nahe w. ★★★→★★★★

Small Einzellage on the slopes at NIEDERHAUSEN producing charming Riesling wines of great finesse. Grosslage: BURGWEG. Owner: Niederhausen-Schlossböckelheim Staatl. Weinbaudomäne.

Hermannshof

See Schmitt, Weingut Hermann Franz

Hermannshöhle Nahe w. ★★★→★★★★

One of the best Einzellagen on the Nahe, at NIEDERHAUSEN, 100% steep and 100% Riesling. In a good vintage great wine of immense elegance is made. Grosslage: BURGWEG. Growers: August E. Anheuser, Niederhausen-Schlossböckelheim Staatl. Weinbaudomäne, Jacob Schneider.

Heroldrebe

Red grape variety, a crossing of Portugieser × Limberger. Like the Helfensteiner it originated in WEINSBERG. Can yield as much as 140 hl/ha of light red wine of no special quality. Needs to be picked late in the season, to avoid an unripe flavour and an excess of tannin. 242ha (598 acre), over half in the Rheinpfalz.

Herrenberg Franken w. (r.) ★★

Small Grosslage at Castell prod. full-bodied Silvaner and Müller-Thurgau, and a small quantity of red wine.

Herrenberg M-S-R w. ★★★

Herrenberg is a common site name, but the Herrenberg Einzellage at OCKFEN on the Saar is one of the best known outside Germany. It is an excellent sloping site producing well-balanced, full wines in good years. Grosslage: SCHARZBERG. Growers: Fischer, Rheinart, Solemacher, Trier Staatl. Weinbaudomäne.

Herrenberg, Weingut Serriger

See Simon, Bert

Herrenberger M-S-R w. ★★★→★★★★

Einzellage of outstanding quality at AYL on the Saar, 100% steep and exclusively Riesling. In good vintages the wine shows great class: it is stylish, well structured and will keep for years. Grosslage: SCHARZBERG. Solely owned by the Bischöfliche Weingüter.

Herrgottsacker Rhpf. w. ★★★

Largest, 120ha (297 acre), Einzellage at DEIDESHEIM. Produces racy Rieslings, lighter than some in the district but stylish, with a balance more often found in the Rheingau. Grosslage: MARIENGARTEN. Growers: Bassermann-Jordan, Josef Biffar, Bürklin-Wolf, Hahnhof, Kern, Mosbacher, Mossbacher-Hof, E. Spindler, Wegeler-Deinhard, J. L. Wolf.

Hersteller

The producer of a wine, not the grower of the grapes. Often found as in "hergestellt in", i.e. "produced in".

Herxheim am Berg Rhpf w. (r.) ★★

Village on a plateau in the n. Rheinpfalz with one of the oldest nature reserves in the region. Good, solid, meaty wines. Grosslage: KOBNERT.

Herzhaft

Hearty. In Germany, describes a wine with pronounced flavour and bouquet, and usually good acidity. A term that might be applied, for example, to a Riesling from MÜNSTER-SARMSHEIM in the Nahe, or from LORCH in the Rheingau.

Hessen
Federal state encompassing the vine-growing regions of the Rheingau and Hessische Bergstrasse. The capital is WIESBADEN. Not to be confused with Rheinhessen in Rheinland-Pfalz. Area under vine 3,329ha (8,226 acre).

Hessische Bergstrasse w.
Smallest of the wine-producing regions, with 389ha (961 acre) under vine. Riesling covers 205ha (507 acre). Müller-Thurgau is widely planted in the n. near Darmstadt. The v'yd holdings are

Bensheimer Kalkgasse
Ruländer · Kabinett
Qualitätswein mit Prädikat
Amtl. Prüf-Nr. 50 012 004 83
Erzeugerabfüllung 0,7 l
WEINGUT DER STADT BENSHEIM / BERGSTRASSE
RITTERPLATZ 2 · 6140 BENSHEIM I

exceptionally small and in most cases vine-growing is very much a weekend occupation. More than 90% of the harvest is delivered to cooperative cellars. For all that, the wines can be excellent and compare in quality with many from the Rheingau, to which they are similar in style. They are seldom found outside the region.

Hessisches Weingut, Landgräflich Rhg.
50ha (124 acre) estate taken over by the Prince and Landgrave of Hessen in 1958, 88% Riesling, in well-known sites at RÜDESHEIM, GEISENHEIM, JOHANNISBERG, WINKEL, RAUENTHAL, ELTVILLE and KIEDRICH. The estate is enthusiastic about the Scheurebe plantations in the Winkeler DACHSBERG, that have produced many award-winning wines. Annual yield is claimed to be some 37,500 cases, sold in Germany and abroad. Address: Grund 1, 6222 Geisenheim.

Heyl zu Herrnsheim, Weingut Freiherr Rhh.
Important NIERSTEIN estate, with buildings dating from the 16th

1981er
Qualitätswein b.A.
Rhein
hessen
Niersteiner Spiegelberg
Müller-Thurgau
ERZEUGERABFÜLLUNG AUS DEM WEINGUT
Freiherr Heyl zu Herrnsheim · Nierstein a. Rh.

century. 28.1ha (69 acre) in the best sites (PETTENTHAL, HIPPING, ÖLBERG, etc.), 60% Riesling, 20% Müller-Thurgau, 16% Silvaner, etc. The estate also owns all the 1.3ha (3.2 acre) of the Niersteiner Brudersberg. Approx. annual production is the equivalent of 21,600 cases, of characterful Riesling and Silvaner wines as well as flavoury Müller-Thurgau. Up to 60% are dry. Sales in Germany and abroad. Address: Mathildenhof, Langgasse 3, 6505 Nierstein.

Himmelreich M-S-R w. ★★★
100% steep, SW-facing Einzellage of nearly 90ha (222 acre) at

GRAACH. The site forms part of the great sweep of v'yds that stretches from BERNKASTEL to ZELTINGEN-RACHTIG. Among Mosel wines, those from the Graacher Himmelreich seem full, fruity, with a stylish acidity. Prices are similar to those of nearby Wehlener SONNENUHR. Grosslage: MÜNZLAY. Growers: "Abteihof", Christoffel, Friedrich-Wilhelm-Gymnasium, Haag, Kees-Kieren, Kesselstatt, Lauerburg, Pauly, Pauly-Bergweiler, J. J. Prüm, S. A. Prüm, Richter, St Johannishof, St-Nikolaus-Hospital, Schorlemer, Schwab, Studert-Prüm, Thanisch, Vereinigte Hospitien, Wegeler-Deinhard, Weins-Prüm.

Himmelreich M-S-R w. ✶✶→✶✶✶
Like the site of the same name at Graach (see previous entry), the Himmelreich Einzellage at ZELTINGEN-RACHTIG forms part of the continuous v'yd that stretches from BERNKASTEL to Zeltingen-Rachtig. Classic Mosel Riesling wines, although the general standard is probably not quite so high as that set by the Graacher Himmelreich. Grosslage: MÜNZLAY. Growers: Ehses-Geller, Mönchof, Nicolay, Pauly-Bergweiler, Selbach-Oster.

Hipping Rhh. w. ✶✶✶
Mainly steep Einzellage overlooking the Rhein at NIERSTEIN, producing top-quality wines of depth and much flavour. Grosslage: REHBACH. Growers: Balbach, Heyl zu Hernsheim, Kurfürstenhof, Hermann Franz Schmitt, Georg Schneider, Sittmann, Strub.

Hitzlay M-S-R w. ✶✶✶
Einzellage on the rural R. Ruwer at KASEL. Like all the Kasel sites, of excellent quality and capable of producing tremendously fresh, well-constructed wine in good years. Grosslage: RÖMERLAY. Growers: Beulwitz, Kesselstatt, Wegeler-Deinhard.

Hochfarbig
High coloured. Describes a white wine which may be oxydized, or made from grapes whose colour in the skins has entered into the must (possibly from Ruländer, Siegerrebe or Roter Traminer grapes) or from grapes that have been attacked by EDELFÄULE. Thus hochfarbig can be either negative or positive in meaning.

Hochgewächs
See Riesling-Hochgewächs.

Hochheim a. Main Rhg. Pop. 15,200 w. ✶✶✶
Small town 5km (3 miles) e. of MAINZ, but one of the best wine-growing communities of the Rheingau. The best sites (DOMDE-CHANEY, KÖNIGIN VICTORIA BERG, KIRCHENSTÜCK) produce powerful Rieslings with a distinct earthy flavour.The English word "HOCK" derives from Hochheim. Grosslage: DAUBHAUS.

Hochmess Rhpf. w. ✶✶
Small Grosslage of some 100ha (247 acre) on the n. edge of BAD DÜRKHEIM, incl. the well-known SPIELBERG site. The best wines are sold under the Einzellagen names but the quality of wine produced by the Grosslage as a whole is high. The Riesling and Scheurebe wines are often excellent.

Hock
Abbreviation for Hochheimer, originally described wines from HOCHHEIM but became a generic term for all white Rhein wine. The heading "Hocks and Moselles" still appears on many restaurant wine lists in the UK. Hock is defined by the EEC as (1) any German table wine that bears the description "Rhein", (2) a German quality wine from any of the following regions: Ahr, Hessische Bergstrasse, Mittelrhein, Nahe, Rheingau, Rheinhessen, Rheinpfalz. Hock must also be produced from Riesling or Silvaner, or their derivatives.

Hoensbroech, Weingut Reichsgraf & Marquis zu Baden
15ha (37 acre) estate nr. HEIDELBERG, incl. sole ownership of the Michelfelder Himmelberg site. Vines are 30% Weissburgunder, 20% Silvaner, 15% each Riesling and Spätburgunder, etc., producing 12,500 cases a year of powerful dry and med-dry wines sold exclusively in Germany and abroad. Address: 6921 Angelbachtal-Michelfeld.

"Hof Sonneck", Weingut Rhg.
9ha (22 acre) family-owned estate dating from 1756 with holdings

in the HÖLLE, Mittelhölle and Goldatzel sites at JOHANNISBERG. 80% Riesling, 20% Spätburgunder. The wines are, to a large extent, matured in cask. Annual production 9,600 cases, sold in Germany and abroad. Address: Sand 14, 6225 Johannisberg.

Höfer, Weingut Dr Josef Nahe
35ha (86 acre) family-owned estate est. in 1775 with holdings at BURG LAYEN, DORSHEIM, MÜNSTER-SARMSHEIM, etc. 30% of the wines

are dry or med-dry and the balance never oversweetened. Sales are in Germany and abroad. Address: Naheweinstr. 2, 6531 Burg Layen.

Hofkammerkellerei Stuttgart, Württembergische Würt.
38ha (94 acre) estate owned by King Carl, Duke of Württemberg, based on new buildings at Germany's largest baroque castle, Schloss Monrepos. It is the oldest estate in Würt. The holdings are on 6 subsidiary estates in various parts of the region. 48% is Riesling, 20% Limberger, 14% Trollinger, etc. 90% of the wines are dry and virtually all are sold locally. Address: 7140 Ludwigsburg.

Hofstück Rhpf. w. (r.) ★★
Grosslage that covers some 1,250ha (3,089 acre) of scattered v'yds nr. DEIDESHEIM and RUPPERTSBERG. Most of the sites are on level land on clay or sandy soil, producing good-quality white wines from the standard Rheinpfalz vine varieties (Riesling, Müller-Thurgau, etc.) and red from Portugieser.

Hohenberg, Weingut Rhpf.
10ha (25 acre) estate at the foot of the Pfälzer Wald, planted 42% Riesling, 12% Weissburgunder, 12% Müller-Thurgau, 12% Spätburgunder, etc. The steep sites are still partly terraced. Tannic, cask matured red wines, and the refreshing (mainly dry) whites win many national prizes. Annual production of 7,700 cases is sold 95% to the German consumer. Address: Dr. Heinz Wehrheim, Weinstr. 8, 6741 Birkweiler.

Hohenlohe Langenburgsche Weingüter, Fürstlich Würt. and Franken
26ha (64 acre) estate, 30% Müller-Thurgau, 17% Riesling, 15% Kerner, etc. Sole owners of the 17ha (42 acre) Karlsberg site on the slopes at Weikersheim in Württemberg. The wines are Franconian in style, with a pronounced earthy flavour. Annual production is 14,300 cases, all sold in Germany. Address: 6992 Weikersheim/Württemberg im Schloss.

Hohenlohe-Öhringen'sche, Fürst zu Würt.
Estate first mentioned in 1360, covering the 22ha (54 acre) of the sloping Verrenberger Verrenberg site (sole ownership) e. of HEILBRONN. Vines are 60% Riesling, 10% Müller-Thurgau, 10% Limberger, etc. The wines are dry (less than 4 g/l sugar), racy and typical of the grape variety. Annual production is 15,800 cases, sold to private customers and restaurants. Address: 7110 Öhringen. Schloss.

Hohenmorgen Rhpf. w. ★★★
One of several excellent Einzellagen at DEIDESHEIM producing top-quality, weighty Rieslings from sloping ground. Grosslage: MARIENGARTEN. Growers: Bassermann-Jordan, Bürklin-Wolf.

Hölle Rhg. w. ★★★
Einzellage at HOCHHEIM, overlooking the R. Main. Produces full, rounded, slightly earthy wines of excellent quality. Grosslage: DAUBHAUS. Growers: Ashcrott'sche Erben, Staatsweingut, Frankfurt am Main Stadt Weingut, Schloss Schönborn, Werner'sches Weingut.

Hölle Rhg. w. ★★★
Sloping Einzellage at JOHANNISBERG making balanced, classic Rheingau Riesling wines. Grosslage: ERNTEBRINGER. Growers: Hessisches Weingut, "Hof Sonneck", Hupfeld, "Johannisberger Rosenhof", Johannishof, Mumm'sches Weingut, Wegeler-Deinhard.

Höllenberg Rhg. r. ★★
Steep Einzellage overlooking the village of ASSMANNSHAUSEN, planted mainly in Spätburgunder. The wine is usually stylish and shows the vine characteristics well. Somewhat expensive. Grosslage: STEIL.

Holschier, Weingut Nikolaus Jakob Rhg.
Small, 2.34ha (5.8 acre) estate with holdings mainly in GEISENHEIM. Vines are 80% Riesling. Production has been limited while the v'yds have been reconstructed and modernized. A small quantity of very successful sparkling wine is made for the estate, using base wine from its holding in the Geisenheimer Mönchspfad site. Vinification is traditional and increasingly meeting a demand for drier wines. Sales are exclusively in Germany, some via STRAUSSWIRTSCHAFT. Address: Hermannstr. 11, 6222 Geisenheim/Rheingau.

Holzgeschmack
"Taste of wood." The flavour that may be picked up by a wine that has been stored in a new cask.

Honigberg Rhg. w. ★★
Grosslage of some 250ha (618 acre), incl. the Winkeler HASENSPRUNG site and SCHLOSS VOLLRADS. Production of good-quality Rheingau Riesling is endemic in Honigberg, so a Riesling sold under the Grosslage name will be closely related to wines sold with an Einzellage name. Good value for money but not cheap.

Honigsäckel Rhpf. w. ★★
A relatively small Grosslage of about 170ha (420 acre) covering three sites near the village of UNGSTEIN (Weilberg, Herrenberg and Nussriegel). Full-bodied wines, typical of the region, from varied soil on steep or gentle slopes.

Hövel, Weingut von M-S-R
Important Saar estate, nearly 200 years old, with cellars dating back to the 12th century. A holding in the SCHARZHOFBERG and sole ownership of the Hütte in OBEREMMEL, total 12ha (30 acre) of steep v'yds, 95% Riesling. Annual production is 10,000 cases of cask matured, typical high-quality Saar wines with pronounced acidity. Sales are in Germany and abroad. Address: Agritiusstr. 5-6, 5503 Konz-Oberemmel.

Hubertuslay M-S-R w. ★★
Mainly steep Einzellage at KINHEIM producing good-quality, charming Riesling wines, possibly lacking the personality of the best of the region. Grosslage: SCHWARZLAY. Growers: Kees-Kieren, Mönchof, Nicolay.

Huesgen GmbH, Adolf
Wine merchants, est. 1735, exporting estate bottlings and their own of QbA, DTW and EEC table wine. Annual turnover is 1m. cases, 90% exported. Address: 5580 Traben-Trabach.

Hupfeld Erben, Weingut H. Rhg.
10ha (25 acre) estate with holdings at JOHANNISBERG (HÖLLE, etc.), WINKEL (HASENSPRUNG, JESUITENGARTEN, etc.), MITTELHEIM, OESTRICH (LENCHEN, etc.), but best known for its ownership of Weingut KÖNIGIN VICTORIA BERG. Address: Rheingaustr. 113, 6227 Oestrich-Winkel.

Huxelrebe
White grape variety, a crossing of Weisser Gutedel × Courtillier musqué by Dr Georg Scheu of Alzey, dating from 1927. If the vine is prevented from its tendency to overcrop the MUST will be above

average in weight, with more acidity than Müller-Thurgau. Because of the high sugar content of the grapes the wine will often reach potential AUSLESE quality, with a light MUSKAT bouquet. Planted in 1,758ha (4,344 acre), mainly in the Rheinhessen and Rheinpfalz.

Hybriden
Hybrid vines: crossings of American and European vines that may be grown only under controlled conditions for experimental purposes. Hybrids are not the same as new crossings (NEUZÜCHTUNGEN) of one European vine with another.

Ice Saints
See Eisheiligen

Ice Wine
See Eiswein

Ihringen Baden w. (r.) ★★
Village in the Bereich KAISERSTUHL-TUNIBERG producing positive wines from a variety of vines, esp. Silvaner, which covers 37% of the area under vine. Müller-Thurgau and various members of the Burgunder (Pinot) family are also grown. Grosslage: VULKANFELSEN.

Immich-Batterieberg, Carl Aug. M-S-R
6ha (15 acre) estate with sites at ENKIRCH, incl. sole ownership of the steep 1.3ha (3 acre) Batterieberg v'yd. 100% Riesling. Annual production 4,400 cases of elegant, racy wine, sold in Germany and abroad. Address: 5585 Enkirch.

Ingelheim am Rhein Rhh. Pop. 19,300 r. (w.) ★★→★★★
Small town known for many years for its agreeable Spätburgunder WEISSHERBST and red wine. Grosslage: Kaiserpfalz.

Innere Leiste Franken w. ★★★
Steep site at WÜRZBURG and one of the relatively few internationally known Franken Einzellagen. Produces splendid, rather earthy Riesling wines with positive, firm style. Not in a Grosslage (see GROSSLAGEFREI). Growers: Bürgerspital, Juliusspital, Würzburg Staatl. Hofkeller.

Invertzucker
Invert sugar. A mixture of glucose and fructose which until 1971 could be used with water to enrich and deacidify cheaper wines. Achieved notoriety in the early 1980s for having been used in the falsification of wine.

Iphofen Franken w. ★★★
Fine old town with many noble and ecclesiastical wine-related buildings dating back to the 16th century. Silvaner, Müller-Thurgau and other vines produce top-quality wines, full of flavour and character. Grosslage: BURGWEG.

Istein, Schlossgut Baden
6ha (15 acre) estate of the rural district of Lörrach near Basel. The typical range of Baden vines produces 4,000 cases annually of dry red and white wines with much EXTRACT sold almost exclusively in Germany. Appropriate to one of the warmest parts of Germany is a Gewürztraminer Auslese with 16.8% actual alcohol. Address: Weingut des Landkreises Lörrach, 7859 Efringen-Kirchen.

Jahrgang
Vintage. Not used in the sense of "harvest", for which the German word is Ernte, but simply to denote wine of any one year. (See pages 19–21 for vintage information.)

Jahrgangssekt
Vintage, quality sparkling wine. A vintage may be given to a quality sparkling wine if at least 85% of the grapes used to make its base wine come from the year stated. Jahrgangssekt is not necessarily either better or worse than non-vintage sparkling wine, but in the eyes of the consumer it can have a certain added individuality.

Jesuitengarten Rhg. w. ★★→★★★
Einzellage close to the R. Rhein at WINKEL producing well-balanced wines, mainly from Riesling. Grosslage: HONIGBERG. Growers: Allendorf, Brentano'sche Guts., Hessisches Weingut, Hupfeld, Johannishof, Wegeler-Deinhard, Zwierlein.

Jesuitengarten Rhpf. w. ★★★
Only 6ha (15 acre) in extent, this Einzellage at FORST has a reputation for refined, well-balanced Riesling wines. More elegant and less fat in flavour than some from the Rheinpfalz, their quality is undenied. The site is widely known outside the region. Grosslage: MARIENGARTEN. Growers; Bassermann-Jordan, Buhl, Bürklin-Wolf, Forster Winzerverein, Mossbacher-Hof, E. Spindler, J. L. Wolf.

Johannisberg Rhg. w. ★★→★★★
Through its Schloss (castle), one of the most famous German wine-producing villages, lying in a fold in the v'yds. Distinguished Riesling wines are made and the Grosslage, ERNTEBRINGER, is probably the best known in the region.

Johannisberg, Bereich Rhg. w.
The Rheingau region and the Bereich Johannisberg cover exactly the same territory – a little under 3,000ha (7,413 acre), alongside the Rhein and Main rivers between LORCHHAUSEN and Wicker, beyond WIESBADEN. Johannisberg has been known for many years as a wine-producing village and its name has become legally attached to the whole of the Bereich. The use of the name Bereich Johannisberg for still wine has been limited, as in many instances the Grosslage name (ERNTEBRINGER, BURGWEG, STEINMÄCHER, etc.) preceded by the appropriate village name has seemed more attractive. Nevertheless, the name has proved popular as a description for sparkling wine made from grapes grown in the district.

Johannisberg, Schloss
See Schloss Johannisberg

"Johannisberger Rosenhof", Weingut Rhg.
5ha (12 acre) estate with holdings in GEISENHEIM, WINKEL and JOHANNISBERG. Vines are 75% Riesling, 10% Spätburgunder, 5% Kerner, etc. The typical Rheingauer wines have been very successful both in regional and national competition, and can be tasted in the estate's wine bar. Annual production is 4,600 cases. No exports. Address: Rosengasse 7, 6225 Johannisberg.

Johannishof, Weingut Rhg.
Estate dating from 1680. 18ha (44 acre) of modernized v'yds in JOHANNISBERG, WINKEL and GEISENHEIM, 95% Riesling. 8 metre (27ft) deep cellars help the maturation of stylish, firm Rheingau wines. Sales in Germany and abroad. Address: 6222 Johannisberg.

Josefinengrund, Weingut M-S-R
Estate owned by Franz REH & Sohn.

Josephshof, Der
See Kesselstatt, Weingut Reichsgraf von

Josephshöfer M-S-R w. ★★★
Small, prestigious Einzellage at GRAACH, owned by the Weingut Reichsgraf von KESSELSTATT. 6ha (15 acre), 90% steep, produce stylish, full-bodied wines that benefit from maturation in bottle. Grosslage: MÜNZLAY.

Jost, Weingut Toni Mrh. and Rhg.
Family-owned estate, est. in 1832, with 10ha (25 acre) on steep or sloping sites at BACHARACH and STEEG in the Mittelrhein and at WALLUF and MARTINSTHAL in the Rheingau. Vines are 70% Riesling, 10% Müller-Thurgau, etc. High production of dry and med-dry wines. Annual production is 7,500 cases. Much is sold in the estate's wine bar, some is exported. Address: Hahnenhof, Oberstr. 14, 6533 Bacharach.

Juffer M-S-R w. ★★★
One of the best-known Einzellagen on the Mosel, at BRAUNEBERG. 100% steep. Produces elegant Riesling wines, less steely than some from BERNKASTEL and more gentle in flavour. Very appealing and can certainly be of top quality. Grosslage: KURFÜRSTLAY. Growers: "Abteihof", Bergweiler-Prüm, Haag, Karp-Schreiber, Kesselstatt, Licht-Bergweiler, Richter, St-Nikolaus-Hospital.

Juffer-Sonnenuhr M-S-R w. ★★★
Small, S-SE facing, steep Riesling Einzellage at BRAUNEBERG, surrounded by the larger Juffer site. Very stylish, top quality wines.

Grosslage: KURFÜRSTLAY. Growers: Fritz Haag, Karp-Schreiber, Max Ferd, Pauly-Bergweiler, Richter, Thanisch.

Julius-Echter-Berg Franken ✹✹✹
Einzellage at IPHOFEN producing wines with firm acidity and much flavour from Riesling, Silvaner and Müller-Thurgau. Grosslage: BURGWEG. Growers: Juliusspital, Wirsching.

Juliusspital-Weingut Franken
Great WÜRZBURG charitable estate, dating from 1576, owned by the Julius hospital. Its 160ha (395 acre) of v'yds incl. holdings in many of Franken's most famous sites: Würzburger STEIN, Escherndorfer LUMP, Rödelseer KÜCHENMEISTER, and at IPHOFEN and RANDERSACKER. Vines are 35% Silvaner, 24% Müller-Thurgau, 11% Riesling, plus many other vine varieties incl. a small amount of Spätburgunder. Maturation in cask (some over 100 years old) 150m (492 ft) long cellar helps to produce wines with depth and body. Annual production is the equivalent of some 107,000 cases. Sales are in Germany and abroad. The wines can also be tasted in the estate's own wine bar. Address: Klinikstr. 5, 8700 Würzburg.

Jung
Young. Implies freshness if applied to a QbA and immaturity in the case of a fine wine.

Jungfernwein
Literally virgin wine: the first wine to be produced from vines in their second year after being planted. The term is no longer allowed as an official description.

Jungkenn, Weingut Ernst Rhh.
Estate owned since 1977 by Dr. Liselotte Sittmann of Weingut Carl SITTMANN, but which has retained its own separate, public identity. Holdings at DIENHEIM, ALSHEIM, OPPENHEIM, and NIERSTEIN, produce 16,600 cases annually of soft, full-bodied Rheinhessen wine, sold in Germany and abroad. Address: Wormser Str. 61, 6504 Oppenheim.

Jungwein
Young wine. Defined by the EEC as a wine with an incomplete fermentation, not yet separated from its yeast deposit.

Kabinett
Before 1971 spelt "Cabinet", originally a description given to wines considered to be particularly fine and worthy of storage in a grower's private cellar, or Cabinet. Since 1971 Kabinett has been the legally established term for the first category of PRÄDIKAT (QmP) wine, the lightest and most delicate of German wines. The old spelling is still permitted as a brand name for sparkling wines, e.g. Deinhard Cabinet, Schloss Wachenheim Grün-Cabinet, Schloss Koblenz Cabinet.

Kaiserstuhl-Tuniberg, Bereich Baden w. (r.)
The warmest and driest BEREICH, facing the v'yds of Alsace across the Rhein. Although the wines are not widely known outside Germany, the Spätburgunder and Ruländer have a good reputation in their homeland. The volcanic soil gives the white wine a positive flavour that is easily recognized.

Kaiserstühler Winzergenossenschaft, Ihringen eG Baden
Largest local cooperative cellar in Germany, with 950 members owning approx. 400ha (988 acre) all at Ihringen. Vines incl. a high proportion of Silvaner (39%) plus Müller-Thurgau (27%), Ruländer (8%), Spätburgunder (21%), etc. Annual production is equivalent to 476,200 cases of full-bodied wine, with the lower acid content (compared to the wines of the n. regions) expected in Baden. Address: Winzerstr. 6, 7817 Ihringen.

Kalb Franken w. ✹✹✹
Well-known Einzellage on the slopes at IPHOFEN producing stylish, firm Müller-Thurgau and Silvaner wines. Grosslage: BURGWEG. Growers: Frankeneg, Popp, Wirsching.

Kallstadt Rhpf. w. ✹✹✹→✹✹✹✹
The northernmost of the string of top-quality Rheinpfalz villages. Splendid, full-flavoured, essentially fruity wines from Riesling, Silvaner, Scheurebe, etc., similar in price to those of FORST and DEIDESHEIM further s. Grosslagen: KOBNERT and FEUERBERG.

Kallstadt eG, Winzergenossenschaft Rhpf.

Small cooperative cellar founded in 1902 whose members own 190ha (470 acre) of v'yds at KALLSTADT (SAUMAGEN, STEINACKER, etc.). Vines are 25% Riesling, 13% Silvaner, 14% Portugieser, 13% Müller-Thurgau, etc. 40% of the wines are dry/med-dry, sold 97% in Germany. Address: Weinstr. 126, 6701 Kallstadt.

Kalte Ente

"Cold duck": a corruption of "Kalte Ende", the cold end to a meal. A drink which, sold commercially, must contain at least 25% sparkling wine or PERLWEIN. Other ingredients are still wine, lemon peel and sugar to taste. In home-made Kalte Ente the proportion of sparkling wine will probably be much higher and will be added, very chilled, immediately before serving.

Kalte Sophie

See Eisheiligen.

Kanitz, Weingut Graf von Rhg.

Estate dating from the 13th century or earlier with 19.5ha (48 acre) of v'yds, all on steep sites at LORCH. Vines are 95% Riesling, organically manured. The wines are elegant and full of flavour. 70% are dry or med-dry. They can be tasted in the wine bar in the estate's 16th-century buildings. Annual prod. is 8,000 cases, sold in Germany and now abroad. Address: Rheinstr. 49, 6223 Lorch.

Kanzem M-S-R w. ★★★

One of a number of very small, pretty, rustic villages on the Saar that can make superb Riesling wines in good years. Grosslage: SCHARZBERG.

Kanzemer Berg, Weingut M-S-R

Small, 5ha (12 acre), high-quality estate, dating from the 16th century or earlier, with a holding in the modernized Kanzemer ALTENBERG site, 90% Riesling. Superb, flowery wines with lingering fruity acidity, that last for years in bottle. The great 1976 vintage produced only 2,000 cases, incl. two different Trockenbeerrenauslesen. Sales in Germany and abroad. Address: Weinstrasse 11, Maximilian v. Othegraven, 5511 Kanzem.

Kanzler

White grape variety, a crossing of Müller-Thurgau × Silvaner from Dr Scheu of ALZEY, planted in 107ha (264 acre), mainly in the Rheinhessen and Rheinpfalz. The yield is often small but the MUST weight is usually higher by about 20° Oechsle than that of Müller-Thurgau. The harvest can take place after the Müller-Thurgau has been picked resulting in full-bodied wines, sometimes of AUSLESE quality or higher.

Karp-Schreiber, Weingut Chr. M-S-R

3ha (7 acre) estate with holdings at BRAUNEBERG (JUFFER), 66% Riesling, 33% Müller-Thurgau and Kerner. Annual production is 3,300 cases of racy, fruity wines of which up to 40% are dry or med-dry. Many successes in regional and national competitions. Sales in Germany and abroad. Address: 5551 Brauneberg.

Karst & Söhne, Weingut, Joh. Rhpf.

10ha (25 acre) estate owned by the Karst family, growers for more than 250 years. Holdings are at BAD DÜRKHEIM (SPIELBERG, FUCHSMANTEL, etc.), 80% Riesling, also 10% highly successful Scheurebe. Annual production is 8,300 cases, 50% exported. Address: Burgstr. 15, 6702 Bad Dürkheim.

Karthäuserhof, Gutsverwaltung M-S-R

Ruwer estate, est. in the 14th century, owners of the 20ha (49 acre) 90% Riesling hill, the KARTHÄUSERHOFBERG, from which it produces some 12,500 cases a year of cask matured wines sold in Germany and abroad. Address: 5500 Trier-Eitelsbach.

Karthäuserhofberg M-S-R w. ★★★

Hill of vines overlooking EITELSBACH on the Ruwer, divided into five, mainly steep, Einzellagen: Burgberg, Kronenberg, Orthsberg, Sang and Stirn. All are owned by the Gutsverwaltung KARTHÄUSERHOF. Grosslage: RÖMERLAY.

Kasel M-S-R w. ★★→★★★

Small village in the compact little Ruwer valley, making topquality Riesling wines in good years. Grosslage: RÖMERLAY.

Kees-Kieren, Weingut M-S-R
Estate of 4.1ha (10 acre) incl. holdings at KINHEIM (HUBERTUSLAY) and GRAACH (DOMPROBST and HIMMELREICH), 100% Riesling. Annual production is some 4,200 cases of racy, light wines, mainly matured in wood in the vaulted cellar built in 1828. Biggest demand is for the KABINETT wines. Sales in Germany, the USA and UK. Address: Hauptstr. 22, 5551 Graach.

Kehrnagel M-S-R W. ★★★
One of several excellent Einzellagen at KASEL, mainly steep and planted with Riesling and Müller-Thurgau. Racy, elegant wines, esp. the Rieslings. Grosslage: RÖMERLAY. Growers: Beulwitz, Bischöfliche Weingüter, Kesselstatt, Simon, Wegeler-Deinhard.

Kellerbesichtigungen
"Cellar visits". For details on visiting cellars, see page 22.

Kellermeister
Cellar master. Responsible for the wine-making and all cellar activity, incl. training apprentices. Today, the younger generation of cellar masters will almost certainly have trained at a viticultural institute.

Kendermann GmbH, Hermann
Export house, est. in 1947. Leading brands are Black Tower Liebfraumilch and a QbA Mosel, Green Gold. Very successful in the USA. Address: Mainzerstr. 57, 6530 Bingen/Rhein.

Kern, Weingut Dr. Rhpf.
Estate dating in its present form from the start of the 19th century, with 5.8ha (14 acre) in top-quality sites in DEIDESHEIM (HERRGOTTSACKER, KIESELBERG, LANGENMORGEN, LEINHÖHLE, GRAINHÜBEL, etc.), RUPPERTSBERG (LINSENBUSCH, REITERPFAD) and in FORST (UNGEHEUER). Planted with 69% Riesling, 10% Kerner, etc. The emphasis is on dry wines, many sold in the estate's wine bar. Address: Schloss Deidesheim, 6705 Deidesheim.

Kerner
White grape variety, a crossing of Trollinger × Riesling from the viticultural institute in WEINSBERG. From 5ha (12 acre) in 1964, plantings had increased to 6,960ha (17,199 acre) in 1985 and Kerner is now found in all 11 wine-producing regions. It grows well in middle-quality sites, suitable for Silvaner, and can ripen late into the season, producing wine in all the quality (QmP) categories. The crop is large and the MUST weight usually 10–15° higher on the Oechsle scale than that of Riesling. Its acidity often causes it to be likened to Riesling, although its flavour is less fine. It is fruity, with a slight MUSKAT bouquet.

Kernig
Term used to describe a wine that has good body and acidity. Associated particularly with Rheingau Rieslings, often with a certain amount of bottle age.

Kesselstatt, Weingut Reichsgraf von M-S-R
Great estate, dating in its present form from 1820 but it has operated as a Weingut for more than 600 years. Consists of four different estates, all owned by Günther and Kathi Reh, at GRAACH ("Der Josephshof"), PIESPORT ("Domklausenhof"), KASEL ("St Irminenhof") and OBEREMMEL ("Oberemmeler Abteihof") 100% Riesling and covering 96ha (237 acre) in some of the best sites of the M-S-R: Graacher JOSEPHSHÖFER (sole owner) and HIMMELREICH. Bernkasteler BRATENHÖFCHEN, Zeltinger SONNENUHR. Piesporter GOLDTRÖPFCHEN and Braneberger JUFFER on the Mosel; at KASEL on the Ruwer and at WILTINGEN and SCHARZHOFBERG on the Saar. Annual prod. is the equivalent of 90,000 cases, sold in Germany and abroad. The Reh family also owns a number of other estates incl. Koch and Felix Müller at Wiltingen, Otto van Volxem at Oberemmel, Ehses-Berres at Zeltingen-Rachtig, D.J.B. Hain at Neumagen-Dhron, Domaine Bertagna (Burgundy), as well as the largest sekt manufacturers in Europe, Faber, of Trier. Address: Liebfrauenstr. 10, 5500 Trier.

G. C. Kessler and Co.
Oldest sparkling-wine producers in West Germany, at Esslingen nr. Stuttgart, est. in 1826 by Georg Christian von Kessler, who had

worked with the Champagne house Veuve Clicquot Ponsardin. Wine sold under the Kessler label is made by FLASCHENGÄRUNG (bottle fermentation) and that of the subsidiary company, Gebrüder Weiss, by vat fermentation. Address: Marktplatz 21–23,7300 Esslingen.

Kesten M-S-R w. ★★
Old village near BRAUNEBERG, whose wines are not often found abroad other than under the Grosslage name Bernkasteler KURFÜRSTLAY. A high proportion of Riesling is grown.

KGaA
Kommanditgesellschaft auf Aktien. Partnership based on shares, as in Deinhard & Co. KGaA.

Kiedrich Rhg. w. ★★★
Small, attractive village on the slopes above ELTVILLE. There has always been a close bond between the vine growers of the region and the remarkable parish church of St Valentin (although it was an Englishman, John Sutton, who restored the church and organ to their present splendour in the 19th century, and established the famous choir). Best-known sites are GRÄFENBERG and SANDGRUB. Grosslage: HEILIGENSTOCK.

Kieselberg Rhpf. w. ★★★
One of the best sites in DEIDESHEIM, making excellent Riesling wines. Grosslage: MARIENGARTEN. Growers: Bassermann-Jordan, Biffar, Buhl, Dr. Deinhard, Kern, Spindler.

Kinheim M-S-R w. ★★
Ancient wine village nr. TRABEN-TRABACH; the v'yds were established by Benedictine monks in the 12th century. The sites face S and SE, planted mainly with Riesling, and produce stylish, elegant wines. Grosslage: SCHWARZLAY.

Kirchberg Franken w. ★★
Kirchberg is one of the most common site names in Germany. The small, 1.5ha (3.7 acre) Kirchberg site at Castell produces excellent, powerfully flavoured, earthy wines. Grosslage: HERRENBERG. Growers incl. Castell'sches Domänenamt.

Kirchenstück Rhg. w. ★★★
One of the best small Einzellagen at HOCHHEIM, producing elegant Riesling wines with fine, balanced acidity. Grosslage: DAUBHAUS. Growers: Aschrott'sche Erben, Staatsweingut, Frankfurt am Main Weingut, Schloss Schönborn, Werner'sches Weingut.

Kitzingen Franken Pop. 20,200 w. ★★→★★★
Town 19km (12 miles) s.e. of WÜRZBURG with attractive old buildings, and for centuries a centre of the Franken wine trade. The 8th-century Benedictine abbey claims one of the oldest (more than 1,000 years old) cellars in Germany. Wines with grip, from Silvaner and Müller-Thurgau. Grosslage: Hofrat.

Kläuserweg Rhg. w. ★★★
One of several excellent Einzellagen at GEISENHEIM on the Rhein, on sloping ground, producing full-bodied Riesling wines with firm acidity. Grosslage: ERNTEBRINGER. Growers: Forschungsanstalt Geisenheim, Hessisches Weingut, Johannishof, Mumm'sches Weingut, Ress, Schumann-Nägler, Vollmer, Wegeler-Deinhard, Zwierlein.

Klingelberger
Name used in the Bereich ORTENAU in Baden for Riesling, after the one-time Klingelberg site at DURBACH in which it was planted.

Klingenberg a. Main Franken r. (w.) ★★
Small town 23km (14 miles) s. of Aschaffenburg on the Main, first mentioned in connection with wine-growing in AD 776. Well known in Germany for its red wine (Portugieser, Spätburgunder). Also produces Müller-Thurgau. No Grosslage.

Kloster
Monastery or convent. In law, Kloster can be included in the title of an estate if the wine is made in the Kloster's own cellar from its own estate-grown grapes. The Cistercian, Carthusian and Benedictine Orders have all been involved in vine-growing in Germany, but the most famous wine-connected Kloster today is undoubtedly the Cistercian KLOSTER EBERBACH in the Rheingau.

Kloster Eberbach
12th-century Cistercian monastery in a valley above HATTENHEIM in the Rheingau. Today, like the Cistercian Clos de Vougeot in Burgundy, it is very much the spiritual home of vine-growing in the region. It is open to the public and provides a venue for many activities promoting wine. It is also a base for the GERMAN WINE ACADEMY.

Klostergut St Lamprecht
See Bergdolt, F. u. G.

Kloster Machern, Weingut M-S-R
The estate Nachf is owned by Michel Schneider covering 50ha (124 acre) at WEHLEN (sole ownership of Abtei, Klosterhofgut and Hofberg) and at ZELL and Merl. Vines are 78% Riesling, 7% Müller-Thurgau and 15% new crossings. Annual production is 44,400 cases and sales on the export market are large. Address: 5550 Bernkastel-Wehlen, 5583 Zell/Mosel.

Klüsserath M-S-R w. ★★
Long, narrow village on the MITTELMOSEL, stretching for 250ha (618 acre) between the BRÜDERSCHAFT Einzellage and the river. Good-quality Riesling wines. Grosslage: ST MICHAEL.

Knebel, Weingut Erwin M-S-R
Small estate nr. KOBLENZ, in the vine-growing Knebel family since 1727. Holdings in all the Einzellagen at WINNINGEN, 70% Riesling. Depending on the vintage, Erwin Knebel will produce the full range of award-winning Mosel wines up to EISWEIN and TROCKENBEERENAUSLESE level. 70% are dry or med-dry. Annual production is 2,400 cases. Address: Am Markt 5, 5406 Winningen.

Knoll & Reinhart, Weinbau-Weinkellerei Franken
Estate dating from 1925 with 3ha (7 acre) in SOMMERACH, RÖDELSEE and IPHOFEN. 33% Silvaner, 30% Kanzler, etc. The success of recent years has been the Kanzler wine. Sales are directly to the German consumer. Grapes are also bought in from neighbouring growers to increase the throughput. Address: Alte Poststr. 6, 8710 Kitzingen 2.

Knyphausen, Weingut Freiherr zu Rhg.
Estate founded in the 12th century by the Cistercians from KLOSTER EBERBACH, acquired by the Knyphausen family in 1818. 20ha (49 acre) incl. holdings at ERBACH (MARCOBRUNN, SIEGELSBERG, etc.), HATTENHEIM (WISSELBRUNNEN) and KIEDRICH. 90% Riesling, 4% Spätburgunder. Annual production 14,000 cases of good-quality wine, typical of the region, sold in Germany and abroad. Address: Klosterhof Drais, 6228 Eltville.

Kobern M-S-R w. ★★
Charming old village nr. KOBLENZ in the Bereich ZELL. Very steep v'yds planted mainly with Riesling give powerfully flavoured, fruity wines. Grosslage: WEINHEX.

Koblenz Mrh and M-S-R Pop. 117,000 w.
Founded in the 1st century after Christ as "Confluentes", Koblenz stands at the meeting point of the Rhein and Mosel. Badly damaged in World War II, the old part of the town has been expertly restored. Near the centre of the town are the 0.2ha (0.5 acre) of one of the smallest Einzellagen in Germany, the Schnorbach-Brückstück, planted mainly in Müller-Thurgau. In the Ehrenbreitsteiner Kreuzberg site, in a charming side valley of the Rhein, good Mittelrhein Riesling wines are made. Koblenz is an important administrative centre for the local wine trade and is the home of v'yd owners, wine exporters and Sekt producers DEINHARD.

Kobnert Rhpf. w. (r.) ★★
Grosslage of some 1,500ha (3,707 acre) that spreads n. from the village of KALLSTADT. As throughout the Bereich MITTELHAARDT/ DEUTSCHE WEINSTRASSE, the quality of wine is high, the range of vine varieties wide and the soil varied.

Koch Erben, Bürgermeister Carl Rhh.
6th generation, 10ha (25 acre) estate, planted with 35% Riesling, 18% Silvaner, 15% Müller-Thurgau, etc., at OPPENHEIM (SACKTRÄGER, KREUZ, etc.) and DIENHEIM. Storage is in wood and vat, and 15% of the annual production of 9,400 cases is dry or med-dry. The

wines mature well in bottle, and are sold mainly in Germany but also abroad. Address; Wormser Str, 62, 6504 Oppenheim.

Koehler-Ruprecht, Weingut Rhpf.

8.5ha (21 acre) KALLSTADT estate, incl. holdings in STEINACKER. Vines are 67% Riesling, plus Kerner, etc., producing concentrated wines full of flavour and character. Spätburgunder is also grown. Maturation is in oak casks and only QmP wines are produced. 65% are dry or med-dry. Because of the micro-climate, AUSLESE can be made every year from one or more of the vine varieties. Annual production is 8,300 cases. The wines are sold in Germany and also abroad. Address: Weinstr. 84, 6701 Kallstadt an der Weinstrasse.

Kommissionär

See Broker

Königin Victoria Berg Rhg. w. ★★★

Small, 5ha (12 acre) Einzellage at HOCHHEIM, named after Queen Victoria and owned by the Weingut Königin Victoria Berg. Grosslage: DAUBHAUS.

Königin Victoria Berg, Weingut Rhg.

Estate concentrated entirely in one site, the Königin Victoria Berg (see previous entry), to which Queen Victoria allowed her name to be officially given in 1857, following a visit to HOCHHEIM in 1850, owned by Weingut H. HUPFELD ERBEN. Production is approximately. 3,300 cases a year of firm full-bodied Riesling wines with a positive, earthy character. Much is exported to the English-speaking countries via the Koblenz wine shippers DEINHARD & COMPANY, under the original Victorian oval label. Address: Rheinstrasse. 2, 6203 Hochheim.

Königswinter Mrh. Pop. 35,000 w.

Today a tourist attraction, Königswinter, nr. Bonn, is known to have produced wines since the 11th century. Its small – and only – Einzellage, Drachenfels, accounts for more than half the 19ha (47 acre) viticultural area of the state of NORDRHEIN-WESTFALEN, producing Müller-Thurgau and Riesling wines with pronounced acidity. Grosslage: Petersberg.

Konsumwein

Wine for everyday drinking. The term is not defined in law but refers to cheap wine blended to a particular style.

Konz M-S-R Pop. 14,700 w. ★★

Town at the confluence of the Saar and Mosel. A high proportion of Riesling is grown, producing fruity, racy wines in a number of good ORTSTEILEN. Grosslage: SCHARZBERG.

Korkgeschmack

Corked. Term used to describe wines with an unclean smell. The causes are not fully understood but they include infection of the cork on the tree by fungus, incorrect storage and inadequate cleaning of cellar equipment.

Kratzig

Describes a wine that "scratches" (kratzt) the throat through too much volatile acid. Such a wine would be in very poor condition and liable to deteriorate further.

Kreuz Rhh. w. ★★★

An Einzellage shared by OPPENHEIM and Dienheim, next to the well-known SACKTRÄGER site and which is almost as distinguished. Grosslage: GÜLDENMORGEN. Growers: Baumann, Guntrum, Koch Erben, Oppenheim Staatsweingut, Schmitt'sches Weingut, Sittmann.

Kreuznach, Bereich Nahe w.

Bereich that covers the v'yds of what used to be known as the Lower Nahe (Untere Nahe) from Bingerbrück upriver to BAD KREUZNACH. The Bereich name is probably used more for administrative purposes than as a description of wine. The type of simple quality wine likely to be sold as Bereich Kreuznach will usually be a little more full in flavour than a wine from the adjacent Bereich SCHLOSSBÖCKELHEIM.

Kronenberg Nahe w. **★★**

1,300ha (3,212 acre) Grosslage surrounding the town of BAD KREUZNACH. The top-quality sites concentrate on Riesling but many other grapes are grown on a wide variety of soils. The best Riesling wines will normally be sold under an Einzellage name, but a Kronenberg wine should still show the blend of body and racy flavour expected from the Nahe.

Krötenbrunnen Rhh. w. (r.) **★**

Large Grosslage covering nearly 1,800ha (4,448 acre). It encompasses some of the v'yds of the well-known wine villages of DIENHEIM, GUNTERSBLUM, ALSHEIM and UELVERSHEIM, as well as four of the sites at OPPENHEIM – Schlossberg, Schloss, Paterhof, Herrengarten. The Krötenbrunnen name is mainly used for inexpensive simple-quality wine (QbA), very much on the same level as that from the adjacent Grosslage GUTES DOMTAL.

Krötenpfuhl Nahe w. **★★**

Small Einzellage at BAD KREUZNACH planted mainly in Riesling, from which excellent, positive, stylish wines are made. Grosslage: KRONENBERG. Growers: August E. Anheuser, Paul Anheuser.

Kröv M-S-R w. **★→★★**

Village near TRABEN-TRABACH, probably best known outside the region for the wines of its Grosslage NACKTARSCH.

Küchenmeister Franken w. **★★★**

Einzellage at RÖDELSEER producing spicy wines, full of flavour, that can rise to considerable heights in a good vintage. Grosslage: Schlossberg. Growers: Juliusspital, Wirsching.

Kupferberg & Cie., KGaA., Christian Adalbert

Est. in 1850 as producers of sparkling wine, Kupferberg quickly moved into the export market, selling, in particular, a "Sparkling Hochheimer Domdechaney", an early forerunner of LAGENSEKT. At the same time, in the 1850s, the brand "Kupferberg Gold" was launched. About two-thirds of Kupferberg's production gains its sparkle in vat, one-third in bottle. For the latter, the yeast deposit from the second fermentation is removed by filtration, avoiding the regular and expensive shaking of each bottle to force the deposit onto the cork for later removal. Owners of Champagne Bricout et Koch S.A., Avize. Annual production is 1m. cases. Address: Kupferberg-Terrasse, 6500 Mainz.

Kupfergrube Nahe w. **★★★→★★★★**

Undoubtedly one of the finest Riesling Einzellagen of the Nahe, and therefore of the whole of Germany. It was created by convict labour in the early part of this century, and literally hewn out of the rocky hillside. In the best years great wines of incredible distinction and complexity are made from the 100% steep slopes. Rightly expensive. Grosslage: BURGWEG. Growers: Niederhausen-Schlossböckelheim Staatl. Weinbaudomäne, Plettenberg, Schlink-Herf-Gutleuthof.

Kupp M-S-R w. **★★★**

100% steep Riesling Einzellage at AYL on the Saar, capable of producing great wines in fine vintages. Grosslage: SCHARZBERG. Growers: Bischöfliche Weingüter, Nell, Rheinart.

Kupp M-S-R w. **★★★**

One of two good Einzellagen on the Saar of the same name, the small, mainly steep Kupp at WILTINGEN produces elegant Riesling wine. Grosslage: SCHARZBERG. Growers: Bischöfliche Weingüter, Felix Müller.

Kurfürstenhof, Weingut Rhh.

Centuries-old estate, acquired by the Seip family in 1950, with 35ha (86 acre) in many of the best sites at NIERSTEIN (BILDSTOCK,

FINDLING, PETTENTHAL, HIPPING, ÖLBERG, etc.), and at NACKENHEIM, DIENHEIM and OPPENHEIM. The estate is also sole owner of the small, 0.6ha (1.5 acre) Goldene Luft site at Nierstein. Fresh, lively wines, showing the grape characteristics well, and incl. surprising quantities of BEERENAUSLESE and TROCKENBEERENAUSLESE from many new vine crossings. Sales in Germany and abroad. Address: Fronhof 7, 6505 Nierstein.

Kurfürstlay M-S-R w. ★

Large Grosslage of more than 1,600ha (3,954 acre), incl. the top-quality wine-producing village of BRAUNEBERG. Wines sold under the Kurfürstlay name should be of adequate quality, reflecting the expected fresh Mosel characteristics, but are unlikely to be very distinguished.

Lack

Lac or varnish. Originally a resinous substance secreted by an insect, the *Coccus lacca,* which yields a fine, red dye. Before the arrival of the capsule, coloured wax seals (Siegellack) were used to protect the corks in bottled wine. The different colour capsules used by Schloss Johannisberg today for its various qualities of wine are still referred to as Rotlack, Grünlack, etc.

Lactic acid

See Milchsäure

Lage

Site: a v'yd that has been recorded in the official v'yd register (the Weinbergsrolle). The smallest unit is the EINZELLAGE, which should be not less than 5ha (12 acre) in size, although there are exceptions. A GROSSLAGE comprises a number of Einzellagen. Only quality (QbA or QmP) wines may bear site names. If they do, at least 85% of the wine must come from the site stated. In the case of a QbA the remaining 15% must have originated in the same region, or for a QmP from the same BEREICH.

Lagensekt

Quality sparkling wine from an EINZELLAGE or GROSSLAGE. There is an increasing interest in Germany in sparkling wines bearing site names, often offered by well-known estates. Lagensekt is usually made by a specialist contract cellar, using a second fermentation in bottle (FLASCHENGÄRUNG) to produce the sparkle. See also MARKEN-SEKT, RIESLINGSEKT.

Lahn Mrh.

Small river that joins the Rhein at Lahnstein, just below KOBLENZ. The v'yds, now much reduced in size and number, are planted mainly with Riesling.

Laible, Weingut Andreas Baden

Long-established family-owned estate of 3.8ha (9 acre) with hold-

ings on the hilly slopes around DURBACH. Vines are 26% Riesling, 18% Traminer, etc. The estate has new cellars, set in the midst of the v'yds, and produces a low yield of fresh, full-bodied and often slightly SPRITZIG wine, sold mainly to private customers in Germany. Address: Am Buehl 71, 7601 Durbach.

Lamm-Jung, Weingut Rhg.

Estate est. in 1948 by Herr Josef Jung from two separate holdings at ERBACH and KIEDRICH. 7.7ha (19 acre) of vines, 73% Riesling. Fruit trees are also grown commercially. Good-quality wine-making. Most of the annual production of some 6,200 cases is collected by private customers directly from the cellars. Address: Eberbacherstr. 50, 6229 Erbach.

Landau in der Pfalz Rhpf. Pop. 36,500 w. ★→★★

Attractive town in the Bereich SÜDLICHE WEINSTRASSE, suffered much through wars and political upheavals over the centuries. Wines are sound but seldom outstanding when compared to the finest in the region. Grosslage: Königsgarten.

Landenberg, Weingut Frieherr von M-S-R

Hoteliers, wine merchants, and owners of 9.9ha (24 acre) of steep, modernized v'yds at Ediger-Eller and Senheim, planted mainly in Riesling, but also and unusually with a small parcel of Gewürztraminer. Sales are in Germany and abroad. Address: Moselweinstr. 60, 5591 Ediger-Eller.

Landgräflich

Belonging to a landgrave, as in Landgräflich Hessisches Weingut at Johannisberg. A landgrave was a count of a country district (his urban counterpart was a burgrave).

Landwein

"Country wine": a category of German table wine created in 1982, the equivalent of *vin de pays*, with a natural alcohol content (before enrichment) at least 0.5% higher than the minimum set for DEUTSCHER TAFELWEIN. A Landwein cannot be sweeter than HALBTROCKEN (i.e. it will contain at most 18 g/l sugar). It is a rustic wine, to be enjoyed in large quantities, accompanying food. Its commercial success so far has been limited.

Lang, Weingut Hans Rhg.

11.5ha (28 acre) estate with holdings in KIEDRICH and HATTENHEIM (incl. WISSELBRUNNEN). 80% Riesling, 10% Spätburgunder. Herr Lang's initial interest was grafting vines; he moved into wine-making in 1959. Annual prod. is 9,000 cases of wine incl. sekt, 30% is dry or med-dry, light and elegant in style. Sales in Germany and abroad. Address: Rheinallee 6, 6228 Eltville-Hattenheim.

Langenbach & Co GmbH. Rhh.

Wine merchants established in 1852, with a 7ha (17 acre) holding in the Wormser LIEBFRAUENSTIFT-KIRCHENSTÜCK, owned by Whitbread & Co PLC, London. Annual turnover just under 1m. cases, sold in Germany and 45 other countries. Address: Alzeyerstr. 31, 6520 Worms.

Langenlonsheim Nahe w. ★★

Small agricultural town between BAD KREUZNACH and BINGEN, could be described as top of the second division in the Nahe. Old-established estates produce good, wholesome wines, seldom found outside Germany. Grosslage: Sonnenborn.

Langenmorgen Rhpf. w. ★★★

Small, 7ha (17 acre) Einzellage on the slopes at DEIDESHEIM, making excellent Riesling wine. Grosslage: MARIENGARTEN. Growers: Bassermann-Jordan, Bürklin-Wolf, Kern.

Laubenheim Rhh. w. ★★

Small town, now within the boundaries of MAINZ. Grosslage: ST ALBAN.

Lauerburg, Weingut J. M-S-R

Small Mosel estate, in the Lauerburg family since 1700. Holdings are 100% Riesling in top-quality sites at Graach (HIMMELREICH), Bernkastel (BRATENHÖFCHEN, DOCTOR). Approximate annual production is 5,900 cases of elegant, top-quality wine that benefits from ageing in bottle. Sales are in Germany and abroad – much through the Alzey wine shippers H. Sichel Söhne. Address: Graacherstr. 24, 5550 Bernkastel-Kues.

Lauffen a. Neckar Würt. r. w. ★★

Small town 10km (6 miles) s.w. of HEILBRONN, esp. well known in the region for its gentle Schwarzriesling wine, but other red and white vine varieties are also grown. Grosslage: Kirchenweinberg.

Lay M-S-R w. ★★
Small Einzellage at BERNKASTEL, planted exclusively in Riesling. Grosslage: BADSTUBE.

Lebendig
Lively. Describes a fresh wine with good acidity and often a noticeable amount of carbon dioxide (slightly SPRITZIG).

Lehmen M-S-R w. ★★
One of many small villages in the Bereich ZELL producing sound, crisp Riesling wines from very steep v'yds. Grosslage: WEINHEX.

Lehranstalt
Teaching institute. Germany's teaching institutes for viticulture and wine-making are respected throughout the world. Among the best known are those at GEISENHEIM and WEINSBERG.

Leicht
Light. This describes a wine that is light in alcohol and low in extract.

Leinhöhle Rhpf. w. ★★★
Mainly sloping Einzellage at DEIDESHEIM from which full-bodied, top-quality Riesling wines are made. Grosslage: MARIENGARTEN. Growers: Bassermann-Jordan, Josef Biffar, Buhl, Dr Deinhard, Hahnhof, Kern, E. Spindler, J. L. Wolf.

Leiwen M-S-R w. ★★
Small, pleasant village in the MITTELMOSEL, probably best known as the home of wine merchants and v'yd owners Franz REH & Sohn. Racy, fruity Rieslings. Grosslage: ST MICHAEL.

Lemberger
See Limberger

Lenchen Rhg. w. ★★★
Large, 145ha (358 acre), mainly level Einzellage at OESTRICH making flowery, balanced Rieslings with finesse and body. Grosslage: GOTTESTHAL. Growers: Eser, Hupfeld, Rheingau eG, Vereinigte Weingutsbestizer, Wegeler-Deinhard.

Lenz-Dahm GmbH, Weingut-Weinhandel M-S-R
Small 2.7ha (7 acre) estate, with holdings at PÜNDERICH. 100% Riesling. Fermentation at low temperatures, use of SÜSSRESERVE, minimum use of sulphur dioxide are the proclaimed characteristics of the wine making. The marketing policy is clear and 80% of the wines are dry or med-dry. Address: Hauptstr. 3, 5587 Pünderich.

Lese
HARVEST

Lesegut
The grapes from which wine is made. Most often found in the phrase "AUS DEM LESEGUT".

Licht-Bergweiler Erben, Weingut P. M-S-R
Mosel estate, in the Licht family for more than 200 years, with holdings at BRAUNEBERG (incl. JUFFER), Wehlener SONNENUHR, Graacher DOMPROBST and at BERNKASTEL, producing some 11,000 cases a year of balanced, elegant wine, matured in wood. Sales in Germany and abroad. Address: Bernkastelerstr. 33, 5551 Brauneberg/Mosel.

Liebfrauenkirche Rhh.
The Church of Our Lady in Worms: the v'yd from which the world-famous LIEBFRAUMILCH originally came adjoins the Gothic church. The v'yd is largely on the site of an old convent – a writer in the early 19th century noted that the soil was much mixed with rubble and therefore somewhat artificial. Today it forms the Liebfrauenstift-Kirchenstück Einzellage, itself part of the LIEBFRAUEN-MORGEN Grosslage.

Liebfrauenmorgen Rhh. w. ★★
Grosslage of more than 1,000ha (2,471 acre) scattered around the cathedral city of WORMS in the extreme s. of the Rheinhessen. V'yds are on level or slightly sloping land. The name Liebfrauenmorgen shares its origin with LIEBFRAUMILCH: both relate to the LIEBFRAUENKIRCHE (Church of Our Lady) in Worms. A MORGEN is an obsolete measure of land.

Liebfrauenstift-Kirchenstück
See Liebfrauenkirche

Liebfraumilch

Also spelt Liebfrauenmilch, meaning the "milk of Our Lady", after the v'yd of the LIEBFRAUENKIRCHE (Church of Our Lady) in Worms from which the wine originally came. A white QbA, produced mainly in the Rheinpfalz and Rheinhessen regions, to a lesser extent in the Nahe and theoretically also in the Rheingau. It must derive predominantly from Riesling, Silvaner, Müller-Thurgau, or Kerner and should taste of these grapes. It may not, however, bear a grape name and must contain more than 18 g/l of residual sugar (the upper limit for HALBTROCKEN wines). Liebfraumilch is the most widely exported of German wines, and since the early 1970s has become among the cheapest. In as much as it is a German quality wine and must pass through a control centre, Liebfraumilch should be at least pleasant and agreeable. However, the quality of the cheapest brand will bear little relationship to the standards set by the old established brands, such as "Blue Nun" and "Madonna".

Lieblich

Medium-sweet. Technically describes a wine with 18–45 g/l residual sugar. Can often be applied to Rheinhessen QbA with low acidity and a gentle, sweet flavour. Such wines contain relatively little alcohol and are, for many, the archetypal German wines, so widely appreciated (especially as LIEBFRAUMILCH) on the export market.

Liebrecht'sche Weingutsverwaltung, Oberstlt. Rhh.

12.5ha (31 acre) estate with holdings in modernized v'yds at BODENHEIM, planted with 53% Riesling, 25% Silvaner and 8% Kerner. Rieslings are particularly distinguished but all the wines do well at the national (DLG) competitions. Annual production: 10,600 cases, sold mainly to the consumer but also exported. Address: Rheinstr. 30, 6501 Bodenheim.

Lieser M-S-R w. ★★

Small village nr. BERNKASTEL-KUES making racy, elegant wines. It takes its name from the stream that flows into the Mosel. The castle at Lieser is the family seat of the v'yd-owning von SCHORLEMER family. Grosslagen: Beerenlay and KURFÜRSTLAY.

Limberger, Blauer

Red grape variety, also spelt Lemberger, occupying 532ha (1,315 acre) in Württemberg (also widely grown in Austria where it is known as Blaufränkisch). It ripens late in the season, shortly before the Spätburgunder, compared to which its wine is lighter, has a higher acid content and is usually inferior in quality. Often sold blended with Trollinger.

Lingenfelder, Weingut Karl & Hermann Rhpf.

10ha (25 acre) estate, planted with 22% Riesling, 17% Müller-Thurgau, 15% Scheurebe, etc., at Freinsheim and Grosskarlbach. Individual wines of considerable charm compare well with those from better known Rheinpfalz villages. Arguably the barrique-aged Spätburgunder is amongst the best in Germany. Annual production of 9,200 cases is sold in Germany and the UK. Address: Hauptstr. 27, 6711 Grosskarlbach.

Linsenbusch Rhpf. w. ★★→★★★

Large, 175ha (432 acre), level Einzellage at RUPPERTSBERG, in which various vine varieties are grown. Its Müller-Thurgau is exceptionally stylish. Grosslage: MARIENGARTEN. Growers: Bassermann-Jordan, Buhl, Bürklin-Wolf, Kern, Ruppertsberger Winzerverein "Hoheburg", E. Spindler, Wegeler-Deinhard.

Longuich M-S-R w. ★★

Small village e. of TRIER, nr. the upstream boundary of the MITTELMOSEL, making distinguished, fruity Rieslings. Grosslage: Probstberg.

Loosen-Erben, Weingut Benedict M-S-R

Small Mosel estate with holdings at ERDEN (TREPPCHEN and PRÄLAT) and ÜRZIG (WÜRZGARTEN). Over the years many fine wines have been made. No SÜSS RESERVE is used, and the wines can be tasted at the estate's "Alter Klosterhof" wine bar in Ürzig. Address: Würzgartenstr. 1, 5564 Ürzig.

Lorch Rhg. w. ★★
Village in the Rhein gorge, opposite the v'yds of the Mittelrhein, at the downstream end of the Rheingau. Riesling predominates. Quality is good, prices are similar to those from villages such as JOHANNISBERG and WINKEL, although the wines probably cannot quite compete with the finest in the region. Grosslage: BURGWEG.

Lorchhausen Rhg. w. ★★
Attractive village immediately adjacent to the v'yds of the Mittelrhein, producing light, elegant Riesling wine. Grosslage: BURGWEG.

Lorettoberg Baden w. ★★
Grosslage s. of FREIBURG in the Bereich MARKGRÄFLERLAND. Many vine varieties (esp. Gutedel) and a high proportion of simple quality wine (QbA), made to modern high standards of vinification. Much of the wine is sold by the vast Central Cooperative Cellars (ZBW) at BREISACH.

Löwensteinhof, Weingut M-S-R
Small 2.6ha (6 acre) estate, 85% Riesling, owned by the Löwenstein family, established as vine growers in WINNINGEN through 13 generations. Sales are exclusively to the consumer, with the dry Riesling Spätlesen being much in demand. Address: 5406 Winningen.

Löwenstein-Wertheim-Rosenberg'sches Weingut, Fürstlich Franken/Baden
Estate that has been producing wine since the 12th century; acquired by the Löwenstein-Wertheim-Rosenberg family nearly 200 years ago. 27ha (67 acre), many in very steep sites, incl. the terraced Homburger Kallmuth by the R. Main. Vines are 42% Silvaner, 19% Müller-Thurgau, 15% Spätburgunder, etc., producing traditional dry Franken wines, and a small amount of red wine sold in Burgundy bottles. No exports. Address: Rathausgasse 5, 6983 Kreuzwertheim.

Lump Franken w. ★★★
Steep, well-known Einzellage at ESCHERNDORF making powerful, soft, Silvaner and Müller-Thurgau wines. Grosslage: KIRCHBERG. Growers: Franken eG, Juliusspital.

Maikammer Rhpf. w. ★
Small town in the n. of the Bereich SÜDLICHE WEINSTRASSE, well known in the region. Sound but not top-quality wines. Grosslage: Mandelhöhe.

Main
River 483km (300 miles) long that flows into the Rhein at MAINZ. En route it provides an erratic line around which the Franken v'yds are planted. It also passes the small but important sites at HOCHHEIM in the Rheingau.

Mainz Rhh. Pop. 186,500
Capital of RHEINLAND-PFALZ and the headquarters of many institutions concerned with wine. It lies mainly in the Bereich NIERSTEIN and much of its sound wine is sold under the Grosslage names of ST ALBAN and DOMHERR. It is also the birthplace of the printer Johannes Gutenberg.

Mainzer Weinbörse
A fair held each year in MAINZ for the wine trade. In 1986 more than 550 wines, incl. sparkling wines, from almost 50 leading estates in Rheinhessen, Rheinpfalz, Nahe, Mosel-Saar-Ruwer, Franken, Rheingau, Baden and Württemberg were available for tasting. The fair is an important event in the German wine-trade year.

Maische
The pulp and juice of the grape, after it leaves the crusher and before it is pressed.

Malic acid
See Äpfelsäure.

Männle, Weingut Heinrich Baden
5ha (12 acre) estate planted 38% in Spätburgunder, plus Müller-Thurgau, Ruländer, Scheurebe and a range of other varieties. 60% of the wines are dry or med-dry, and customers value the red cask

matured wine from Spätburgunder highly. Sales are mainly directly to the German consumer. Annual production is 3,300 cases. Address: 7601 Durbach-Sendelbach.

Marcobrunn Rhg. w. ✦✦✦→✦✦✦✦
One of the best-known Einzellagen in the Rheingau, covering some 5ha (12 acre) nr. ERBACH. The mainly Riesling wines need time in bottle to show their very considerable best, but are somewhat expensive compared to those from neighbouring sites. Grosslage: DEUTELSBERG. Growers: Staatsweingut, Knyphausen, Oetinger, Reinhartshausen, Schloss Schönborn, Simmern'sches.

Mariengarten Rhpf. w. ✦✦
Grosslage of some 400ha (988 acre) in the heart of the Bereich MITTELHAARDT/DEUTSCHE WEINSTRASSE. It covers v'yds in three well-known wine villages – WACHENHEIM, FORST and DEIDESHEIM. A high percentage of Riesling is grown. Although the Grosslage wines are not expected to be in the same class as those from the best Einzellagen, they should still show similar characteristics of Riesling style with a slightly earthy Rheinpfalz flavour.

Marienhof, Weingut M-S-R
Estate owned by Franz REH & Sohn.

Marienthal, Staatliche Weinbaudomäne Ahr
The RHEINLAND-PFALZ state-owned cellars in the Ahr valley, with 18.7ha (46 acre) of v'yds. Vines are mainly Spätburgunder and Portugieser. Wines are matured in cask and no wine from warmer climates is added to deepen their colour. In Germany they have a loyal following, but their relatively low alcohol and tannin content limits their appreciation abroad. Annual production is 6,700 cases. Address: Klosterstrasse, 5481 Marienthal.

Markant
Characteristically striking. Describes a wine with positive features, that are typical of origin and vine variety, and are therefore easy to recognize and recall.

Markensekt
Quality sparkling wine sold under a brand name. Most German sparkling wine is Markensekt, and the number of consumers who ask for a sparkling wine with a regional or site name (LAGENSEKT) is still relatively small. Unlike the wine lover who will want, and find, endless variations in still wine, the German sparkling-wine drinker prefers consistency of price and quality. For him, geographical origin is unimportant. He will ask for a RIESLINGSEKT when he wants a top-quality sparkling wine, but it, too, will probably bear a brand name, such as Deinhard Lila Imperial, Jubilar Brut from Rilling or Riesling Brut from Kupferberg & Cie.

Markenwein
"Branded wine": wine sold under a (usually) registered name by one company or group of companies. The aim is to supply the same style of wine year after year, even if the blend varies from one market to another. The large number of German branded wines reflects the attempts over many years to overcome the difficulties of the German language, particularly in English-speaking countries. Some of the best-known brand names are applied to a range of wines (e.g. Goldener Oktober). Others, such as Black Tower and Green Label are more closely associated with one wine. The efforts of the leading brand owners on the export markets, and the financial support they have given to their wines, are largely responsible for the success of German wine abroad.

Markgräflerland, Bereich Baden w. (r.)
Bereich that stretches from FREIBURG to Lörrach nr. the Swiss border. Its wines are well known in s. Germany, esp. those made from Gutedel.

Martinsthal Rhg. w. ✦✦
Small, out-of-the-way village at the WIESBADEN end of the Rheingau producing admirable Riesling wines, somewhat overshadowed by those of neighbouring RAUENTHAL. Grosslage: STEINMÄCHER.

Matheisbildchen M-S-R w. ✦✦
Einzellage at BERNKASTEL producing full-bodied, firm Riesling wines. Grosslage: BADSTUBE.

A-Z Mat-Meh

Matheus-Lehnert, Weingut J. M-S-R
5.5ha (14 acre) Mosel estate – the Matheus family has been growing vines for many generations. The mainly steep holdings, planted
90% in Riesling, are at PIESPORT (GOLDTRÖPFCHEN), DHRON and
TRITTENHEIM. Annual production is almost 6,600 cases of cask-
matured award winning wines. Sales are in Germany and abroad.
Address: In der Zeil 1, 5559 Neumagen-Dhron.

Mäuerchen Rhg. w. ★★★
Mainly level Einzellage on the outskirts of GEISENHEIM, producing
elegant, fruity wines. Grosslage: BURGWEG. Growers: Forschungsanstalt Geisenheim, Hessisches Weingut, Holschier, Rheingau eG,
Schloss Schönborn, Schumann-Nägler, Vollmer, Zwierlein.

Maximin-Grünhaus M-S-R w. ★★★→★★★★
Small hamlet on the Ruwer. All its excellent 32ha (77 acre) of
mainly Riesling v'yd is owned by C. V. SCHUBERT'SCHE Gutsverwaltung. Grosslage: RÖMERLAY.

Maximinhof
See Studert-Prüm, Stephan

Mayschoss-Altenahr, Winzergenossenschaft Ahr
Oldest cooperative cellar in Germany founded in 1868. Its 280
members supply grapes from 20ha (49 acre) at Altenahr and 90ha
(222 acre) at Mayschoss planted with 40% Spätburgunder, 15%
Portugieser, 30% Riesling and 15% Müller-Thurgau. Light, gentle
red wines and firm whites are sold almost exclusively in Germany.
Address: Bundesstr. 42, 5481 Mayschoss.

Meaty
Describes a full-bodied, rich but not sweet wine, with sufficient acidity to balance the weight. Might be applied to a Riesling SPÄTLESE
from the Rheinpfalz in a good year.

Meddersheim Nahe w. ★★
Very much a Riesling growing village of the upper reaches of the
Nahe. Most of the grapes are delivered to the excellent Winzergenossenschaft RHEINGRAFENBERG, named after the well known,
eponymous Einzellage. Grosslage: Paradiesgarten.

Medium-dry
See Halbtrocken

Meersburg a. Bodensee Baden Pop. 5,100 r. w. ★★
Beautiful old walled town on the banks of the BODENSEE and a
major tourist attraction. Steep, lakeside v'yds produce good Spätburgunder, lively Müller-Thurgau and well-balanced Ruländer.
See also next entry.

Meersburg, Staatsweingut Baden
59.1ha (146 acre) estate established in 1802, owned by the state of
Baden-Würtemberg. The v'yds are mainly on the shores of the
BODENSEE, facing Switzerland. Vines are 46% Spätburgunder, 39%
Müller-Thurgau, etc. The range of wines is impressive, incl. BEERE-
NAUSLESEN and EISWEINE from both red and white grapes. The rule
of the estate, laid down in 1801, "non in quanto, sed in quale"
("not in quantity, but in quality"), is followed closely. Annual
production is 41,600 cases, sold mainly in Germany. Address:
Seminarstr. 6, 7758 Meersburg.

Meerspinne Rhpf. w. (r.) ★→★★
Grosslage of some 795ha (1,964 acre) at the s. end of the Bereich
MITTELHAARDT/DEUTSCHE WEINSTRASSE. The reputation of its wines
is inevitably overshadowed by those of the adjacent Grosslage HOF-
STÜCK, with its sites at DEIDESHEIM.

Mehrhölzchen Rhg. w. ★★
Grosslage of some 350ha (865 acre) in the central Rheingau covering individual sites at HALLGARTEN and OESTRICH. As usual in the
region, the finest wines are sold under the site names. The Grosslage name is used for sound but not top-quality wine. A very high
proportion of Riesling is grown.

Mehring M-S-R w. ★★
Village on the Mosel some km. downstream from TRIER, overlooked by its steep or sloping v'yds. In the steep sites, Riesling
makes flowery, firm wines with good acidity. Grosslagen: ST
MICHAEL for the better, SSW-facing sites; Probstberg for the rest.

Mertesdorf M-S-R w. ★★
Small Ruwer village whose best-known wines are sold under the name of its satellite hamlet MAXIMIN-GRÜNHAUS. Prestigious Riesling wines of great elegance. Grosslage: RÖMERLAY.

Mettenheim Rhh. w. ★★
Small village marking the s. end of the RHEINTERASSE. Grosslagen: KRÖTENBRUNNEN and RHEINBLICK.

Metternich Sektkellerei GmbH, Fürst von
Sparkling-wine manufacturers founded in 1971 by Söhnlein Rheingold KG to sell wine under the Fürst von Metternich name, a right acquired by Söhnlein in 1934. Vintage "Fürst von Metternich Brut", although based on Riesling wine, has less acidity than some of the best German sparkling wines but is full bodied. Address: Söhnleinstr. 1-8, 6200 Wiesbaden-Schierstein.

Meyer Wineries GmbH, Peter
Wine merchants heavily involved in exports to the UK and USA, concentrating on LIEBFRAUMILCH and inexpensive QbA. Annual turnover is 1.25m. cases. Owners of the von SCHORLEMER estates. Address: Cusanusstr. 14, 5550 Bernkastel-Kues.

Meyerhof, Weingut M-S-R
Estate owned by Hermann Freiherr v. SCHORLEMER GmbH.

Michelmark Rhg. w. ★★→★★★
Einzellage at ERBACH making Riesling wines with pronounced fruity acidity that benefit from bottle age. Grosslage: DEUTELSBERG. Growers: Nikolai, Oetinger, Reinhartshausen, Richter-Boltendahl, Tillmanns, Wagner-Weritz.

Michelsberg M-S-R w. ★
One of the best-known Grosslagen in Germany, covering more than 1,300ha (3,212 acre) in the neighbourhood of PIESPORT. Some of the individual sites, such as Piesporter TREPPCHEN and Trittenheimer ALTÄRCHEN, extend over 200ha (494 acre) or more; others cover less than a hectare. The quality varies greatly, with much rather ordinary Müller-Thurgau wine being made and sold as Piesporter Michelsberg. However, as soon as the word Riesling appears on the label, one should have a wine with good Mosel style and fruit. No top-quality wine will be sold under the name Michelsberg; its reputation has been somewhat tarnished in recent years.

Milchsäure
Lactic acid. Not normally present in MUST but formed during alcoholic fermentation and, infrequently in German wine, by a malolactic fermentation (see ÄPFELSÄURE).

Mild
Describes a wine that is balanced but has relatively low acidity. It is not a quality definition and is neutral in implication. Might well be applied to a Müller-Thurgau from the Bereich SÜDLICHE WEINSTRASSE (Rheinpfalz). It is often popularly used as an alternative to LIEBLICH.

Milz, Weingut M-S-R
The Milz family has been making wine since 1520. Today the 8.1ha (20 acre) estate has holdings at NEUMAGEN, DHRON, TRITTENHEIM (ALTÄRCHEN, APOTHEKE) and OCKFEN, and enjoys sole ownership of the 0.8ha (2 acre) Neumagener Nusswingert, the 0.5ha (1.18 acre) Trittenheimer Felsenkopf and the 0.25ha (0.6 acre) Trittenheimer Leiterchen – all three sites very steep and 100% Riesling. The wines, matured in the estate's 300-year-old cellar, have won many prizes. Approx. annual production is 7,250 cases, sold in Germany and abroad. Address: Laurentiushof, 5559 Trittenheim.

Mittelhaardt/Deutsche Weinstrasse, Bereich Rhpf. w. (r.)
Bereich that covers some of the best v'yds in Germany. The quality of the wines is very high and most are sold under the Einzellage or Grosslage name. The Bereich name is rarely found on a label.

Mittelheim Rhg. w. ★★
Small village joined to its neighbour WINKEL, looks across the Rhein to INGELHEIM in the Rheinhessen. The proportion of Riesling grown is high. Grosslagen: shares HONIGBERG with Winkel; the remainder is in ERNTEBRINGER.

Mittelmosel M-S-R

Middle Mosel: area almost the same as that covered by the Bereich BERNKASTEL.

Mittelrhein

Region of 747ha (1,846 acre) whose steep v'yds closely follow the course of the Rhein upstream from KÖNIGSWINTER, just s. of BONN. The attractive terraced v'yds have almost all been rebuilt in recent years to form uninterrupted, more easily worked slopes. The romantic and sometimes dramatic scenery is well known to many visitors, but the wine seldom leaves the region except in the back of

Weingut Toni Jost

BACHARACH AM RHEIN

MITTELRHEIN
Bacharacher Schloß Stahleck
Riesling Spätlese
Qualitätswein mit Prädikat
Erzeugerabfüllung · A. P. Nr. 1 698 041 033 83   0.75 l

tourists' cars or as branded sekt. Riesling covers 75% of the area under vine and its wine can reach great heights, although general the quality is not so distinguished as that from the neighbouring Rheingau, of which it often seems a slightly more steely, earthy version. In the region n. of BRAUBACH the wine resembles that from the Lower Mosel. Mittelrhein Riesling makes excellent sparkling wine.

Mittlere Nahe

Area covering the best v'yds of the Nahe between BAD KREUZNACH and SCHLOSSBÖCKELHEIM. Not an official wine designation, but a description used in the region.

Mönchof, Weingut M-S-R

5.5ha (14 acre) 100% Riesling estate, owned by the Eymael family since 1802, but with ecclesiastical origins in the early 16th century. Holdings are at ÜRZIG (WÜRZGARTEN), ERDEN (TREPPCHEN), ZELTINGEN-RACHTIG (HIMMELREICH), WEHLEN and KINHEIM (HUBERTUSLAY). The annual production of 5,800 cases of slaty, cask matured wines are sold in Germany and increasingly abroad. Address: 5564 Ürzig.

Monsheim Rhh. w. ★

Wine village nr. the border with the Rheinpfalz, with a technically advanced cooperative cellar. Grosslage: DOMBLICK.

Monzingen Nahe w. ★★

Village with wines once thought to be of sufficient quality to warrent shipment to the East Indies and back to encourage maturation. V'yds are steep with a high proportion of Riesling. Grosslage: Paradiesgarten.

Morgen

A measure of land, now obsolete, that varied from region to region but was usually a little less than an acre (.405 hectare): thought to have equalled the amount of land that a man could plough in a Morgen (morning). The word is still recalled in site names such as Güldenmorgen and Hohenmorgen.

Morio-Muskat

White grape variety, a crossing of Silvaner × Weissburgunder, grown on 2,641ha (6,526 acre), mainly in the Bereich SÜDLICHE WEINSTRASSE where the vine was developed and in the Rheinhessen. It can yield up to 200hl/ha or more and often forms part of good commercial blends, to which its pronounced bouquet brings a certain attraction. If the grapes are left until after the Silvaner harvest they can make full-bodied, balanced wines. Morio-Muskat now accounts for 2.6% of the total area under vine, but its planting is unlikely to increase. The particularly strong bouquet and flavour can become cloying and the wine lacks true distinction.

Mosbacher, Weingut Georg Rhpf.

Estate of 9.3ha (23 acre) with holdings in most of the best sites at FORST (UNGEHEUER, PECHSTEIN, MUSENHANG, etc.) and at DEIDESHEIM (HERRGOTTSACKER) and WACHENHEIM. The percentage of Riesling is high (80%) and the wines achieve many successes at regional and national competitions. Cask matured, Riesling dry wines are much in demand by private customers in Germany. Annual production is 7,500 cases. Address: Weinstrasse 27, 6701 Forst an der Weinstrasse.

Mosel

Famous wine river that rises in the Vosges mountains and flows some 500km (310 miles) later into the Rhein at KOBLENZ, having been joined en route by many tributaries incl. the Ruwer and the Saar. The 130 or so picturesque wine villages that line its banks are easily reached from the Koblenz-Trier motorway or from the Hunsrück Hohenstrasse (B327).

Minor roads follow both sides of the river closely for most of the distance from Trier to Koblenz, and much of the riverside journey can also be made by train.

Mosel-Saar-Ruwer w.

Probably the best known of the wine-producing regions, with 12,701ha (31,385 acre) under vine, mainly Riesling (55%), Müller-Thurgau (23%), Elbling (9%) and Kerner (6%). Many of the v'yds are on very steep, slaty sites that provide ideal ripening conditions for Riesling. Because of the difficult terrain, viticultural costs are

far greater than in the flat or rolling countryside of the Rheinhessen or Rheinpfalz. However, in recent years most of the old walled terraces that could only bear a small number of vines have been replaced by more economically worked v'yds, and 72% of the vine-growing area has now been modernized. Over 25% of the crop is delivered to cooperative cellars, and this percentage is increasing. The balance is either bottled by the grower or sold in bulk to the wine trade. There are many distinguished estates, most of them upstream from ZELL, either on the Mosel itself or on its tributaries, the Saar and the Ruwer. A Riesling wine from the M-S-R has a high level of tartaric acid which gives it style, freshness and the possibility of developing well in bottle over many years. A "good" year will be one in which these characteristics are pronounced and much late-picked (SPÄTLESE) wine can be made.

Mosel-Saar-Ruwer eG, Zentralkellerei M-S-R

See Zentralkellerei Mosel-Saar-Ruwer eG.

Moseltaler

A name created in 1986 for quality wines from the Mosel-Saar-Ruwer made from Riesling, Muller-Thurgau, Elbling and Kerner, which are typical of the region. They must contain between 15 and 30 g/l residual sugar, and have a total acidity of at least 7 g/l.

Mossbacher-Hof, Weingut Rhpf.

11ha (27 acre) estate with holdings in important Einzellagen at FORST (UNGEHEUER, PECHSTEIN, MUSENHANG, JESUITENGARTEN, etc.) and DEIDESHEIM (HERRGOTTSACKER), planted with a high proportion of Riesling (90%). 75% of the wines are dry, 10% med-dry. Elegant acidity is the characteristic. Sales mainly in Germany. Address: 6701 Forst.

Most, Mostgeweicht

See Must

Muffig

Musty. Wines that have been stored in unclean containers or bottled with corks that have also been incorrectly stored can develop a dirty smell. If the fault is not too serious, the smell can be removed by treatment in bulk.

Mülheim M-S-R w. ★★★

Village on the Mosel with a high proportion of Riesling in its v'yds, making elegant, lively wines. Somewhat overshadowed by its neighbours, BERNKASTEL and BRAUNEBERG. Grosslage: KUR-FÜRSTLAY.

Müller KGaA, Mattheus

One of the oldest sparkling-wine producers in Germany, est. in 1838, and taken over by Seagram in 1984. "MM Extra", the best known of the company's brands today, gains its sparkle in vat. Mattheus Müller owns Gebrüder Hoehl GmbH, whose best-known brand is Hoehl Diplomat. Address: 6228 Eltville.

Müller GmbH and Co. KG, Rudolf M-S-R

Wine merchants, sparkling-wine producers and owners of 14.5ha (36 acre) on the Saar at OCKEN, SCHARZHOFBERG, SAARBURG and KANZEM (98% Riesling) and on the Mosel at ÜRZIG and REIL (80% Riesling). 50% of the THANISCH estate in Bernkastel belongs to Rudolf Müller. Best known of the Rudolf Müller wines is the widely exported "Bishop of Riesling", a Bereich Bernkastel Riesling QbA. Address: 5586 Reil.

Müller-Dr Becker, Weingut Rhh.

22.5ha (56 acre) estate nr. the border with the Rheinpfalz dating from 1625, planted 20% Müller-Thurgau, 20% Riesling, and many other varieties. Sales only in Germany. Address: Vordergasse 16, 6523 Flörsheim-Dalsheim.

Müller-Scharzhof, Weingut Egon M-S-R

Great estate, owned by Egon Müller, dating in its present form

from 1797 but with origins reaching back over 700 years. 8.5ha (21 acre) of top-quality Saar v'yds incl. 7ha (17 acre) in the heart of the superb SCHARZHOFBERG. 2ha (5 acre) of the Scharzhofberg holding is planted in ungrafted Riesling, and only QmP in good vintages is sold under the Scharzhofberger name. 95% of the total area under vine is Riesling.

In good years the wines are known for their great finesse and ability to last in bottle. Approximate annual production of bottled wine is 5,000 cases, sold in Germany and abroad. Address: 5511 Wiltingen.

Müller-Thurgau

White grape variety, the great work-horse vine of Germany, covering 25,292ha (62,499 acre) in all 11 wine-growing regions. Named after its developer, Prof. Dr Müller from the Thurgau in Switzerland, it was originally thought to be a crossing of Riesling × Silvaner but is now considered to be a crossing of two clones of Riesling. It regularly produces a large crop, usually with low acidity, early in the autumn. The low acid content and the tendency of the grapes to rot makes a late harvest difficult.

Müller-Thurgau cannot compare in quality with Riesling but it makes perfectly sound, agreeable wine, usually of no great distinction. On some good estates, however, the wine is surprisingly elegant. It is more often the backbone of cheap commercial blends when it is best drunk within a year or so of being bottled.

Müllerrebe

Red grape variety, a mutation of Spätburgunder, also deceptively known as Schwarzriesling and found in France as Pinot Meunier. Planted in 1,473ha (3,640 acre), mainly in Württemberg, it produces wine with a good deep colour but rather lacking in acidity and, therefore, elegance.

Müllheim Baden w. (r.) ★★

Centre of the Bereich MARKGRÄFLERLAND. Wine making predominantly in the hands of cooperative cellars. Well known for Gutedel from sloping v'yds. Grosslage: Burg Neuenfels.

Mumm'sches Weingut, G. H. v. Rhg.

70ha (173 acre) estate, est. in the early 19th century, lying above SCHLOSS JOHANNISBERG where it owns Burg Schwarzenstein and a restaurant with a fine view of the Rheingau. The estate is also sole owner of the 3.8ha (9 acre) Hansenberg and 4ha (10 acre) Schwarzenstein sites at JOHANNISBERG, and has holdings in RÜDESHEIM (BERG ROTTLAND, BERG SCHLOSSBERG, BERG ROSENECK, etc.), ASSMANNSHAUSEN, GEISENHEIM and WINKEL, planted with 86% Riesling. All wines are cask-matured and the aim is the Rheingau Riesling virtues of good acidity and fruit. Approx. annual production is 60,800 cases, sold in Germany and abroad. Address: Schulstrasse 32, 6222 Geisenheim.

Mundelsheim Würt. r. w. ★★

Prosperous-looking, picturesque village with often photographed, steep, and sometimes terraced, y'ds. 60% are planted in red vine varieties (Trollinger, Schwarzriesling, and Spätburgunder). Grosslage: Schalkstein.

Münster-Sarmsheim Nahe w. ★★★

A small village some 3km (2 miles) s. of BINGEN, which produces top-quality Riesling wine from its DAUTENPFLÄNZER Einzellage. The "Sarmsheim" does not appear on the label. Grosslage: SCHLOSSKAPELLE.

Münzlay M-S-R w. ★★

Grosslage of more than 500ha (1,236 acre) around ZELTINGEN-RACHTIG, GRAACH and WEHLEN, on both sides of the R. Mosel. Most of the v'yds are very steep, producing a relatively small crop from Riesling grown on slaty soil. The best wines will normally be sold under the individual site names (Wehlener SONNENUHR, Zeltinger SONNENUHR, Zeltinger HIMMELREICH, etc.). Wine that is sold carrying only the Grosslage name, Munzlay, should still be quite stylish, but will probably lack the finesse of one of the wines becoming an Einzellage name on the label.

Musenhang Rhpf. w. ★★★

Sloping Einzellage at FORST making top-quality, stylish, meaty Riesling wines. Grosslage: MARIENGARTEN. Growers: Bassermann-Jordan, Forster Winzerverein, Hahnhof, Mosbacher, Mossbacher-hof.

Muskat

Name applied to many different and sometimes unrelated vine varieties. Some are European in origin, others are hybrids. Both red and white Muskat grapes are possible. The common factor of all Muskat wine is a distinctive bouquet that can range from the flowery and delicate to the overblown and sickly. The most widely

grown "Muskat" in Germany is Morio-Muskat. Gelber Muskateller with 42ha (104 acres) and Muskat-Ottonel, 21ha (52 acre) are
found mainly in Baden and Württemberg.

Must

Grape juice. Its quality is judged by weight, which for practical
purposes means its sugar (and thus its potential alcohol) content
and its degree of acidity. Must weight (Mostgewicht) is measured
in Germany against the OECHSLE scale. The legal minimum must
weight for each quality of German wine ranges from 44° Oechsle
for DEUTSCHER TAFELWEIN in the n. regions to 150° for a TROCKEN-
BEERENAUSLESE. Thus, although the importance attached to the
actual ALCOHOL content of a wine is not as great in Germany as in
other countries, great value is placed on the potential alcohol content as expressed by the sugar content of the must. From must,
wine and SÜSSRESERVE are made.

Nackenheim Rhh. w. ★★★

Small town on the Rhein, nr. MAINZ, birthplace of Carl Zuck-
mayer. The area under vine is not large but the red sandstone produces excellent wine with character and style. Grosslagen:
SPIEGELBERG, GUTES DOMTAL.

Nacktarsch M-S-R w. ★

Relatively small Grosslage of some 400ha (988 acre) in the MITTEL-
MOSEL, devoted entirely to the v'yds of the village of KRÖV. A high
proportion of Riesling is grown on extremely steep sites and the
wine, like that from the neighbouring villages, has all the welcome
Mosel characteristics of freshness and fruitiness. None of the individual Kröver site names is as well known, particularly to the
German consumer, as that of Nacktarsch – a name which, if translated, means exactly what you would expect.

Nägler, Weingut Dr Heinrich Rhg.

6.5ha (16 acre) estate with holdings in RÜDESHEIM (BERG ROTTLAND,
BERG SCHLOSSBERG, BERG ROSENECK, Bischofsberg, Drachenstein
and Magdalenenkreuz). Vines are 86% Riesling, 9% Ehrenfelser,
5% Spätburgunder. Yield is strictly limited. The range offered
covers four vintages. Approximate annual production is 5,100
cases, sold in Germany and abroad. Address: Friedrichstr. 22,
6220 Rüdesheim.

Nahe w. (r.)

Region of 4,610ha (11,392 acre) with a relatively small number of
growers making what is generally accepted as some of the finest
wine in Germany. Many of the v'yds are on gentle or steep slopes
and Riesling occupies the best sites. Wines made in the attractive
area between BAD KREUZNACH and SCHLOSSBÖCKELHEIM resemble
those of the Mosel or Saar. They can be extremely elegant, with a

wonderfully balanced fruity acidity. The Nahe is very much an
agricultural as well as a viticultural region and many vine-growers
are involved in farming as well.

Often the growers are also wine-makers and bottle their
produce themselves rather than sell their grapes, or their wine in
bulk, to others. Some 40% of a vintage is said to be sold directly

to the consumer by estate-bottlers. The best-known on the export market, but not the best wine of the region is that of the Grosslage Rüdesheimer ROSENGARTEN. At all quality levels, Nahe wine is normally good value for money.

Nahe-Winzer Kellereien eG Nahe

Central cooperative cellar whose members supply grapes from 730ha (1,804 acre) throughout the Nahe. 20% Silvaner, 30% Müller-Thurgau and 26% Riesling, etc. Sales are in Germany and abroad. Address: Winzenheimerstr. 30, 6551 Bretzenheim.

Narrenkappe Nahe w. ***

One of several sloping Einzellagen at BAD KREUZNACH producing essentially racy Riesling wines with fine, fruity acidity. Grosslage: KRONENBERG. Growers: August E. Anheuser, Paul Anheuser, Finkenauer, Schlink-Herf-Gutleuthof, Plettenberg.

Nassverbesserung

Wet-sugaring: the addition of a solution of sugar and water to QbA and DTW (not QmP), to increase the alcohol content and reduce acidity. Although it is often the most satisfactory way of improving the quality of wine made from unripe grapes in poor vintages, it has been forbidden since March 1984. The EEC objection to Nassverbesserung lay not in the method, or indeed in the quality of the result, but in the fact that the total quantity of liquid was increased (by a maximum of 10% for QbA and 15% for DTW) over its original volume.

Naturgewächs

Before 1971 a synonym for NATURREIN.

Naturrein

According to the 1930 German Wine Law, a wine in which the alcohol content had not been increased by added sugar could be called "naturrein". As a result, wines that would have benefited from more alcohol were sometimes left thin and unbalanced so as to be able to claim "purity". The use of the term was prohibited by the 1971 Wine Law.

Naturwein

A NATURREIN wine.

Neckar

River that rises nr. the Danube and flows, some 402km (250 miles) later, into the Rhein at Mannheim. Its Württemberg v'yds are not as continuous as those of the Mosel but are often equally as steep and as costly to maintain. Many lie well away from the river, diminishing somewhat the river's importance to vine-growing.

Neckerauer, Weingut K. Rhpf.

Old-established estate n. of BAD DÜRKHEIM covering 16ha (40 acre) 30% Riesling, selling Weisenheimer wines from a wide range of vines suitable to the sandy clay soil. The annual production of 13,100 cases shows a low yield, concentrated on QmP. All styles are made, 50% dry and med-dry. The amount of Riesling will be increased. Sales are mainly in Germany. Address. Ritter von Geisslerstr. 9, 6714 Weisenheim am Sand.

Neef M-S-R w. *→**

Small village between COCHEM and ZELL producing positive Riesling wines. Surprisingly for this part of the river, Elbling is also grown. Grosslage: Grafschaft.

Neidischer Herbst

Envious autumn. Term used, almost inexplicably to describe a vintage with a small yield.

Neipperg, Weingüter u. Schlosskellerei Graf von Würt.

Estate dating back to the 12th century, with the von Neipperg family still in command. 18.6ha (46 acre) are planted with red vine varieties (Limberger, Schwarzriesling, Spätburgunder, Trollinger), 13ha (32 acre) with white vine varieties (Riesling, Traminer, Muskateller, Müller-Thurgau). Emphasis in listing and selling the wines is given to the vine variety and PRÄDIKAT (e.g. Riesling Spätlese Schwaigerner Ruthe). 97% are dry or med-dry, sold in Germany. The estate also owns Château Canon la Gaffelière, Clos l'Oratoire, Château La Mondotte and Château Peyreau in St-Emilion, Bordeaux. Address: 7103 Schwaigern.

Nell, Georg-Fritz von M-S-R
16ha (40 acre) Trier estate, owned by the von Nell family since 1803, with sole ownership of the Trierer Benediktinerberg and Kurfürstenhofberg sites as well as holdings at WILTINGEN, AYL and BERNKASTEL, 80% Riesling. The wines are concentrated in flavour

and benefit from bottle age. Approx. annual production is relatively low (11,400 cases), sold in Germany (particularly the drier wines) and with great success abroad. Address: Weingut Im Thiergarten 12, 5500 Trier.

Nervig
Nervous. A term similar in meaning to KERNIG, or the French *nerveux*. Describes a wine in which the balance of alcohol, extract and acid is very good. Such a wine will be vigorous (not flat and tired), firm and impress by its style. Not a description that is often used, but could be applied to good Riesling wines.

Neuer Wein
New wine. The consumer in Germany has as yet no great interest in drinking his own Neuer Wein within weeks of the vintage, but is as partial to Beaujolais Nouveau as anybody else. Nevertheless, cheap wines from early-ripening vine varieties are on sale by November, but they are not given great prominence.

Neuleiningen Rhpf. w. ★★
Fine old fortified village with a Mediterranean atmosphere perched on a hilltop in the n. of the Rheinpfalz, overlooking its sloping v'yds. The wines are not great but characterful and flavoury, Rieslings and Silvaners are made. Grosslage: Höllenpfad.

Neumagen M-S-R w. ★★→★★★
Ancient wine village nr. PIESPORT, producing racy wines, mainly from Riesling. Grosslage: MICHELSBERG.

Neus, Weingut J.
See Sonnenberg, Weingut.

Neustadt Rhpf. Pop. 50,500 w. (r.) ★★→★★★
Busy wine-town in the s. of the Bereich MITTELHAARDT/DEUTSCHE WEINSTRASSE. Produces good, meaty wine. Grosslagen: MEERSPINNE, Rebstöckel, Pfaffengrund.

Neutral
Wine term, used mainly within the trade, often applied to QbA or DTW with no excesses of flavour or bouquet, made from grapes such as Elbling, Silvaner and sometimes Riesling. A neutral flavour is often unrelated to quality, except in a base wine from which sparkling wine is to be made, in which case it is normally considered an advantage.

Neuzüchtungen
New crossings of one European vine with another, e.g. Scheurebe, a crossing of Silvaner × Riesling. (Crossing of European and American vines are HYBRIDEN.)

Neveu, Weingut Freiherr von Baden
Estate of some 15ha (37 acre), acquired by the von Neveu family in 1832, planted 44% in Riesling, 21% Müller-Thurgau, 15% Spätburgunder, etc. Sole owners of DURBACHER Josephsberg. The full-

bodied, firm wines, with a touch of natural gas are bottled by the huge Zentralkellerei (ZBW) at Breisach. Annual production is 8,300 cases. 10% is exported. Address: 7601 Durbach.

Nicolay, C.H. Berres Erben, Weingut Peter M-S-R

Mittelmosel estate dating in its present form from the 19th century, with an old vaulted cask cellar. 15.1ha (37 acre) of holdings at ÜRZIG (WÜRZGARTEN, and sole ownership of Goldwingert), ERDEN (TREPPCHEN and PRÄLAT), ZELTINGEN-RACHTIG (HIMMELREICH), WEHLEN and KINHEIM (HUBERTUSLAY). Vines are 96% Riesling, 4%

DIE BERÜHMTEN WEINGÜTER DIESER ARTEIN SIND GRÖSSTENTEILS IN UNSEREM BESITZE

QUALITÄTSWEIN
MIT PRÄDIKAT

1981
Ürziger Würzgarten
Riesling Kabinett

NICOLAY *sche Weingüts Verwaltung*
C.H. BERRES ERBEN *Bengg-Mosel*

Erzeuger-Abfüllung

e 750 ml

Müller-Thurgau. Annual production is 14,000 cases of individually cask-matured wines that reflect the sometimes subtle variations between one site and another. Sales are in Germany and abroad. A cellar selling wines from other estates is attached to the Weingut. Address: Gestade 15, 5550 Bernkastel-Kues.

Niederhausen Nahe w. ★★★→★★★★

Small village surrounded by steep, game-filled woods and top-quality v'yds producing some of the most elegant Riesling wines of the region. Unusually for the Nahe there is a small plantation of Traminer. Home of the Staatliche Weinbaudomäne (see next entry). Grosslage: BURGWEG.

Niederhausen-Schlossböckelheim, Verwaltung der Staatlichen Weinbaudomäne Nahe

The Nahe State Wine Cellars are one of the great wine estates of the world, est. in 1902, with 45ha (111 acre) in SCHLOSSBÖCKELHEIM (KUPFERGRUBE, FELSENBERG), NIEDERHAUSEN (HERMANNSHÖHLE, sole owners of Hermannsberg, etc.), TRAISEN (BASTEI), ALTENBAMBERG, MÜNSTER-SARMSHEIM and DORSHEIM, etc. Vines are 93% Riesling (the estate, in its role as vine-breeder, has five registered clones of Riesling on sale and in use in Germany). Cool fermentation, skilled vinification and maturation in wood, guided by an outstanding cellar-master, results in Riesling wines of incredible delicacy and complexity. Annual production is 23,300 cases. Sales are in Germany and abroad. Address: 6551 Oberhausen.

Nierstein Rhh. Pop. 6,000 w. ★★★

Small town dedicated to wine-making, 20km (12 miles) from MAINZ in the heart of the RHEINTERRASSE, with many old vaulted cellars and a wine festival each August. The 150 or so growers incl. some of the best-known wine names in Germany. Grosslagen: SPIEGELBERG, AUFLANGEN and REHBACH (and GUTES DOMTAL for one site only, the Pfaffenkappe).

Nierstein, Bereich Rhh. w. (r.)

Best-known Bereich of the Rheinland in export markets, covering the fine v'yds of the RHEINTERRASSE n. and s. of NIERSTEIN, as well as those in much of the rolling hinterland away from the river. A wine sold as Bereich Nierstein will not be of great quality but it will be soft, light, pleasantly fruity and likely to contain a high proportion of Müller-Thurgau. It will also be cheap. If it is very cheap, then that is how it will taste.

Nies'chen M-S-R w. ★★★

Mainly steep, SSW-facing Einzellage at KASEL on the Ruwer producing spicy Riesling wines with a positive fruity, crisp style. Sometimes suffers from frost. Grosslage: RÖMERLAY. Growers: Beulwitz, Bischöfliche Weingüter, Kesselstatt, Simon, Wegeler-Deinhard.

Nikolai, Weingut Heinz Rhg.

5.2ha (13 acre) estate, owned by the Nikolais for four generations, with holdings in ERBACH (MICHELMARK, etc), KIEDRICH (SANDGRUB) and HALLGARTEN. Vines are 85% Riesling, 10% Scheurebe, 5% Kerner. The Riesling wines reflect the classic Rheingau virtues of good acidity and spiciness, 45% dry or med-dry. Approximate annual production is 4,200 cases. Address: Ringstr. 14, 6228 Eltville 2.

Nobling

White grape variety, a crossing of Silvaner × Gutedel from the state viticultural institute at FREIBURG, planted in 164ha (405 acre), mainly in Baden. It can be harvested at the same time as Silvaner, is often heavier by some 10° Oechsle and has greater acidity. Given the right conditions it will produce SPÄTLESE and AUSLESE wines with a positive flavour and fine bouquet.

Nonnenberg, Weingut Rhg.

Estate of 7ha (17 acre) with sole ownership of Rauenthaler Nonnenberg, planted 85% Riesling. No herbicides are used and the soil is left unploughed. Half the Riesling wine is dry or med-dry and most of the annual production of 4,600 cases is sold by wine merchants A. Weigand of Bingen, much to private customers. Address: 6229 Martinsthal.

Nordheim Franken w. ★★

Village nr. VOLKACH, e. of WÜRZBURG, with the largest area under vine in Franken, incl. the massive 250ha (618 acre) Vögelein site. Powerful, soft, long-flavoured Silvaner and Müller-Thurgau wines, many sold directly by the producers. Grosslage: Kirchberg.

Nordrhein-Westfalen

Federal State, within whose s. border lie 21ha (52 acre) of Mittelrhein v'yd nr. Bonn. The capital is Düsseldorf.

Norheim Nahe w. ★★★

Village with small Einzellagen producing wines with good acidity and flavour. Riesling from the DELLCHEN site can produce great wine in good years. Grosslage: BURGWEG.

Nussbrunnen Rhg. w. ★★★

Small Einzellage at HATTENHEIM making full-bodied Riesling wines. Grosslage: DEUTELSBERG. Growers: Reinhartshausen, Ress, Schloss Schönborn, Simmern'sches Rentamt.

Nussdorf Rhpf. w. ★

Village in the Bereich SÜDLICHE WEINSTRASSE nr. LANDAU IN DER PFALZ, producing sound, inexpensive wines. Grosslage: Bischofskreuz.

Oberemmel M-S-R w. ★★★

Village set in pleasant country nr. WILTINGEN in the Saar valley, making finely tuned, racy Riesling wine. Grosslage: SCHARZBERG.

Obermosel, Bereich M-S-R w.

Upper-Mosel Bereich, facing the v'yds of Luxembourg across the river. Produces simple, agreeable and refreshing quality wine from Elbling, much of it converted into sparkling wine.

Oberwesel Mrh. w. ★★

Ancient wine village in the s. Mittelrhein, 40km (25 miles) from KOBLENZ in the Rhein gorge. All its v'yds are extremely steep, planted almost 100% Riesling and produce racy, firm wines. Grosslage: Schloss Schönburg.

Ockfen M-S-R w. ★★★

Saar village well known for centuries for its BOCKSTEIN and HERRENBERG sites. Top-quality, flowery, racy Riesling wine. Grosslage: SCHARZBERG.

Oechsle, Oechsle scale

Christian Ferdinand Oechsle (1774-1852), a prolific inventor and musician, was born, lived and died in Württemberg. He developed the Oechsle scale, which compares the weight of a MUST with that of water. The Oechsle figure is the specific gravity of the must with the decimal point moved three places to give a whole number. Thus

90° Oechsle is equivalent to a specific gravity of 1.090, i.e. 1 litre of the must in question would be 90 grams heavier than 1 litre of water at 20°C.

Oesterreicher
Synonym for Silvaner, a grape variety believed by some to have come to Germany from Austria (Oesterreich).

Oestrich Rhg. w. ★★★
Small Rhein town halfway between RÜDESHEIM and the outskirts of WIESBADEN, making firm, full-bodied Riesling wines that rise to greatness in fine years. Grosslagen: GOTTESTHAL, MEHRHÖLZCHEN.

Oetinger'sches Weingut, Robert von Rhg.
Estate with 7.5ha (19 acre) of vines, 73% Riesling, at ERBACH (MICHELMARK, SIEGELSBERG, MARCOBRUNN, etc.) and KIEDRICH (SANDGRUB). Annual production is 4,600 cases of wines with powerful acidity, 75% dry or med-dry. No export. Address: Rheinallee 1–3, 6228 Eltville-Erbach.

Offenburg, Weingut der Stadt Baden
Ancient charitable estate, founded in 1301, taken over by the town of Offenburg in 1936. Its 30.5ha (75 acre) of vines are 36% Müller-Thurgau, 17% Riesling, 17% Spätburgunder, plus a range of other varieties. Approx. annual production is 22,900 cases of fresh wines with good acidity, typical of the Bereich ORTENAU. No exports. Address: St Andreas-Hospital-Fonds, Steingrube 7, 7601 Ortenberg.

Offene Weine
See Ausschankwein

OHG
Offene Handelsgesellschaft. Describes a business general partnership, as in Weingut Bercher OHG.

Ökologische Weinbau
Ecological wine production has been increasing since the 1970s. It is practised according to certain guide lines by at least 50 growers, and mention of its use appears in price lists. Only organic manures are acceptable, and insecticides and fungicides are forbidden, as is the use of asbestos filter sheets in the cellar. Spontaneous alcoholic fermentation (no added yeasts), malo-lactic fermentation and cask maturation are recommended. Sulphur dioxide is kept to two-thirds of that allowed by EEC law. The WALTHARI system of wine making takes this a stage further.

Ökonomierat
Agricultural Counsellor. Honorary title awarded for services to agriculture in its broadest sense. Appears in the title of a number of estates, e.g. Weingut Ökonomierat August E. Anheuser, Weingut Ökonomierat Max-G. Piedmont.

Ölberg Rhh. w. ★★★
S-facing Einzellage at NIERSTEIN producing full-bodied, stylish wines. Grosslage: AUFLANGEN. Growers: Balbach, Gessert, Guntrum, Heyl zu Herrnsheim, Kurfürstenhof, Hermann Franz Schmitt, Georg Schneider, Schuch, Sittmann, Strub.

Opel, Weingut Irmgard von Rhh.
Estate at Schloss Westerhaus, with a 13ha (32 acre) solely owned Einzellage of the same name, and 187ha (462 acre) of agricultural land. Vines are 51% Riesling, 14% Spätburgunder, 12% Müller-Thurgau, etc. Over 80% of the wine is dry or med-dry, and is matured in cask. The 1983 Spätburgunder Auslese Weissherbst with 15.1% of alcohol will last for years. Annual production of 6,700 cases (incl. Opel Brut Riesling Sekt) is sold in Germany and abroad. Address: Schloss Westerhaus, 6507 Ingelheim.

Oppenheim Rhh. Pop. 4,700 w. ★★★
Small wine-producing town on the RHEINTERRASSE, headquarters of a number of important estates and exporting houses and with a well-known viticultural institute (see next entry). Its attractions incl. the much-photographed St Katharinen-Kirche and the Deutsches Weinbaumuseum (German Viticultural Museum). Grosslagen: GÜLDENMORGEN, KRÖTENBRUNNEN.

Oppenheim, Staatsweingut der Landes- Lehr- und Versuchsanstalt Rhh.
Research and training institute, founded in 1895 and owned by the

state of Rheinland-Pfalz. The institute owns 40ha (99 acre) of v'yds at OPPENHEIM (SACKTRÄGER, KREUZ, Herrenberg, Zuckerberg.), DIENHEIM and NIERSTEIN (PATERBERG, PETTENTHAL, ÖLBERG). Vines are 41% Riesling. Because of the estate's experimental role there are also many new crossings. The v'yds are maintained to an exemplary standard and emphasis is laid on retaining the individual grape variety character in the wines. Annual production is 16,700 cases. Many awards have been won at regional and national competitions. Sales are mainly in Germany. Address: Zuckerberg 19, 6504 Oppenheim.

Optima

White grape variety, a crossing of (Silvaner × Riesling) × Müller-Thurgau, planted in 499ha (1,233 acre), mainly in the n. regions of the M-S-R and Rheinhessen. The yield is similar to that of Riesling (about 70hl/ha) and wine of Auslese quality can be made provided the acidity is not too low.

Orbel Rhh. w. ✳✳✳

One of the many excellent Einzellagen on the slopes at NIERSTEIN, making full-flavoured, weighty wines. Grosslage: AUFLANGEN. Growers: Gessert, Guntrum, Hermann Franz Schmitt, Georg Schneider, Sittmann, Strub, Wehrheim.

Ordensgut Rhpf. w. (r.) ✳

Grosslage at the n. end of the Bereich SÜDLICHE WEINSTRASSE. Many vine varieties and sound, quality wines.

Originalabfüllung

Estate bottling. A term used until 1971 to describe unsugared (NATURREIN) wines that had been produced and bottled by the grower. Cooperative cellars could also sell their wines as Originalabfüllungen. The term ERZEUGERABFÜLLUNG has in part superseded Originalabfüllung, although it can be applied equally to a sugared or unsugared wine.

Originalabzug

Identical in meaning to ORIGINALABFÜLLUNG.

Ortega

Early-ripening white grape variety, a crossing of Müller-Thurgau × Siegerrebe from WÜRZBURG in Franken, planted in 1,208ha (2,985 acre), mainly in the Rheinpfalz, Rheinhessen and M-S-R. It produces good, powerfully scented wine up to KABINETT quality. Insufficient acidity makes it unsuitable for late-picking. Benefits from early bottling followed by a period of maturation.

Ortenau, Bereich Baden w. (r.)

Bereich that stretches s. from Baden-Baden at the foot of the Black Forest. It produces wines of very good quality, esp. from Riesling (known locally as Klingelberger), that are beginning to be found on the export market.

Ortsteil

Part of a larger community, e.g. the village of ERBACH in the Rheingau is an Ortsteil of the town of ELTVILLE.

Osthofen Rhh. w. (r.) ✳✳

Small town with many rustic wine bars and cellars, 10km (6 miles) n. of WORMS in the Bereich WONNEGAU. Very good wines are produced, probably missing the style of those from further n. in the Bereich NIERSTEIN. Well known in Germany but less so on the export market. Grosslagen: Pilgerpfad, Gotteshilfe.

Othegraven, Maximilian v.

See Kanzemer Berg, Weingut

Oxidativ

A wine that shows signs of oxydation, but is not yet fully oxydized, is described as "oxidativ". Its opposite, a wine from which contact with the air has been kept to a minimum, is "reduktiv". Most German wines fall into this latter category.

Palatinate

See Rheinpfalz

Pappig

Describes a wine with excessive sweetness that is FLACH.

Parzelle

Plot. For administrative purposes Einzellagen are often subdivided into smaller parcels of land which are named and numbered. However the Einzellage remains the smallest geographical unit that can be mentioned on a wine label.

Paterberg Rhh. w. ★★→★★★
Largest Einzellage, 148ha (366 acre), at NIERSTEIN, producing stylish, good-quality wine. Grosslage: SPIEGELBERG. Growers: Guntrum, Georg Schneider, Sittmann, Strub, Wehrheim.

Pauly KG, Weingut Otto M-S-R
Estate of some 3ha (7 acre) dating back more than 300 years, owned by Otto-Ulrich and Axel Pauly. The steep holdings are at GRAACH (DOMPROBST, HIMMELREICH), WEHLEN (SONNENUHR) and BERNKASTEL (LAY and Johannisbrünnchen). Vines are 95% Riesling. Approx. annual production is 3,750 cases of typical, top-quality, fresh Mosel wines, sold in Germany and increasingly abroad. Address: Bernkastelerstr. 5–7, 5550 Graach.

Pauly, Otto Ulrich
See "Abteihof", Weingut

Pauly-Bergweiler, Weingut Dr. M-S-R
Three well-known Mosel families are united in this estate: Prüm, Bergweiler and Berres from Ürzig. The estate owns 11.3ha (28 acre) with holdings in BERNKASTEL (GRABEN, SCHLOSSBERG, etc.), GRAACH (HIMMELREICH, DOMPROBST), WEHLEN (SONNENHUHR,

MOSEL · SAAR · RUWER

Der Weinbergsbesitz von
Dr. Pauly
umfaßt Lagen in Bernkastel, Graach, Wehlen, Zeltingen, Erden und Brauneberg.

Qualitätswein mit Prädikat

Erzeuger-Abfüllung

A. P. Nr.
2 576 185 033 84

750 ml

1983
Graacher Himmelreich
Riesling Eiswein
Weingut Dr. Pauly-Bergweiler
Zach. Bergweiler-Prüm Erben-Bernkastel

etc.), ZELTINGEN-RACHTIG, ERDEN and BRAUNEBERG. Vines are 96% Riesling. No SÜSSRESERVE is used, and fermentation is temperature controlled. Approx. annual prod. is 12,000 cases, sold 50% in Germany and 50% abroad. Address: Zach. Bergweiler Prüm Erben, Gestade 15, 5550 Bernkastel-Kues.

Pechstein Rhpf. w. ★★★
Mainly level Einzellage at FORST making full-bodied Riesling wines. Grosslage: MARIENGARTEN. Growers: Bassermann-Jordan, Bürklin-Wolf, Forster Winzerverein, Mosbacher, Mossbacher-Hof, Spindler, J. L. Wolf.

Perle
White grape variety, a crossing of Gewürztraminer × Müller-Thurgau, with rosé-coloured grapes that produce a light, gentle white wine. It is planted in 273ha (675 acre), mainly in the Rheinhessen and in Franken where much work has been carried out improving the vine at the state viticultural institute at WÜRZBURG.

Perll, August Mrh.
100-year-old estate with 3.8ha (9 acre), 68% Riesling, in the very steep v'yds of the Bopparder Hamm, overlooking the Rhein upstream from KOBLENZ. The slate-grown, racy, lively Riesling wines enjoy remarkable success at national competitions. Production is 4,200 cases a year, sold mainly to the German consumer. Address: Oberstr. 81, 5407 Boppard.

Perlwein
Semi-sparkling wine, the result of a second fermentation in a pressurized tank or simply of impregnation with carbon dioxide. The bottling and labelling must be such that the wine will not be confused with a sparkling wine. At best, Perlwein is a cheap and

pleasant drink but it usually lacks the style and the ability to retain its sparkle once opened that is characteristic of good-quality sparkling wine.

Pettenthal Rhh. w. ★★★

One of the best, mainly steep Einzellagen at NIERSTEIN. The wine is full of flavour from the red sandstone and clay soil. Grosslage: REHBACH. Growers: Balbach, Baumann, Gessert, Guntrum, Heyl zu Herrnsheim, Kurfürstenhof, Hermann Franz Schmitt, Schneider, Schuch, Wehrheim.

Pfeffingen, Weingut Rhpf.

Estate a few km n. of BAD DÜRKHEIM with 11.5ha (28 acre) of modernized v'yds in UNGSTEIN (Herrenberg and Weilberg). Vines are 70% Riesling, 10% Müller-Thurgau, etc. Family commitment to the estate is total – both the daughter and son-in-law are qualified "Weinbauingenieure" (vine growers and wine makers) – and the wines win many awards at regional and national competitions. Annual production is 7,500 cases with a high proportion of QmP, incl. dry and med-dry wines. Sales in Germany and abroad. Address: Fuhrmann-Eymael, 6702 Bad Dürkheim.

Pfleger, Weingut Jakob Rhpf.

Organically manured estate of 7.5ha (19 acre), with holdings at HERXHEIM AM BERG, Freinsheim, and KALLSTADT (STEINACKER), planted with 40% Scheurebe, 20% Riesling, 10% Ruländer and 10% Müller-Thurgau. Annual production is 6,100 cases, 40% dry or med-dry. Sales mainly to the consumer, but also some exports. Many prize winning wines. Address: Weinstr. 38, 6719 Herxheim.

Pfleger, Weingut Werner Rhpf.

5ha (12 acre) estate, established as recently as 1983, with holdings at HERXHEIM AM BERG, Freinsheim and Dackenheim. Practically all the wines are QmP from a range of white and red vine varieties. Many top prize winners. Annual production is 3,700 cases, sold to the consumer. Address: Weinstr. 34, 6719 Herxheim am Berg.

Phylloxera

Known as the "Reblaus" in Germany where it first appeared in 1874. Phylloxera (full title *Phylloxera vastatrix*) is an aphid that causes swellings or growths on the roots of European vines (*Vitis vinifera*), which then rot in winter, so destroying the root system.

Piedmont, Weingut Ökonomierat Max-G. M-S-R

Fourth-generation family estate nr. the confluence of the Saar and Mosel. 6ha (15 acre) of v'yds, all in FILZEN. Vines are 90% Riesling, producing excellent spicy wines in good years. Approx. annual production is 4,200 cases of QmP, cask-matured, 60% of Kabinet quality. Sales in Germany and abroad. Address: Saartal. 1, 5503 Konz-Filzen.

Piesport M-S-R w. ★★→★★★

One of the best-known village names on the Mosel, particularly when linked to its Grosslage MICHELSBERG or its Einzellage GOLD-TRÖPFCHEN. While the high quality of the best Piesporter Rieslings cannot be disputed, equally good wines at lesser prices can often be found elsewhere on the Mosel. Unfortunately, some of the non-Riesling wines that appear on the market with Piesport in their name, originating from the wider boundaries of the Grosslage Michelsberg, do the excellent and ancient wine-producing village little credit.

Pilgerpfad Rhh w. (r.) ★→★★

Grosslage of over 1,000ha (2,471 acre) in sandy, clay soil producing agreeable wines without the flair of the best from the RHEINTERRASSE.

Pittersberg Nahe w. ★★

Sloping Einzellage at MÜNSTER-SARMSHEIM producing fruity wines with good body but usually less finesse than those made up-river at SCHLOSSBÖCKELHEIM. Grosslage: SCHLOSSKAPELLE. Growers incl. Niederhausen-Schlossböckelheim Staatl. Weinbaudomäne.

Plettenberg'sche Verwaltung, Reichsgräflich von Nahe

50.8ha (126 acre) estate with 18th-century origins. Holdings are at BAD KREUZNACH (BRÜCKES, NARRENKAPPE, etc.), SCHLOSSBÖCKELHEIM (KUPFERGRUBE and FELSENBERG), Bretzenheim, Winzenheim, ROX-

HEIM and NORHEIM, planted 65% Riesling, 20% Müller-Thurgau, etc. The approximate annual production is the equivalent of 28,600 cases of seriously made wine, which is mainly dry or med-dry. Sales are international. Address: Winzenheimerstr., 6550 Bad Kreuznach.

Plump

Describes a wine with high extract, possibly an excessive alcohol content and certainly too little acid. With modern wine-making methods, in which acidity and freshness are retained, plump wines are not so common as they were 20 years ago. The Rheinpfalz, Rheinhessen, Franken and Baden are more likely to produce wines that are plump than regions further north.

Pokal

Large glass with a content of 200 or 250ml in which "open wine" (AUSSCHANKWEIN) is served.

Pommern M-S-R w. ★★

Known by the Romans as Pomaria on account of its apple orchards, the village of Pommern is appreciated today for its fruity, stylish Riesling wines from approx. 66ha (163 acre) of v'yd. Grosslage: GOLDBÄUMCHEN.

Popp KG, Weingut Ernst Franken

Wine merchants with 14ha (35 acre), receiving grapes from growers in a further 20ha (49 acre) at Iphofen, Rodelseer, etc. Vines are 50% Müller-Thurgau, 25% Silvaner, plus the red wine variety, Schwarzriesling. Sales are abroad and in Germany, much via the company's two wine bars. Address: Rödelseer Str. 14-15, 8715 Iphofen.

Portugieser, Blauer

After Spätburgunder, the most widely planted red vine variety in Germany, covering 3,183ha (7,866 acre) of which more than half lie in the Rheinpfalz. The yield is large, the MUST weight is low and the acidity high. It is suggested that the Portugieser is often picked too early in the season, and that if it were gathered after the Müller-Thurgau a more satisfactory wine would result. As red wine, the colour seems light to the non-German, but the Portugieser makes an attractive WEISSHERBST in the Rheinpfalz.

Prädikat

A quality distinction. See Qualitätswein mit Prädikat (QmP).

Prädikatsweingüter, Verband Deutscher

An association of QmP-producing estates, with origins going back to the last century. The aim of the association, which has approx. 160 members, is to promote the sale of estate-bottled QmP. Some members (e.g. Schloss Vollrads, Weingut Rappenhof) include the association's emblem, a bunch of grapes forming the body of an eagle with outspread wings, on their labels.

Prälat M-S-R w. ★★★→★★★★

Very small, 2.2ha (5.44 acre), top-quality Einzellage at ERDEN, planted exclusively in Riesling. Great wines in the best years. Grosslage: SCHWARZLAY. Growers: Loosen-Erben, Nicolay, St Johannishof, Weins-Prüm.

Prämierung

See Bundesweinprämierung

Probe

Tasting. For details of wine tastings in Germany, see page 22.

Prüfungsnummer

See Amtliche Prüfung

Prüm, Weingut Joh. Jos. M-S-R

One of the most prestigious estates on the Mosel, best known for the 4.5ha (11 acre) holding in the Wehlener SONNENUHR, which the estate has done so much to make famous. A further 9.5ha (23 acre) are in other sites at WEHLEN and at GRAACH (HIMMELREICH and DOMPROBST), ZELTINGEN-RACHTIG (SONNENUHR) and BERNKASTEL, (GRABEN, BRATENHÖFCHEN). The grapes (mainly Riesling) are usually gathered as late as possible. The wines are made with immense care and attention to detail to ensure they reach their full potential. Although the KABINETT wines in off-vintages can surprise by their style and positive SPRITZIG flavour, the estate is best known for its incredibly luscious AUSLESEN. Approx. annual production is 10,000 cases. Sales are worldwide. Address: Uferallee 19, 5550 Bernkastel-Wehlen.

Prüm Erben, Weingut S.A. M-S-R
Estate of 5.5ha (14 acre) est. in 1911 when the original Prüm family property was divided among the heirs (Erben). S.A. Prüm owns holdings at WEHLEN (SONNENUHR, etc.), BERNKASTEL, GRAACH (HIMMELREICH, DOMPROBST) and ZELTINGEN-RACHTIG (SCHLOSSBERG). 100% Riesling. The aim is to make racy, elegant wines, 30% are dry or med-dry. No SÜSSRESERVE. Approx. annual production is 5,600 cases and 60-80% is exported. Address: Uferallee 25-26, 5550 Bernkastel-Wehlen.

Pünderich M-S-R w. ★★
Small, picturesque wine village, just inside the boundaries of the Bereich BERNKASTEL nr. ZELL. Much good, sound wine is sold under the Grosslage name, vom HEISSEN STEIN. Elegant, fruity Riesling wines appear under the various Einzellage names.

Qualitätsschaumwein
Quality sparkling wine. A sparkling wine may only be described as Qualitätsschaumwein in the EEC if it has fulfilled the conditions of production laid down in its country of origin. In Germany most quality sparkling wine (more widely known as SEKT) is sold under a brand name (MARKENSEKT). Sales are increasing of Sekt from a specified region (SEKT b.A) bearing a vintage, a regional name and sometimes a site name, made from a single vine (usually Riesling – RIESLINGSEKT), but as yet they are a small fraction of total Sekt production. A SEKT b.A can bear a site, a village or a district (BEREICH) name, if 85% of the base wine was grown in the place state. The remaining 15% must come from the same region (ANBAUGEBIET). The best Qualitätsschaumwein is stylish, crisp, clean and fruity.

Qualitätswein eines bestimmten Anbaugebietes (QbA)
Quality wine from a specified region (bestimmtes Anbaugebiet). In the eyes of the law, the category of a quality wine is only established once it has passed the official examination (AMTLICHE PRÜFUNG). To qualify for consideration it will have been made from legally recommended or authorized vine varieties and its MUST weight will have reached certain minimum levels, depending on the vine variety and region of origin. It will not have been blended with wine from another region. Some 95% of German wine is classified as quality wine. In contrast, 87% of Italian and 64% of French wines are table wines.

Qualitätswein mit Prädikat (QmP)
"Quality wine with distinction": wine made from grapes with sufficient natural sweetness to need no sugar added during vinification. The six levels of Prädikat are KABINETT, SPÄTLESE, AUSLESE, BEERENAUSLESE, EISWEIN and TROCKENBEERENAUSLESE. Any of these distinctions may be won by a wine from MUST of a certain minimum weight, provided it achieves the necessary "marks" at an official control (AMTLICHE PRÜFUNG) centre. The grapes will also have been harvested according to a procedure, established in law. appropriate to the particular Prädikat.

The minimum must weights – and therefore potential alcohol level – for each Prädikat vary depending on the region and the wine variety. Those for Riesling in the M-S-R, for example, are:

M-S-R Riesling	Minimum must weight in degrees Oechsle	Potential alcohol content by volume
Kabinett	67	8.6
Spätlese	76	10.0
Auslese	83	11.1
Beerenauslese	110	15.3
Eiswein	110	15.3
Trockenbeerenauslese	150	21.5

A Beerenauslese, Eiswein or Trockenbeerenauslese from the M-S-R is always a sweet wine, but the acidity prevents it from becoming cloying. Normally, an Auslese from the Mosel is also sweet, but the amount of residual sugar in a Spätlese or Kabinett wine can vary from very little (perhaps 4 g/l) to more than 30 g/l. In top-quality estates the sweetness in wines below Auslese level may not be very noticeable because it is usually just sufficient to balance the acidity and enhance the delicacy of the wine.

Randersacker Franken w. ★★★
Village a few km from WÜRZBURG, with buildings that date back to the 14th century. Its steep sites produce fine, powerfully flavoured Silvaner wine and elegant Rieslings. Like all Franken wine, relatively expensive. Grosslagen: EWIG LEBEN, Teufelstor.

Randersacker eG, Winzergenossenschaft Franken
Cooperative cellar with 258 members supplying grapes from 122ha (301 acre) of v'yds in RANDERSACKER (TEUFELSKELLER, etc.), SOMMERHAUSEN and WÜRZBURG. Vines are 44% Müller-Thurgau, 28% Silvaner, etc. Approx. annual production is equivalent to 142,000 cases. 80% is sold locally. No exports. Address: Maingasse 33, 8701 Randersacker.

Rappenhof, Weingut Rhh.
Estate dating from the 17th century, owned by Dr Reinhard Muth. 36ha (89 acre) of white and red vine varieties, incl. Riesling (41%), Müller-Thurgau (12%) and Silvaner (11%). A fascinating list of wines from ALSHEIM (FRÜHMESSE, etc.), GUNTERSBLUM, DIENHEIM

and NIERSTEIN. 50% are dry – the Weissburgunder is esp. attractive. Interesting experiments of ageing in new casks are being carried out. Annual production is 25,000 cases. Address: Bachstr. 47-49, 6526 Alsheim.

Rassig
Racy. Describes a wine with pronounced but pleasant acidity and style, as is often found in the M-S-R region.

Rauenthal Rhg. w. ★★★→★★★★
Important wine village on the slopes above ELTVILLE, not far from WIESBADEN. Its best-known Einzellage is BAIKEN. Typical Rauenthaler wines have excellent acidity and need bottle age to show their best. Grosslage: STEINMÄCHER.

Rebe
Vine, e.g. Huxelrebe, Müllerrebe.

Rebholz, Weingut Ökonomierat Rhpf.
9ha (22 acre) estate owned by a family involved in vine-growing for some 300 years. Holdings, 25% terraced, are at SIEBELDINGEN and Birkweiler. Vines are 31% Riesling, 14% Müller-Thurgau, 20% Spätburgunder, etc. The estate was the first to produce a TROCKENBEERENAUSLESE from Müller-Thurgau (in 1949) and is noted for individual wines with real quality in an area where this is not usual. SÜSSRESERVE is not used and much dry wine is made. QbA musts are enriched only if absolutely necessary and then downgraded to DEUTSCHER TAFELWEIN. Address: Weinstrasse 54, 6741 Siebeldingen.

Refractometer

Small hand-held instrument, widely used during the harvest, which measures refraction of light through a sample of grape juice, giving a quick measurement of MUST weight.

Regner

White grape variety, a crossing of Luglienca bianca (a table grape) × Gamay früh (a red grape), planted in 163ha (403 acre), mainly in the Rheinhessen. The main harvest is usually shortly before that of Müller-Thurgau but the grapes can be left on the vine to produce SPÄTLESE wine. Acidity is low but the quality is good. The wine is described as "traditional" (i.e. no extreme flavours) with a gentle Muskat bouquet.

Reh & Sohn GmbH & Co. KG, Franz M-S-R

Family business of wine merchants, exporters and (dating from the 17th century) estate owners, with an overall output of 1.5m. cases a year. The family owns the Weingut Josefinengrund with holdings at LEIWEN and TRITTENHEIM (APOTHEKE, ALTÄRCHEN) and the Weingut Marienhof at PIESPORT (GOLDTRÖPFCHEN, TREPPCHEN, GÜNTERSLAY and all of the steep little Gärtchen site), DHRON. Sales are mainly abroad. Address: Römerstr. 27, 5559 Leiwen.

Rehbach Rhh. w. ★★

Small Grosslage of some 65ha (161 acre) overlooking the Rhein above NIERSTEIN. Its Einzellagen incl. the distinguished HIPPING and PETTENTHAL and also one of the smallest individual sites in Germany, the 0.6ha (1.5 acre) Goldene Luft.

Reichensteiner

White grape variety, a crossing of Müller-Thurgau × (Madeleine Angevine × Calabreser-Fröhlich) from the state viticultural institute at GEISENHEIM. Planting increased from 5ha (12 acre) in 1970 to 358ha (885 acre) in 1985. The yield is similar to that of Müller-Thurgau, the MUST weight heavier by 5-10° Oechsle and acidity is also greater. The flavour of the wine is neutral and pleasant. Given the right weather conditions, a late harvest is possible.

Reichsfreiherr

Title received from the Kaiser, appears in the name of various estates, e.g. Weingut des Reichsfreiherrn von Ritter zu Groenesteyn.

Reichsgraf

Count, appointed by the Kaiser. The inheritor of the title would be a Graf but not a Reichsgraf.

Reichsrat

A state representative, at national level, in the formation of national law. Found in the title of, for example, the Rheinpfalz wine grower Weingut Reichsrat von Buhl.

Reif

Ripe. Describes a wine that is full, mature. See also FLASCHENREIFE (bottle ripeness).

Reil M-S-R w. ★★

One of the best-known Mosel villages, downstream from TRABEN-TRABACH, making very good Riesling wine. The original home of the exporting house and estate owner Rudolf MÜLLER. Grosslage: vom HEISSEN STEIN.

Rheinhartshausen

See Schloss Rheinhartshausen

Reintonig

Describes a wine that smells and tastes absolutely clean.

Reiterpfad Rhpf. w. ★★★

Sloping Einzellage at RUPPERTSBERG producing good-quality, elegant Riesling and Silvaner wines. Grosslage: HOFSTÜCK. Growers: Bassermann-Jordan, Biffar, Buhl, Bürklin-Wolf, Dr Deinhard, Kern, Ruppertsberg Winzerverein "Hoheburg", Spindler.

Rentamt

Originally the local authority for financial administration within a state, later used to describe a similar office on a large country estate. Appears, for example, in the title of Fürst von Metternich-Winneburg'sches Domäne Rentamt at Schloss Johannisberg.

Repperndorf Franken w. ★

Wine village nr. KITZINGEN. Its v'yds are alleged to have been planted by Charlemagne. Now known mainly as the site of the large regional cooperative cellar that handles a third of the Franken grape harvest. Grosslage: Hofrat.

Ress KG, Balthasar Rhg.

Family estate and wine merchants under the name Stefan B. Ress KG., founded more than 100 years ago. Leaseholders since 1978 of SCHLOSS REICHHARTSHAUSEN, plus holdings in many well-known sites incl. BERG ROTTLAND, BERG SCHLOSSBERG, etc., at RÜDESHEIM; KLÄUSERWEG at GEISENHEIM; HASENSPRUNG at WINKEL; DOOSBERG at OESTRICH; NUSSBRUNNEN and WISSELBRUNNEN at HATTENHEIM; SANDGRUB at KIEDRICH; and at HOCHHEIM; ERBACH, ASSMANNSHAUSEN, etc. totalling 20.4ha (51 acre). Vines are 83% Riesling, 5% Spätburgunder, etc. Estate-bottled wines total some 20,000 cases a year, sold in Germany and abroad. Address: Rheinallee 7, 6228 Eltuille.

Restsüsse

Residual sugar in a wine, the result of an incomplete fermentation or the addition of SÜSSRESERVE. A certain amount of unfermented, or residual, sugar is characteristic of German wines. It is the fine balance of acid, alcohol and restrained sweetness that gives them charm and delicacy.

Restzucker

Unfermented sugar in a wine which provides the residual sweetness (RESTSÜSSE) for which it is, in practice, a synonym.

Reverchon, Weingut Edmund M-S-R

Estate with 27.3ha (67 acre) at Filzen (sole owner of Herrenberg), OCKFEN (BOCKSTEIN, etc.), WILTINGEN (GOTTESFUSS) and KONZ, 90% Riesling. Light, lively Saar wines, 70% dry or med-dry sold in Germany and abroad. Address: Saartalstr. 3, 5503 Konz-Filzen.

Rhein

The great river that rises in the Swiss Alps, flows through the heart of the German wine-growing regions and on to the North Sea, some 1,300km (800 miles) from its source. Along the way it is fed by the Neckar, Main, Nahe, Mosel and Ahr. For centuries the river served as the best route for moving wine from the regions where it was produced to customers in Germany and, via Rotterdam, abroad. In the last 25 years the uncertainties of river transport have put this traffic into the motorway system, but the Rhein remains important to wine for climatic reasons, as a tourist attraction and as a factor, directly or indirectly, linking many of the v'yds of Germany.

Rheinart Erben, Weingut Adolf M-S-R

Saar estate owned by Herr Heinzgünter Schmitt of H. Schmitt Söhne, with holdings at OCKFEN (BOCKSTEIN, HERRENBERG), AYL (KUPP) and WILTINGEN (SCHLANGENGRABEN). Vines are 80% Riesling. Approx. annual production is 23,000 cases, sold in Germany and abroad. A bottle-fermented sparkling wine is also produced from the estate's Riesling base wine. Address: Weinstrasse 25, 5559 Longuich.

Rheinberg Kellerei GmbH

Wine exporters, est. in 1939, owned by Edeka, the largest trading group in W. Germany. QbA under well-known names but also more than 100 QmP, many from the Rheinhessen and Rheinpfalz. Annual turnover is 4.2m. cases. Address: Mainzerstr. 162-170, 6530 Bingen.

Rheinblick Rhh. w. ★★

Grosslage incl. within its boundaries the Alsheimer FRÜHMESSE. Many of the v'yds are on steep or sloping sites and the quality of wine is often higher than that sold under other Grosslage names from the region.

Rheinfront

See Rheinterrasse.

Rheinfront eG, Bezirks-Winzergenossenschaft Rhh.

Cooperative cellar with 450 members holding 272ha (672 acre) in many of the best sites in NIERSTEIN and the surrounding district. Vines are 34% Müller-Thurgau, 31% Silvaner, 7% Scheurebe, etc. Much is sold in bulk to the wine trade, the balance to the consumer in Germany. Address: Karolingerstr. 6, 6505 Nierstein.

Rheingau w. (r.)

Compact region of 2,940ha (7,265 acre), incl. some of the best v'yds in West Germany. 80% of the vines are Riesling. There are some 2,250 growers, 84% of whom have v'yd holdings of less than 1ha. About 400 bottle their own wine, and it is among these that the greatest and well-known estates are found. It is from their presence and wine-making over the centuries that the reputation of Rheingau Riesling derives. The Rheingau climate and soil produce Rieslings that have the elegance of a Mosel or a fine Nahe wine but with more body and depth of flavour. They can vary from straight-

RHEINGAU RHEINGAU

Produce of Germany

Schloss Reinhartshausen

A. P. Nr. 32 071 037 79   e 750 ml

1978er Erbacher Hohenrain Riesling

Qualitätswein mit Prädikat Eiswein - Auslese

SCHLOSS REINHARTSHAUSEN · 6229 ERBACH

forward, simple quality wines to complex Auslesen and yet remain successful throughout. Rheingauer wines are not the cheapest in Germany but they are often less expensive than wines of similar standing from Baden, Württemberg or Franken, and are seldom overpriced.

The circuitous Rheingauer Riesling Route that runs the length of the region makes it easy to visit the widely known wine villages by road, and for those with more time and an inclination to walk there is a well-signposted path through the v'yds.

Rheingau eG, Gebietswinzergenossenschaft Rhg.

Cooperative of 330 members, in a region where the cooperative system is not at its strongest. Members own 150ha (371 acre) in KIEDRICH (SANDGRUB), OESTRICH (LENCHEN) and GEISENHEIM (MÄUERCHEN), as well as ELTVILLE, ERBACH, WINKEL, LORCHHAUSEN, MARTINSTHAL and HOCHHEIM. Vines incl. Riesling (80%), Müller-Thurgau (8%) and Spätburgunder (2%). Approx. annual production is equivalent to 154,700 cases of good wines, typical of the region. 10% is sold abroad via export houses. Address: Erbacher Str. 31, 6228 Eltville.

Rheingrafenberg eG, Winzergenossenschaft & Weinkellerei Nahe

Relatively small cooperative cellar with 120 members supplying grapes from 156ha (385 acre), Riesling 55%, Müller-Thurgau 20%. Annual production is equivalent to 214,300 cases. Sales are mainly in Germany – none in bulk. Address: Naheweinstr. 63, 6553 Meddersheim.

Rheinhell Rhg. w. ✱✱✱

Einzellage on an island in the Rhein called the MARIANNENAU after Princess Marianne of Prussia who bought the nearby SCHLOSS REIN-HARTSHAUSEN in 1855, now solely owned by her descendants. The site benefits from a mild microclimate and is planted with Riesling, Weissburgunder and Kerner. Grosslage: DEUTELSBERG.

Rheinhessen w. (r.)

Largest of the wine regions with 25,167ha (62,190 acre) of vines, incl. many new crossings – Scheurebe, Faber, Huxelrebe, etc. – from the viticultural institute at ALZEY in the heart of the region. For consistently the best Rheinhessen Riesling or Silvaner wines one must look to the RHEINTERRASSE nr. NIERSTEIN, with its fine sites overlooking the river, or possibly to the v'yds at BINGEN where the Rhein meets the Nahe. Away from the RHEINTERRASSE the v'yds often occupy slightly sloping ground overlooking farmland. The wines from such sites tend to be softer than those from the Nahe or the M-S-R but have a useful ability to combine the flavour from the soil with that of the new vine varieties. Most Rheinhessen wine is sold under a Grosslage or Einzellage name and some 70% is sold in bulk by the growers to the wine trade for bottling. Approx. 3,000 growers bottle their own wine, and among these will be found some of

the best estates in Germany. At the other extreme, Rheinhessen also produces very cheap wine, which should be agreeable as a light drink but will probably have very little character.

Rheinhessen Silvaner Trocken
A QbA produced individually by about a hundred growers and sold under a common black and orange label.

Rheinland-Pfalz
Federal State with 67% of the planted viticultural area of West Germany, covering the Rheinpfalz, Rheinhessen, Nahe, Ahr and most of the Mosel-Saar-Ruwer and Mittelrhein. The capital is MAINZ.

Rheinpfalz w. (r.)
Region of 22,869ha (56,512 acre), also known as the Palatinate, that stretches from the frontier with France to the Rheinhessen border. The n. part, the Bereich MITTELHAARDT/DEUTSCHE WEINSTRASSE, has a dry, warm climate, and the success and reputation of its wine, judged by the prosperity of the region's villages, has been noted by writers over the centuries. There are a number of leading estates, situated mainly between KALLSTADT and RUPPERTSBERG, with a high proportion of Riesling in their v'yds, making wine to the very finest standard. In a great year magnificent meaty wines are produced, often deep in colour and with great flavour, that only begin to be at their best eight years or so after the vintage. "Off" years produce slimmer wines, with attractive acidity and fruit, that show well the characteristics of the vine variety. The wines from the s. Rheinpfalz, the Bereich SÜDLICHE WEINSTRASSE,

are of lesser calibre than those from further n. but are good value for money. The countryside is essentially rural and vine-growing is clearly the most important type of farming. The v'yds lie mainly on the level land or on gentle slopes, overlooked by wooded hills rising to 600m (1,968 feet) or more. Visitors to the Pfalz will find living inexpensive, comfortable but unsophisticated.

Rheinterrasse Rhh. w.
Name given to the v'yds alongside the Rhein from the village of BODENHEIM in the n. to Mettenheim in the s. With the possible exception of those at BINGEN, all the Rheinhessen sites are on the slopes of the Rheinterrasse, with its two particularly famous small

towns of OPPENHEIM and NIERSTEIN. The proportion of Riesling and Silvaner planted is greater than elsewhere in the region, and the wines can have much weight and depth of flavour. The Rheinterrasse was previously known as the Rheinfront.

Rhodt unter Rietburg Rhpf. w. ★

Picturesque wine village nr. EDENKOBEN, below Schloss Ludwigshöhe, summer residence of Ludwig I of Bavaria. Produces interesting, good-value-for-money wines from many vine varieties. A number of long-established growers and the large RIETBURG GEBIETSWINZERGENOSSENSCHAFT, also the vineyard with the oldest vines in Germany – 300-year-old Traminers. Grosslage: ORDENSGUT.

Richter, Weingut Max Ferd. M-S-R

Family-owned estate dating from 1680 with 15.3ha (38 acre) at TRABEN-TRABACH, WEHLEN (SONNENUHR), GRAACH (HIMMELREICH), BERNKASTEL, MÜLHEIM (sole owners of Helenenkloster), VELDENZ, BRAUNEBERG (JUFFER), etc. Vines are 85% Riesling. Annual production is 15,000 cases. The top-quality wines are cask-matured. 50% are dry or med-dry. Sales are to the trade in Germany and abroad. No SÜSSRESERVE is used and EISWEIN is a speciality, even in the non-Eiswein years, such as 1976 or 1986. The estate also sells under the Dr Dirk Richter-Wine-Selection label. Address: Hauptstr. 37/85, 5556 Mülheim.

Richter-Botendahl, Weingut Rhg.

100-year-old family-owned estate with 15ha (37 acre) in WALLUF ELTVILLE, RAUENTHAL, ERBACH and KIEDRICH. Vines are 86% Riesling, 7% Müller-Thurgau, 5% Spätburgunder, etc. Approx. annual production is 6,500 cases of typical, modern Rheingau wines, mainly dry and med-dry, sold in Germany and abroad. Address: Walluferstr. 25, 6228 Eltville.

Richtershof, Weingutsverwaltung M-S-R

11ha (27 acre) estate with holdings at MÜLHEIM and VELDENZ, including sold ownership of the tiny 0.38ha (0.9 acre) Carlsberg site, one of the smallest in Germany. Although Riesling is the principal vine, Müller-Thurgau has been grown for over 60 years. Light, fresh, long-lasting wines. Address: Hauptstr. 81-83, 5556 Mülheim.

Riedel, Weingut Jakob Rhg.

Small estate with 17th-century origins. 3.5ha (9 acre) at HALLGARDEN (SCHONHELL, etc.) are 100% Riesling. Bottling is early to retain freshness. The wines are predominantly dry. Annual production is 2,500 cases, sold in Germany. Address: Taunusstr. 1, 6227 Hallgarten.

Rieslaner

White grape variety, a crossing of Silvaner × Riesling from WÜRZBURG grown in 47ha (116 acre) mainly in its region of origin, Franken, With a MUST weight of less than 90° Oechsle (12% alcohol) the wine tastes thin. Acidity is high, and the grapes ripen late in the season. At its best the wine is very stylish and fairly neutral in flavour. Other vines perform more successfully and produce better wine more easily.

Riesling, Weisser

White grape variety that produces the finest German wine. It is planted in 19,615ha (48,471 acre) – just under 20% of the total area under vine. Where the finest v'yds are to be found, in the Mittelhaardt in the Rheinpfalz, in the Rheingau, in the middle Nahe and on the Mosel, the percentage of Riesling grown will be high, for the Riesling in Germany demands a top-quality site. Depending on location the harvest will take place in October, November or even December for certain speciality wines. One of the main characteristics of Riesling is the elegant acidity that makes the flavour of the wine last in the mouth, and gives it the ability to develop over many years in bottle. Riesling flavour is positive and yet restrained, unlike that of a full-blown Traminer. It is therefore able to transmit the taste that comes from the soil, without imposing any strong additional flavour upon it. As a result the variations between a Riesling from one region and those from another are clearly differentiated. All qualities of Riesling wine can be produced, depend-

ing on the vintage and the site, from table wine to the richest
TROCKENBEERENAUSLESE.

Rieslingsekt
Quality sparkling wine from the Riesling grape. Although the number of German sparkling wines that indicate a vine variety on the label is still small, interest in Rieslingsekt is increasing, because it shows well the qualities of freshness and style enjoyed in German still wine. (See also LAGENSEKT, MARKENSEKT.)

Riesling-Hochgewächs
A QbA wine in the Ahr, Mosel-Saar-Ruwer, Mittelrhein, Nahe, Rheinhessen, and Rheinpfalz regions may be described as "Riesling-Hochgewächs", if the original must weight, reached the equivalent of 1.5 degrees alcohol by volume more than the minimum laid down for standard Riesling Qba. In addition, the wine must reach the enhanced level of quality required by the control (AP) authorities.

Rietburg eG, Gebietswinzergenossenschaft Rhpf.
Large cooperative cellar of 1,150 members founded in 1958, covering 1,100ha (2,718 acre) in villages between NEUSTADT and LANDAU. The range of vines is wide, incl. 30% Müller-Thurgau, 20% Silvaner, 10% Riesling, 10% Ruländer, 10% Kerner etc. Annual prod. amounts to the equivalent of almost 1.4m. cases, covering all the styles of wine possible under German wine law. Sales are 80% in Germany, 20% abroad. Address: 6741 Rhodt u.d. Rietburg.

Rivaner
Synonym for Müller-Thurgau used mainly in Luxembourg, but also by the Zentralkellerei Mosel-Saar-Ruwer eG, when selling certain of its Müller-Thurgau wines in the Benelux countries.

Rödelsee Franken w. ★★→★★★
Village nr. KITZINGEN producing top-quality wines that are spicy, powerful and long-flavoured. In recent years many of the v'yds, known to have been in production in the 13th century, have been reconstructed, modernized and replanted, mainly in Silvaner and Müller-Thurgau. Grosslage: Schlossberg.

Römer
Wine glass or rummer. In the n. regions the standard Römer used for the sale of wine by the glass contains 200ml; in Franken, Württemberg and Baden a 250ml Römer is used. The stem is usually green or amber and the bowl is clear but sometimes engraved. The liquid content is, by law, always marked. Finer Römer of varying sizes are produced for private use.

Römerlay M-S-R w. ★★
Grosslage covering the v'yds on the Mosel around TRIER and those of the little Ruwer valley, incl. EITELSBACH and KASEL. Very high proportion of Riesling.

Ronde, Weingut Sanitätsrat Dr M-S-R
Old-established estate at NEUMAGEN, DHRON and TRITTENHEIM (APOTHEKE, ALTÄRCHEN). Vines are 88% Riesling, 8% Müller-Thurgau and – unusually – 4% Ruländer, of which the M-S-R has only 9ha (22 acre) in total. The wines from steep, slaty sites are matured exclusively in wood and frequently win prizes at regional competitions. Annual production is 9,100 cases, sold in Germany and abroad. Address: Römerstr. 9, 5559 Neumagen.

Rosengarten Nahe w. ★
Best-known Grosslage in the Nahe valley, covering more than 600ha (1,483 acre). None of the individual sites is among the best in the region and much use is made of the Grosslage name, combined with that of the village of RÜDESHEIM – not to be confused with the town of the same name in the Rheingau. A Rüdesheimer Rosengarten will usually be a blend of Silvaner and Müller-Thurgau, similar to a wine from the Bereich BINGEN in the Rheinhessen across the R. Nahe but with more acidity.

Roséwein
Pale pink wine made from red grapes, closer in style to white wine than to red. See WEISSHERBST.

Rotberger
Red grape variety, a crossing of Riesling × Trollinger.

Rotenfels Nahe w. ★★★
Einzellage at TRAISEN that takes its name from the nearby rock face, the Rotenfels (at 214 metres (702ft) the highest cliff in Europe n. of the Alps). Produces steely Riesling wines of great character. Grosslage: BURGWEG. Growers incl. Crusius.

Rothenberg Rhh. w. ★★★
20ha (49 acre) Einzellage adjacent to Niersteiner PETTENTHAL on the slopes of the RHEINTERRASSE at Nackenheim. The red slate and sandstone soil can produce wines of real elegance, charm and style. Grosslage: SPIEGELBERG. Growers: Gunderloch-Usinger, Guntrum.

Rothenberg Rhg. w. ★★★
Sloping, modernized Einzellage at GEISENHEIM that produces big, balanced Riesling wines with a slight, attractive taste of the soil. Grosslage: BURGWEG. Growers: Forschungsanstalt Geisenheim, Holschier, Vollmer, Wegeler-Deinhard, Zwierlein.

Rotling
A rosé coloured wine produced by blending red and white grapes or their pulp – not a blend of wine or MUSTS.

Rotwein
Red wine.

Roxheim Nahe w. ★★
Village a few km n.w. of BAD KREUZNACH producing Riesling and Silvaner wines well regarded in the region for their style. Cannot be compared to the best from the Nahe. Usually appropriately priced. Grosslage: ROSENGARTEN.

Rüdesheim Nahe w. ★
Village nr. BAD KREUZNACH, often linked with the Grosslage ROSENGARTEN, a Nahe answer to Niersteiner GUTES DOMTAL. The sites at Rüdesheim itself are planted in Müller-Thurgau and Silvaner, producing sound wines. Not to be confused with Rüdesheim in the Rheingau.

Rüdesheim a. Rhein Rhg. Pop. 10,300 ★★★→★★★★
Town 25km (15 miles) s.w. of WIESBADEN, a major target for tourists and widely known for its street of wine bars, the Drosselgasse – tolerable only to the most gregarious. Its v'yds, protected from the north by the Niederwald (wood) and facing s. across the Rhein to BINGEN, enjoy a good microclimate but can suffer in drought years. Full-flavoured, splendid, positive wines. Grosslage: BURGWEG.

Ruländer
Vine variety planted in 3,123ha (7,717 acre), produces good, full-bodied, soft white wines from blue grapes. Known also as Grauburgunder, and as Pinot Gris in France. In Baden and the Rheinpfalz, where the style of wine is softer than that made further north, the Ruländer seems to reflect the regional character particularly well. It should be planted in a good site where MUST levels can reach a least 80° Oechsle to avoid being thin and uninteresting. Ruländers, with their somewhat "barnyard" bouquet, do not have the elegance of the paler-coloured Riesling, but as a SPÄTLESE or AUSLESE they can impress by their power and fullness.

Ruppertsberg Rhpf. w. (r.) ★★→★★★
Village nr. DEIDESHEIM producing attractive Riesling and Silvaner wines and very stylish Scheurebe. Probably not among the very finest in the Bereich MITTELHAARDT/DEUTSCHE WEINSTRASSE – they often lack the depth and intensity of the best of FORST or DEIDESHEIM – but are usually cheaper. Grosslage: HOFSTÜCK.

Ruppertsberger Winzerverein "Hoheburg" eG Rhpf.
Cooperative cellar with 209 members supplying grapes from 204ha (504 acre), mainly at RUPPERTSBERG (REITERPFAD, LINSENBUSCH, etc.). Vines are 45% Riesling, 22% Müller-Thurgau, 10% Silvaner, etc. Annual production is 238,100 cases, sold principally in Germany. Efficient, modern wine-making in a top-quality part of the Rheinpfalz. Address: Übergasse 23, 6701 Ruppertsberg.

Ruwer
River that rises in the high ground of the Hunsrück and flows some 40km (25 miles) later into the Mosel nr. the village of Ruwer, close to TRIER. In good years the Ruwer v'yds can produce great Riesling

wines, positive and firm in flavour, similar in weight to those of the other important river in their shared Bereich, the Saar, but the slaty character is less pronounced. The little Ruwer valley is characterized by a handful of villages of ancient origin, famous wine estates overlooked by woods and walnut trees, and some of the most interesting wines of the M-S-R region.

Saar

Tributary of the Mosel that rises in the Vosges mountains and enters the Bereich SAAR-RUWER upstream from SAARBURG. On either side of the river, beyond the v'yds, the landscape is wooded and attractive and has been an area for relaxation for the people of TRIER since the time of the Roman occupation. The slate soil of the v'yds is harder than that of the Mosel and gives the wine a strong, steely flavour. Great wines from a number of fine estates are made in good years.

Saar-Ruwer, Bereich w.

The Bereich that covers the Saar and Ruwer v'yds.

Saarburg M-S-R Pop. 5,800 w. ★★→★★★

Ancient town known for its old buildings and half-timbered houses, its bell foundry and its wine. It lies on the R. Saar at the upper end of the vine-growing area. Many of the sites are owned, in part or in whole, by well-known estates. Saarburger Riesling wines in good years are among the best on the Saar. They have a positive slaty Riesling flavour, with a strong bouquet to match. Prices are comparable to those from Mosel villages such as WEHLEN, BERNKASTEL and BRAUNEBERG. Grosslage: SCHARZBERG.

Saarland

Federal State with 98ha (242 acre) of v'yds, incl. those of the Bereich MOSELTOR nr. the German–Luxembourg–French frontier. (The rest of the M-S-R is in the state of RHEINLAND-PFALZ.) The capital is Saarbrücken.

Sackträger Rhh. w. ★★★

Sloping Einzellage on the outskirts of OPPENHEIM producing refined wines, outstanding in good years. Grosslage: GÜLDENMORGEN. Growers: Baumann, Dahlem, Guntrum. Carl Koch, Oppenheim Staatsweingut, Schuch, Sittmann.

Saftig

Juicy. Describes a wine with good acidity and a fruity flavour, that lasts in the mouth. Might apply to a well-made Riesling Spätlese from the RHEINTERRASSE.

St Alban Rhh. w. ★

Grosslage of just under 1,000ha (2,471 acre) between MAINZ and NACKENHEIM that takes its name from the St Alban monastery at Mainz, once a large landowner in the district. Makes sound, easy-to-drink Rheinhessen wines.

St Johannishof, Weingut M-S-R

Quality 9.2ha (23 acre) Riesling estate with holdings at BERNKASTEL, WEHLEN (SONNENUHR, etc.), GRAACH (HIMMELREICH) and ERDEN (PRÄLAT, TREPPCHEN). The estate makes the full range of Mosel wines. 80% are cask matured. Annual production is 8,300 cases. Address: Dr Loosen, 5550 Bernkastel.

St Michael M-S-R w. ★→★★

Large Grosslage of more than 2,200ha (5,436 acre). The best-known sites are around the villages of KLÜSSERATH and LEIWEN, where the vines are mainly Riesling. There are also significant plantations of Müller-Thurgau.

St-Nikolaus-Hospital M-S-R

An old peoples' home dating from 1465 with 8ha (20 acre) at BRAUNEBERG (JUFFER), BERKASTEL (GRABEN, etc.), GRAACH (HIMMELREICH), WEHLEN (SONNENUHR), etc. The wines win top prizes in the DLG competitions, with the med-dry wines appealing particularly to the estate's German customers. Annual production is 7,100 cases. Address: Cusanusstr., 5550 Bernkastel-Kues.

St Rochuskapelle Rhh. w. ★

Grosslage of more than 2,400ha (5,931 acre) in the n.e. corner of the Rheinhessen. Some of the v'yds lie alongside the R. Nahe and the wines often have more acidity than those made further s. in the region. Best-known individual site within the Grosslage is the SCHARLACHBERG at BINGEN.

St Ursula Weingut & Weinkellerei GmbH
Wine merchants, probably best known for the excellent Goldener Oktober range of QbA. Owners of Weingut VILLA SACHSEN. Annual sales are 2,500,000 cases. Address: Mainzerstr. 184, 6530 Bingen.

Salm-Dalberg'sches Weingut, Prinz zu Nahe
Oldest wine producing cellar in Germany dating from 1200. 6.9ha (17 acre) are planted in villages near Bad Kreuznach. 50% of the wines are dry. Most are spritzig, elegant and fruity. 5,000 cases are sold annually, 25% on the export market and the balance in Germany. Address: Schloss Wallhausen, 6511 Wallhausen.

Samtrot
Red grape variety, a mutation of the Müllerrebe, planted in 51ha (126 acre), almost entirely in Württemberg.

Sandgrub Rhg. w. ★★★
Einzellage in two clearly defined and separate sections s. of KIEDRICH, planted mainly in Riesling. Produces stylish, good-quality wine that improves with bottle age. Grosslage: HEILIGENSTOCK. Growers: Groenesteyn, Hessisches Weingut, Knyphausen, Lamm-Jung, Nikolai, Oetinger, Reinhartshausen, Ress, Rheingau eG, Richter-Boltendahl, Sohlbach, Tillmanns, Wagner-Weritz, Weil.

Sanitätsrat
Award given to medical practitioners up to 1918 nationally, and thereafter by some individual states. Appears, for example, in the title of the Neumagen/Mosel estate Weingut Sanitätsrat Dr Ronde.

Saumagen Rhpf. w. ★★
Once a Grosslage, now an Einzellage at KALLSTADT producing wine from the ordinary to the outstanding, but particularly known for its Silvaners. Translated, Saumagen means sow's stomach – the name of a well-known local Rheinpfalz sausage dish. Grosslage: KOBNERT. Growers: Winzergenossenschaft Kallstadt.

Säure
Acidity. Because of the cool nights when the grapes are ripening, the acid level of German wine, at 5-9 g/l, is considerably higher than that of most wines produced in a warmer climate. As a result the wine has a unique freshness that is carefully retained during vinification and maturation. The main acids in German wine are tartaric (WEINSÄURE) and malic (ÄPFELSÄURE). The amount present depends on the ripeness and variety of grape. Top-quality wines such as a BEERENAUSLESE or an EISWEIN often have particularly high acidity, balanced by a large amount of residual sugar. Such wines need years of maturation in bottle to reach their peak and for the acidity to soften. Wines with relatively low acidity (e.g. Müller-Thurgau) are usually best drunk young. The addition of acids to German wine is illegal, but DEACIDIFICATION is allowed.

Schaefer, Weingut Karl Rhpf.
Estate dating from 1843 with 17ha (42 acre) of holdings at DÜRKHEIM (SPIELBERG, etc.) and WACHENHEIM (FUCHSMANTEL). Vines are 75% Riesling. All qualities of wine are matured in cask in the old vaulted cellar and are expected to develop in bottle. 60% of the Rieslings are dry. In recent years the Dürkheimer wines have been particularly successful, both at national competitions and in commercial terms. Annual production is 10,000 cases, sold in Germany and abroad. Address: Weinstr. süd 30, 6702 Bad Dürkheim.

Schales, Weingut Rhh.
200-year-old estate, run with great commitment by the sixth generation of the Schales family. Dalsheim, at the s. end of the Rheinhessen, is not well known outside Germany but the range of wines produced by the estate is wide. A number of vine varieties are grown on 35ha (86 acre) of holdings, and many wines of AUSLESE and higher quality are produced from vines such as Kanzler, Optima, Siegerrebe and Huxelrebe. The aim is freshness and the ability to develop over years in bottle. Approx. annual production is 25,000 cases, 35% are dry or med-dry. Each April the estate holds a mammoth trade tasting, at which some 100 wines are on

show. An impressive and progressive producer. Address: Alzeyerstr. 160, 6521 Flörsheim-Dalsheim.

Scharlachberg Rhh. w. ★★→★★★

Well-known Einzellage at BINGEN on mainly sloping ground, overlooking the R. Nahe. The wines are close in style to those of the Lower Nahe, or even the Rheingau, with attractive acidity and charm. Grosslage: ST ROCHUSKAPELLE. Grower: Villa Sachsen.

Scharzberg M-S-R w. ★★

Grosslage of about 1,600ha (3,954 acre) covering the whole viticultural area of the Saar, where many may feel that the archetypal German wine is produced. A light, elegant, fruity acidity is its main characteristic – more positive and less subtle than a wine from the MITTELMOSEL. Wines using the Scharzberg name are not the cheapest but are usually of much better quality than those sold at rockbottom prices from the Grosslage Bernkasteler KURFÜRSTLAY.

Scharzhofberg M-S-R w. ★★★→★★★★

27ha (67 acre) mainly steep v'yd nr. WILTINGEN on the Saar with the status of a village or community, so that its wine is sold under the single name "Scharzhofberg". Marvellously elegant Riesling wine, full of character in good years. Often one of the great wines of Germany. Growers: Bischöfliche Weingüter, Hövel, Kesselstatt, Koch, Egon Müller, Bernd. van Volxem. Grosslage: SCHARZBERG.

Schatzkammer

Literally treasure room. A part of a cellar set aside for storing the finest, and by implication the oldest, wines. Some estates list a number of rare wines from their Schatzkammer.

Schaumwein

Sparkling wine that meets certain technical standards but is basically cheap and cheerful. Approx. 10% of sparkling wine produced in Germany is classified simply as Schaumwein. The balance is QUALITÄTSSCHAUMWEIN. See also SEKT.

Schenkenböhl Rhpf. w. (r.) ★★

Grosslage of about 600ha (1,483 acre) on either side of the DEUTSCHE WEINSTRASSE between BAD DÜRKHEIM and WACHENHEIM. The individual sites are mainly flat or gently sloping with a good proportion of Riesling. They form part of the finest v'yds of the Rheinpfalz, so that a wine sold under the Grosslage name is still likely to be very stylish and full of quality.

Scheurebe

White grape variety, a very successful crossing of Silvaner × Riesling, named after its developer Dr Georg Scheu. It now covers 4,385ha (10,836 acre), spread throughout all the vine-growing regions. Planted in a good site, suitable for Silvaner, the Scheurebe can produce SPÄTLESE wine of absolute top quality. Lesser wines have a pronounced flowering-currant bouquet, but this is not so marked in fine AUSLESE wines for which Scheurebe also has a considerable reputation. The acidity in unripe Scheurebe grapes is so pronounced that the resulting wine is best used for blending with NEUTRAL, soft wines.

Schillerwein

ROTLING QbA and QmP produced in Württemberg may be called Schillerwein. The name has nothing to do with the poet Friedrich Schiller, a Württemberger by birth, but arises from the wine's varying shades of rosé colour. ("Schillern" means to change colour.) In the past, red and white vine varieties were intermingled in the v'yds and both were harvested and vinified together.

Schlangengraben M-S-R w. ★★

Einzellage at WILTINGEN planted in Riesling and Müller-Thurgau, producing fruity, stylish wines. Well known, but not the best site on the Saar. Grosslage: SCHARZBERG. Growers: Rheinart, Schlangengraben/Schorlemer, Bernd. van Volxem.

Schlangengraben, Weingut M-S-R

Estate owned by Hermann Freiherr v. SCHORLEMER GmbH.

Schleinitz'sche Weingutsverwaltung, Freiherr von M-S-R

Family-owned estate of 4.5ha (11 acre) at the underrated wine-producing end of the Mosel nr. KOBLENZ. Holdings are all at KOBERN, on one of the prettiest parts of the river. Vines are 100% Riesling, producing an impressive list of wines incl. six AUSLESEN and two BEERENAUSLESEN. Styles range from wines with pronounced steely acidity to softer wines with more body and fruit. Many have won awards at national competitions. Approx. annual production is 3,700 cases, sold 90% to private customers. Address: Kirchstr. 17, 5401 Kobern-Gondorf.

Schlink-Herf-Gutleuthof, Vereinigte Weingüter Nahe

Combination of three estates that were founded in 1952, 1830 and 1807 respectively, with 60ha (148 acre) mainly at KREUZNACH (NARRENKAPPE, BRÜCKES, etc.) but also at SCHLOSSBÖCKELHEIM (KUPFERGRUBE), WINZENHEIM and ROXHEIM. Vines are 35% Riesling, 16% Weissburgunder, 15% Müller-Thurgau, etc. The wines follow the pattern of good-quality Nahe wine production from dry QbA to rich BEERENAUSLESE. 40% are exported, the dry and med-dry wines in burgundy bottles.

The estates are also part of the 60-member ERZEUGERGEMEINSCHAFT Simmerner Hof. Address: Planigerstr. 154, 6550 Bad Kreuznach.

Schloss

Castle or palace. Wine that bears the name of a Schloss (e.g. Schloss Johannisberg, Schloss Vollrads) must have been made entirely from grapes grown in the castle's v'yds. It may then be called a Schlossabfüllung (castle-bottling) as opposed to the usual ERZEUGERABFÜLLUNG (estate or producer bottled). The word Schloss also often forms part of an Einzellage name (Serriger Schloss Saarfelser Schlossberg) or a district name (Bereich Schloss Böckelheim), so "Schloss" on a label does not necessarily mean that the wine comes from an individual castle or estate.

Schloss Böckelheim, Bereich Nahe w.

District covering the Nahe region upstream from BAD KREUZNACH, incl. the well-known sites at NIEDERHAUSEN and the village of SCHLOSSBÖCKELHEIM. Many of the v'yds are widely separated. The quality of wine is generally good and will not be as cheap as a Bereich NIERSTEIN, esp. when made from Riesling.

Schloss Deidesheim

See Kern, Weingut Dr

Schloss Groenesteyn, Weingut des Reichsfreiherrn von Ritter zu Groenesteyn Rhg

Important estate dating from the 14th century and owned by the Groenesteyn family since 1640. 33ha (82 acre), 92% Riesling, concentrated in RÜDESHEIM (BERG ROTTLAND, BERG ROSENECK, BERG SCHLOSSBERG, etc.) and Kiedrich (GRÄFENBERG, Wasserros, SANDGRUB), producing approx. 25,000 cases annually. Wines are matured in wood and are among the best in the region. 50% is exported. All are offered as Schloss Groenesteyn followed by the wine name. Address: 6229 Kiedrich-Rheingau.

Schloss Johannisberg, Fürst von Metternich-Winneburg'sches Domäne Rentamt Rhg

Great estate of 35ha (86 acre), planted 100% in Riesling, with an approx. annual production of 25,000 cases. The estate was

recorded as the first (in 1716) to plant Riesling on its own, unmixed with other vine varieties. Maturation in wood in the cool cellars helps to produce the fine, weighty wines for which the Schloss is famous. Different coloured capsules are used for the various quality categories. In recent years many of the QbA and KABINETT wines have been medium-dry. SPÄTLESE wines are made only in outstanding years and, in common with other Rheingau estates, an AUSLESE is a rarity. Most of the buildings, restored after serious damage in World War II, date from the 17th century. Schloss Johannisberg is legally an ORTSTEIL and the wine is sold without any individual site names, in Germany and abroad. Address: 6222 Geisenheim-Johannisberg.

Schloss Kosakenberg
See Zwierlein, Weingut Freiherr von

Schloss Lieser, Weingut M-S-R
Estate owned by Hermann Freiherr v. SCHORLEMER GmbH.

Schloss Neuweier, Weingut Baden
7ha (17 acre) estate in the Bereich ORTENAU, planted with 81% Riesling. 60% of the wines are dry. 4,400 cases are sold annually in Germany but also abroad. Address: Mauerbergstr. 21, 7570 Baden-Baden.

Schloss Ortenberg, Weinbauversuchsgut Baden
Estate founded in 1950 as an experimental institute. Its 7.5ha (19 acre) of v'yds are planted with 20% Riesling, 20% Müller-Thurgau, 15% Traminer and Gewürztraminer, plus a range of varieties, reflecting the estate's research work. The wines (85% white, of which some 40% are dry) are matured in cask or stainless steel, according to their individual needs. Annual production of 5,000 cases is sold mainly to the German consumer. Address: Burgweg 19a, 7601 Ortenberg.

Schloss Reichhartshausen Rhg. w. ★★★
A much-restored castle, originating in the 12th century, now regarded as an ORTSTEIL, with 3ha (7 acre) of v'yd owned entirely by Balthasar RESS.

Schloss Reinhartshausen, Administration Prinz Friedrich von Preussen Rhg.
70ha (173 acre) estate with origins believed to date back to Charlemagne. Present owners are the great-grandchildren of Kaiser Wilhelm II. Holdings are at ERBACH (incl. MARCOBRUNN, MICHELMARK, SIEGELSBERG and sole ownership of Schlossberg), on MARIANNENAU island in the Rhein incl. sole ownership of Erbacher RHEINHELL, and at HATTENHEIM (WISSELBRUNNEN, NUSSBRUNNEN, etc.), KIEDRICH, RAUENTHAL and RÜDESHEIM. Vines are 88% Riesling plus Weissburgunder, Spätburgunder, etc. Apart from the fine traditional wines expected of a great Rheingau estate, the Schloss also makes an interesting Weissburgunder and Chardonnay TROCKEN. Annual production is 75,000 cases, sold in Germany and abroad. Address: 6228 Erbach/Rheingau.

Schloss Saarfelser Schlossberg M-S-R w. ★★→★★★
Mainly steep Einzellage at SERRIG nr. the upper end of the Saar vine-growing area. Sole owner is the VEREINIGTE HOSPITIEN at TRIER. Produces scented, positive, light, stylish Riesling wines that can be superb in good years. Grosslage: SCHARZBERG.

Schloss Saaleck Franken
In 1964 the town of HAMMELBURG bought the ancient v'yds around Schloss Saaleck, now covering 30ha (74 acre). Vines are 50% Müller-Thurgau, 20% Silvaner, 10% Bacchus, etc., producing approximately 7,500 cases a year of powerful, dry wines bottled in the Franken BOCKSBEUTEL and 5,000 cases in litre bottles. Sales are mainly in Germany. Address: Städt. Weingut, 8783 Hammelburg.

Schloss Saarstein, Weingut M-S-R
11ha (27 acre) estate planted 93% in Riesling, at the edge of the vine growing area on the Saar, and taken over by Dieter Ebert, a refugee from Eastern Europe in 1956. 8,300 cases are produced annually of firm, spritzig wine, sold in Germany and abroad. Address: 5512 Serrig.

Schloss Schönborn, Domänenweingut Rhg.

75ha (185 acre) estate owned by the distinguished church and political von Schönborn family, which acquired its first Rheingau v'yds in 1349. The Weingut's present holdings, based on HATTEN-HEIM, are at OESTRICH (DOOSBERG), RÜDESHEIM (BERG SCHLOSSBERG),

GEISENHEIM (MÄUERCHEN), WINKEL (HASENSPRUNG), HOCHHEIM (HÖLLE, DOMDECHANEY, etc.), JOHANNISBERG, ERBACH (MARCOBRUNN) and HATTENHEIM itself (NUSSBRUNNEN, and sole ownership of Pfaffenberg). Vines are 86% Riesling and more will be planted. Maturation is in wood, producing full, big-scale Riesling wines, and a small amount of Spätburgunder with good varietal characteristics and no residual sugar. Sales are worldwide. Address: Hauptstr. 53, 6228 Eltville-Hattenheim.

Schloss Staufenberg, Markgräflich Badis'ches Weingut Baden

The Margrave of Baden (the title corresponds in rank to an English Marquess) owns four wine estates, one of which, based on the 11th-century Schloss Staufenberg, is set in splendid hilly wooded country overlooking the village of DURBACH. The 27ha (67 acre) of steep v'yds are planted mainly in Riesling (40%), Müller-Thurgau (28%) and Spätburgunder (17%), etc. The Riesling wines are firm but rounded. Two-thirds of the red wines are dry or med-dry. Annual production is 14,350 cases, 10% sold abroad. The estate's wine bar has distant but spectacular views of the Vosges mountains. Address: 7601 Durbach.

Schloss Vollrads, Graf Matuschka-Greiffenclau'sche Güterverwaltung Rhg.

Remarkable and possibly most famous private estate in Germany, its 50ha (124 acre) protected by the woods that shelter the Rhein-

gau above WINKEL. The Greiffenclau family is known to have been selling wine in the 12th century, and built Schloss Vollrads at the start of the 14th century. Today, Schloss Vollrads is an ORTSTEIL, regarded in law as a "community". Like SCHARZHOFBERG and STEINBERG, it sells its annual production of approx. 33,300 cases

(45% abroad) with no additional village or v'yd name. Planted 98% in Riesling, the Schloss, with its v'yds somewhat higher than many in the Rheingau, produces wines with pronounced acidity and fine fruit. The estate uses different coloured CAPSULES to indicate variations in the style and quality of its wines. They are predominantly dry or med-dry.

As well as its own Weingut, Schloss Vollrads also owns the Graues Haus restaurant in Winkel, where a range of wines from many different Rheingau growers is served. In 1979 Graf Matuschka-Greiffenclau bought the Weingut Fürst Löwenstein in Hallgarten. Wines that do not reach the Graf's high standards are sold in bulk to the wine trade and are not allowed to bear the Löwenstein or Vollrads name. Address: 6227 Oestrich-Winkel.

Schloss Westerhaus
See Opel, Weingut Irmgard von

Schlossabfüllung
Castle bottled. See SCHLOSS.

Schlossberg M-S-R w. ★★
Schlossberg is a common site name in Germany. The Einzellage at BERNKASTEL on the Mosel, half steep, half sloping, is not in the Bernkastel first division but produces stylish wines, mainly from Riesling. Grosslage: KURFÜRSTLAY. Growers: Pauly Bergweiler, Schorlemer, Schwab, Selbach-Oster, Wegeler-Deinhard.

Schlossberg M-S-R w. ★★★
Steep Einzellage at ZELTINGEN-RACHTIG, next to the SONNENUHR, producing elegant Riesling wines. Grosslage: MÜNZLAY. Growers: Kesselstatt, S. A. Prüm, Schorlemer, Vereinigte Hospitien.

Schlossböckelheim Nahe w. ★★→★★★★
Small but important wine-making community producing elegant, fresh Riesling wines to the highest standards. Set in rural surroundings, upstream from BAD MÜNSTER AM STEIN-EBERNBURG, it is still largely undiscovered by tourists. The Schloss (castle) is now a ruin. Grosslage: BURGWEG.

Schlosskapelle Nahe w. ★★
Grosslage on the left bank of the R. Nahe s. of BINGEN. Best-known sites are at MÜNSTER-SARMSHEIM and DORSHEIM, where full-bodied, meaty Riesling wines with much style are made.

Schlotter, Weingut Valentin Rhg.
120-year-old estate with cellars tunnelling 80m (262 feet) into the steep v'yd slopes at ASSMANNSHAUSEN. Holdings are 4ha (10 acre) at Assmannshausen (HÖLLENBERG, etc.) and 5.5ha (14 acre) at RÜDES-HEIM (BERG ROTTLAND, BERG SCHLOSSBERG, BERG ROSENECK, etc.). The aim is to make lively, elegant, spicy Riesling wines at Rüdesheim and red wines, mainly from Spätburgunder, at Assmannshausen, with little tannin but good, fruity acidity. The estate favours maturation in wood and some of the casks are more than 100 years old. Annual production is 5,800 cases, sold to private customers and also abroad via the exporting house KENDERMANN in Bingen. Address: Lorcherstr. 13, 6220 Rüdesheim.

Schmitt, Weingut Hermann Franz Rhh.
30ha (74 acre) estate established in 1549 by the direct ancestors of the present owners. Among the well-situated holdings at NIERSTEIN are parts of ÖLBERG, HIPPING, PETTENTHAL, ORBEL and sole ownership of the 2.5ha (6 acre) Zehnmorgen site. Vines are 75% Riesling, 10% Silvaner, 10% Müller-Thurgau, etc. Style, body and good acidity are the hallmarks of the estate wines, and they are matured in wood. The dry Riesling Spätlesen and Auslesen have been very successful. Annual production is 16,600 cases, 30% exported. Address: Hermannshof, Kiliansweg 2, 6505 Nierstein.

Schmitt, Weingut Robert Franken
300-year-old family estate of 6.5ha (16 acre) (Randersackerer TEUFELSKELLER, etc.) producing mainly fully-fermented wines. No ANREICHERUNG. Annual production is 5,400 cases. Address: Maingasse 13, 8701 Randersacker.

Schmitt-Dr Ohnacker, Weingut Rhh.
150-year-old, family-owned estate of 12.5ha (31 acre), all at GUN-TERSBLUM. The character of the wines is very much influenced by

119

the very varied soil. Most wines spend 3-8 months in casks, some of which are 100 years old. Fermentation is controlled and special efforts are made to retain the individuality of each wine. Approx. annual production is 12,200 cases, sold in Germany and abroad – mainly through H. SICHEL SÖHNE GMBH of Alzey. Address: Neustr. 6, 6524 Guntersblum.

Schmitt'sches Weingut, Gustav Adolf Rhh.
Estate owners, est. in 1618, wholesale wine merchants and, since the 1930s, an exporting house. 100ha (247 acre) of holdings in NIERSTEIN (PETTENTHAL, ÖLBERG, HIPPING, KRANZBERG, etc.), OPPENHEIM, DIENHEIM, DEXHEIM, GUNTERSBLUM and Gau-Bischofsheim, planted 65% in traditional vines (Riesling, Silvaner, etc.). Approx. annual production is 50,000 cases (a low yield) of estate-bottled wines, 66% exported to more than 60 countries. Address: Wilhelmstr. 2-4, 6505 Nierstein.

Schneider, Weingut Georg Albrecht Rhh.
Family-owned estate with origins reaching back over seven generations. 15ha (37 acre) of holdings at NIERSTEIN, incl. PATERBERG, BILDSTOCK, FINDLING, ORBEL, ÖLBERG, PETTENTHAL and HIPPING – all top-quality sites. Vines are 40% Riesling, 25% Müller-Thurgau, 13% Silvaner, etc. Approx. annual production is equivalent to 11,250 cases. Only the better-quality wines are bottled; the rest is sold in bulk. The reputation of the estate is for fine, "nervig", fruity wines, sold in Germany and abroad. Address: Oberdorfstr. 11, 6505 Nierstein.

Schneider, Weingut Jacob Nahe
Estate owned by the Schneider family – who are livestock farmers as well as vine growers – for more than 400 years. 12.5ha (31 acre) in fine sites at NIEDERHAUSEN (HERMANNSHÖHLE, etc.) and NORHEIM are planted 96% in Riesling. Organic manuring, late picking and individual cask maturation after a temperature-controlled fermentation produce spicy, elegant wines. 60% are dry. Sales are mainly to private customers. Address: Winzerstr. 15, 6551 Niederhausen.

Schneider Nachf., Michel M-S-R
See Kloster Machern, Weingut.

Schneider GmbH, Ludwig Rhpf.
Family-owned estate and wine merchant business, with a fine old half-timbered, heavily beamed inn. The holdings, all at St Martin s. of NEUSTADT, are planted with the wide range of vine varieties usual in the s. Rheinpfalz. The estate is part of the 120ha (296 acre) "St Martinus" ERZEUGERGEMEINSCHAFT. No exports. Address: "Altes Schlösschen", Maikammererstr. 7, 6731 St Martin.

Schnepfenflug an der Weinstrasse Rhpf. w. (r.) ★★
Grosslage of more than 500ha (1,236 acre) on level land nr. the well-known wine villages WACHENHEIM and FORST, growing many different vine varieties. Not to be confused with Schnepfenflug vom Zellertal in the n. Rheinpfalz.

Scholl & Hillebrand GmbH
Exporting house established in 1880 selling Rheingau estate- and non-estate-bottled wines. Address: Geisenheimerstr. 9, 6220 Rüdesheim.

Schönburger
Grape variety, a crossing of Spätburgunder × an Italian table grape, grown at present on 67ha (166 acre), mainly in the Rheinhessen and Rheinpfalz. The grapes, which are luscious to taste and a marvellously delicate pink in colour, produce a white wine with a bouquet reminiscent of Traminer, a high MUST weight (15° Oechsle more than Riesling) and a dangerously low acidity. AUSLESE wine can be made from grapes infected with EDELFÄULE (noble rot).

Schönhell Rhg. w. ★★★
Einzellage at HALLGARTEN making full-bodied, balanced Riesling wines. Grosslage: MEHRHÖLZCHEN. Growers: Engelmann, Eser, Hallgarten/Rhg. eG, Ress, Riedel, Vereinigte Weingutsbesitzer, Wegeler-Deinhard.

Schoppenwein
Synonym for AUSSCHANKWEIN.

Schorlemer, Clemens Freiherr von M-S-R
  See Schorlemer GmbH

Schorlemer GmbH, Hermann Freiherr v. M-S-R
  Combination of five estates owned by Herr Peter Meyer of the
Weinkellerei and exporting house Peter Meyer Wineries GmbH in
Bernkastel. The estates are Weingut Meyerhof, Weingut Schloss
Lieser, Weingut Schlangengraben, Weingut Franz Duhr Nachf.,
Weingut Clemens Freiherr von Schorlemer, with holdings at BERN-
KASTEL (GRABEN, etc.), GRAACH (HIMMELREICH, DOMPROBST,
ABTSBERG), ZELTINGEN-RACHTIG (SCHLOSSBERG, SONNENUHR), OCKFEN
(BOCKSTEIN) and sole ownership of Sandberg at WILTINGEN. 98%
Riesling. As well as typical, racy Riesling wines the estates also
produce sparkling wine from some of their individual site holdings.
Annual prod. is 25,000 cases, sold worldwide with the help of Peter
Meyer-Horne KG. Address: Cusanusstr. 14, 5550 Bernkastel-Kues.

Schubert'sche Gutsverwaltung, C. v. M-S-R
  Fine estate of 33ha (82 acre) with origins dating back to 966,
bought by the von Schubert family in 1882. The holdings are three
solely owned Einzellagen at MAXIMIN-GRÜNHAUS – Bruderberg,
Herrenberg and Abtsberg – planted with 95% Riesling. As well as
the modernized v'yds there is land for cattle raising, fruit farming
and hunting. Very distinguished, racy wines are made – incl. a
Trockenbeerenauslese in 1983. Up to 40% of the total annual production of 25,100 cases is dry or med-dry. Sales are in Germany and
abroad. Address: 5501 Grünhaus/Trier.

Schuch, Weingut Geschwister Rhh.
  Well-known family-owned estate of 16ha (40 acre), dating from
1817. Holdings are at NIERSTEIN (ÖLBERG, PETTENTHAL, FINDLING,
etc.), OPPENHEIM (SACKTRÄGER) and DIENHEIM, planted 50% in

Riesling, plus a typical Rheinhessen range of new crossings. The
wines, incl. some dry and med-dry, show the grape characteristics
well. Approx. annual production is 16,600 cases, sold in Germany
and abroad. Address: Oberdorfstr. 22, 6505 Nierstein.

Schultz-Werner, Weingut Oberst Rhh.
  Family-owned estate dating from 1833, with holdings at Gau-
bischofsheim nr. MAINZ. Vines are 40% Riesling, 24% Müller-
Thurgau, 11% Silvaner, etc. The wines receive individual attention,
appropriate to the vine variety; all are fairly full-bodied and retain a
lively acidity. 60% are dry or med-dry. Approx. annual production is
11,900 cases. 40% is exported. Address: Bahnhofstr. 10, 6501
Gaubischofsheim.

Schumann-Nägler, Weingut Rhg.
  Old family-owned estate, with 18ha (44 acre) at GEISENHEIM (MÄUER-
CHEN, KLÄUSERWEG, etc.) and WINKEL. 97% Riesling. The annual pro-
duction is 13,500 cases of typical, well-balanced Riesling wines, sold
in Germany and abroad. Address: Nothgottsstrasse 29, 6222
Geisenheim.

Schuster, Weingut Eduard Rhpf.
  15ha (37 acre) estate founded by the Schuster family in 1840. Holdings are at KALLSTADT (STEINACKER), UNGSTEIN, BAD DÜRKHEIM and

HERXHEIM. Planted 50% in Riesling, 20% Silvaner, 9% Müller-Thurgau, etc. The aim is to maintain the wine's individuality, grape and vintage characteristics. Maturation is in 80–120-year-old casks. Annual production is 9,800 cases, sold in Germany and abroad. Address: Neugasse 21, 6701 Kallstadt.

Schwab, Weingut Leo M-S-R

3ha (7 acre) 100% Riesling estate at BERNKASTEL (SCHLOSSBERG, etc.), GRAACH (HIMMELRIECH, DOMPROBST), and WEHLEN (SONNE-NUHR), producing 2,400 cases annually of cask matured wines. Many top awards in the DLG competitions. Address: Weingartenstr. 56, 5550 Bernkastel-Kues.

Schwarze Katz M-S-R w. ⋆

Best-known Grosslage of the lower Mosel, nr. ZELL, covering some 630ha (1,557 acre). A very high proportion of Riesling is grown on the steep slopes, except in the NNE-facing Kaimter Marienburger site. Here, in less favourable growing conditions, more new crossings than Riesling are found. None of the individual sites is so well known as the Grosslage name Schwarze Katz (black cat). The wine is usually sound and often sold with a label showing a large black cat, arching its back, making Schwarze Katz almost a brand name.

"Schwarzer Adler", Weingut Baden

Estate of 6ha (15 acre) with a further 35ha (86 acre) attached to it in the form of an ERZEUGERGEMEINSCHAFT. The 41ha (101 acre) are planted 25% Ruländer, 20% Müller-Thurgau, 20% Spätburgunder, etc. Most of the wines are fully fermented, made to accompany food, particularly in leading German restaurants. Owner Franz Keller is a well-known publicist for German dry wines, and runs an import business strong in Bordeaux wine. Address: Badbergstr. 23, 7818 Vogtsburg.

Schwarzerde Rhpf. w. ⋆→⋆⋆

Grosslage of more than 1,100ha (2,718 acre) in the n. Rheinpfalz, with no widely known vine-growing villages. The wines will be very pleasant, agreeable and easy to drink but will lack the distinction of those produced in the central section of the Mittelhaardt a few km further s.

Schwarzlay M-S-R w. ⋆⋆

Grosslage of more than 1,200ha (2,965 acre) in the MITTELMOSEL, incl. the wine villages ÜRZIG, ERDEN, KINHEIM, TRABEN-TRABACH and ENKIRCH. Many of the sites are planted 100% in Riesling. A good-quality Mosel Grosslage.

Schwarzriesling

See Müllerrebe

Schwarzwald

Probably the best-known forest in Europe. It protects many of the Baden v'yds, esp. those of the Bereich ORTENAU. The sites reach up to the edge of the forest, sharing the steep slopes with orchards. Wonderfully rural and pretty, where it is not the victim of acid rain.

Schweich M-S-R w. ⋆⋆

Village nr. TRIER, at the start of the steep-sided Mosel gorge that follows an almost uninterrupted but erratic course down to KOBLENZ. Produces fresh and fruity wines. Grosslage: PROBSTBERG.

Schweinhardt Nachf., Weingut Bürgermeister Willi Nahe

Estate of 23.8ha (59 acre) trading under the Schweinhardt name since 1859, with holdings at LANGENLONSHEIM, between BAD KREUZNACH and BINGEN. Vines are 36% Riesling plus a range of other varieties incl. Rülander, Müller-Thurgau, Scheurebe. Approx. annual production is 14,500 cases. A range of bottle shapes is used depending on the sweetness/colour/style of the wine. No exports. Address: 6536 Langenlonsheim.

Seal

See Siegel

Sekt

Short German word for QUALITÄTSSCHAUMWEIN, originating in the early 19th century. Since 1975 the word Sekt has no longer been reserved for quality sparkling wine produced in Germany. In German-speaking countries one therefore finds Französischer

(French) Sekt, Italienischer (Italian) Sekt, etc. Sparkling-wine production in Germany amounts to about 23m. cases a year.

Selbach-Oster, Weingut Geschwister M-S-R
Small, 4.6ha (11 acre) estate, owned by the Selbach family – involved in vine-growing since 1661. The 100% Riesling holdings are at ZELTINGEN-RACHTIG (HIMMELREICH, SCHLOSSBERG and SONNENUHR), WEHLEN, GRAACH (DOMPROBST and ABTSBERG) and BERNKASTEL (BRATENHÖFCHEN). Wines are matured in oak casks and are typical of the Mosel – crisp, racy, fruity. A dry Auslese is listed. Annual production is 4,100 cases, sold in Germany and abroad. Address: Uferallee 23, 5553 Zeltingen.

Septimer
A crossing of Gewürztraminer × Müller-Thurgau, grown in 30ha (74 acre) mainly in the Rheinhessen. The dark pink grapes make white, full-bodied and very soft wine. Yield and acid content are low and MUST weight is high. Of some interest to estate bottlers who wish to extend the range of wine they can offer, but not generally popular.

Serrig M-S-R w. ★★→★★★
Village, almost at the furthest extremity of the v'yds, upstream on the Saar. Steely Riesling wines are made on a number of top-quality estates. Often a source of excellent base wine for sparkling-wine production. Grosslage: SCHARZBERG.

Sichel Söhne GmbH, H.
Important exporter of good-quality German wine to 81 countries. Founded in 1857, Sichel is best known for the leading and long-established brand Blue Nun Liebfraumilch but also has connections with a number of important estates. 75% of total annual sales of 2.3m. cases is to the USA and UK. Address: Werner von Siemensstr. 14-18, 6508 Alzey.

Siebeldingen Rhpf. w. ★→★★
Village tucked below the foothills of the Haardt range w. of LANDAU IN DER PFALZ. Quite well known; the wines should be good, without the weight and intensity of those of the Bereich MITTELHAARDT/DEUTSCHE WEINSTRASSE. Vines are mainly Müller-Thurgau, Silvaner, Morio-Muskat. Grosslage: Königsgarten.

Siegel
Seal. Now used to indicate the awards, sometimes in the form of a seal but also through strip labels, granted by the DEUTSCHE LANDWIRTSCHAFT GESELLSCHAFT and other organizations.

Siegelsberg Rhg. w. ★★★
Einzellage nr. the Rhein at ERBACH producing racy Riesling wines. Grosslage: DEUTELSBERG. Growers: Eltville Staatsweingut, Knyphausen, Oetinger, Reinhartshausen, Wagner-Weritz.

Siegerrebe
White grape variety, a crossing of Madeleine Angevine × Gewürztraminer from ALZEY in the Rheinhessen, planted in 262ha (647 acre). Bees and wasps often totally destroy the crop, but if the grapes escape attack they can produce a MUST of considerable weight, some 15–20° Oechsle greater than that of Müller-Thurgau. The acidity is low and the wine has an extremely strong bouquet. Siegerrebe is sometimes bottled as a single-vine wine of great quality but is more often used to add interest to commercial blends.

Silvaner, Grüner
Once the most widely grown vine in Germany, now found in 8,050ha (19,892 acre), being steadily replaced by Müller-Thurgau and other vines. The wine is NEUTRAL in flavour and does not hide the character that comes from the soil and site. In a good year it can make top-quality SPÄTLESE wine, esp. on the RHEINTERRASSE around NIERSTEIN and in Franken. Simple Silvaner wine is often blended with Riesling, Morio-Muskat and Scheurebe. Silvaner has many synonyms. Usually spelt Sylvaner outside Germany.

Simmern'sches Rentamt, Freiherrlich Langwerth von Rhg.
Important, 45ha (111 acre) estate, owned by the von Simmern family since 1464, with fine old cellars and administrative buildings. Holdings are at ERBACH (MARCOBRUNN), HATTENHEIM (NUSS-

123

BRUNNEN, etc.), RAUENTHAL (BAIKEN, etc) and ELTVILLE, planted 94% in Riesling. Serious Rheingau wine-making produces top-quality, long-lived wines. Approx. annual production is 32,700 cases, sold in Germany and abroad. Address: Kirchgasse, 6228 Eltville.

Simon, Bert M-S-R

Estate of 32.3ha (80 acre), formed in 1968 from v'yds previously owned by Freiherr von SCHORLEMER and incl. more holdings added since. Today the estate is sole owner of the Herrenberg, Würtzberg and König Johann Berg sites at SERRIG and of the Staadter Antoniusberg at the upstream edge of the Saar vine-growing region. Further holdings are at Niedermennig, EITELSBACH (Marienholz), MERTESDORF and KASEL (KEHRNAGEL, NIES'CHEN and Herrenberg). Vines are 85% Riesling, 8% Müller-Thurgau and, unusually for the M-S-R, Weissburgunder (4%) which, in particular, produces interesting KABINETT wine. The estate made excellent, stylish wine, in the difficult 1982 vintage. Annual production is 22,000 cases, sold 50% in the USA, 15% in the UK and 35% in Germany. Address: Weingut Serriger Herrenberg, Römerstr., 5512 Serrig.

Sittmann, Weingut-Weinkellerei Carl Rhh.

Largest privately owned estate in the Rheinhessen, est. in 1879, with some 80ha (198 acre) at OPPENHEIM (SACKTRÄGER, etc.), DEINHEIM, ALSHEIM (incl. FRÜHMESSE) and NIERSTEIN. The estate produces a full range of typically regional wines. The Sittmanns are wine merchants and exporters as well as v'yd owners and sales of the annual production of 830,000 cases of German and estate bottled wines are worldwide. Address: Wormserstr. 61, 6504 Oppenheim.

Slaty

The soil of the M-S-R, Ahr and Mittelrhein is varied, but many of their v'yds contain slate. Its pervading greyness, both in the soil and on the house roofs, combined with the similarly coloured basalt from the nearby Eifel hills, can make the Mosel a sombre place when the sun does not shine. However, Riesling wines from slate sites have elegance and finesse, and a particular flavour that by association has become known as slaty.

Sobernheim Nahe w. ★→★★

Village upstream from SCHLOSSBÖCKELHEIM making good, lively Riesling and flowery Müller-Thurgau wines. Grosslage: Paradiesgarten.

Sohlbach, Weingut Georg Rhg.

4.6ha (11 acre) estate, est. in 1860 but with a 300-year-old cask cellar. Holdings are all at KIEDRICH (80% Riesling, 10% Spätburgunder). Spätburgunder WEISSHERBST has a loyal following among the estate's private customers and 50% of the Rieslings are dry or med-dry. 12% of the annual production of 3,300 cases is exported to the UK. Address: Oberstr. 15, 6229 Kiedrich.

Söhnlein Rheingold KG, Kellereien

Sparkling-wine producers, est. in 1864. Their "Söhnlein Rheingold" was launched personally in 1876 by Richard Wagner, a friend of the Söhnlein family. The company's main brand today, in terms of volume, is "Söhnlein Brilliant", which sells at approx. DM 5.00 per bottle in Germany. See also Fürst von METTERNICH SEKTKELLEREI GmbH. Address: Söhnleinstr. 1-8, 6200 Wiesbaden-Schierstein.

Solemacher, Weingut Freiherr von M-S-R

5.3ha (13 acre) Saar estate owned by the family of Max Freiherr Raitz v. Frentz for more than 100 years, rebuilt after total destruction in World War II. Holdings are at SAARBURG and in the well-known village of OCKFEN (BOCKSTEIN, HERRENBERG), planted 90% in Riesling. Annual production is 5,700 cases, although this can vary greatly from vintage to vintage. Sales are in Germany and abroad. Address: Kunoweiher 39, 5510 Saarburg.

Sommerach Franken w. ★★

Village downstream from VOLKACH, with some 250ha (618 acre) of v'yds and the oldest cooperative cellar in Franken, founded in 1901. Known for its asparagus and its strongly flavoured Müller-Thurgau and Silvaner wine. Grosslage: Kirchberg.

Sommerhausen Franken w. ★★

Small village upstream from WÜRZBURG, with sweeping, modernized v'yds reaching down to the Main. Produces good-quality Müller-Thurgau and Silvaner wines. Grosslage: ÖLSPIEL.

Sonnenberg, Weingut Rhh.

Mainly red-wine producing estate, founded in 1881, with 8.6ha (21 acre) of vines in the long-established enclave of Spätburgunder around INGELHEIM, facing MITTELHEIM and OESTRICH across the

Rhein. Annual prod. is 8,100 cases, incl. 4,700 cases of Spätburgunder from 5.3ha (13 acre) and 2,400 cases of Portugieser. The wines are dry and are much admired in Germany. But have a low tannin content compared to those from France. Sales at home and abroad. Address: J. Neus, Bahnhofstra. 96, 6507 Ingelheim.

Sonnenhof, Weingut Würt.

20ha (49 acre) family-owned estate n.w. of STUTTGART. Although the estate is only 10 years old, vine-growing has been in the Fischer family since 1522. 62% of production is in powerful, soft red wine from Trollinger, Spätburgunder and Limberger. White wines are mainly from Riesling, Müller-Thurgau and Kerner. Grapes are also bought in at harvest time, producing an annual output for the cellars of some 20,800 cases. 90% of the wine is dry or med-dry. Sales are mainly in Germany, with a start being made abroad. Address: Bezner-Fischer, 7143 Vaihingen-Gündelbach.

Sonnenuhr M-S-R w. ★★★→★★★★

Two Einzellagen of this name lie side by side above the Mosel. One forms part of the v'yds of ZELTINGEN-RACHTIG, the other comes within the boundaries of WEHLEN. Both are well situated, 100% steep, 100% Riesling and make top-quality wine. The Wehlener Sonnenuhr in particular has a reputation for wines of great finesse and fruit, more gentle than those from neighbouring BERNKASTEL sites but with a wonderfully luscious flavour, that can reach the peak of wine-making on the river. Grosslage: MÜNZLAY. Growers in Zeltingen-Rachtig: Ehses-Berres, Ehses-Geller, Friedrich-Wilhelm-Gymnasium, Kesselstatt, Schorlemer, Selbach-Oster, Vereinigte Hospitien, Weins-Prüm. Growers in Wehlen: "Abteihof", Christoffel, Kesselstatt, Lauerburg, Licht-Bergweiler, Pauly, Pauly-Bergweiler, J. J. Prüm, S. A. Prüm, Richter, St. Johannishof, St.-Nikolaus-Hospital, Schorlemer/Meyerhof, Schwab, Studert-Prüm, Vereinigte Hospitien, Weins-Prüm, Wegeler-Deinhard.

Sorte

Variety, species. (See next entry.)

Sortencharakter

Character of the vine variety. The style of a wine from any one v'yd will change each year to a greater or lesser extent, depending on the vintage. Within these variations those qualities that originate in the soil and the variety of grape will normally remain more or less constant. If the character of the vine variety is pronounced, this is usually considered a good thing. With the richest wines of AUSLESE quality and upwards, the vine character is sometimes replaced by that of noble rot (EDELFÄULE).

Sparkling Hock

Sparkling wine from the Rhein. In the 1840s, as the German sparkling-wine industry was expanding, both KUPFERBERG and DEINHARD sold sparkling wines with names the British could easily understand, among which were "Sparkling Hock" and "Sparkling Moselle". Although Sparkling Moselle is still common today, and a number of Sparkling wines are made from Rhein wine, Sparkling Hock as a description has become rare.

Sparkling wine

See Qualitätsschaumwein, Schaumwein, Sekt

Spätburgunder, Blauer

Red grape variety, more commonly known elsewhere as Pinot Noir. In Germany it needs a good site to produce 90 hl/ha or more from its best clones, with MUST weights of at least 80° Oechsle (10% alcohol). A German Blauer Spätburgunder usually has less tannin than a French Pinot Noir and is sometimes offered on the German market with a certain amount of sweetness. As a QbA, the alcohol content will be increased by the addition of sugar. Prepared in this way it can more closely resemble a Pinot Noir from Burgundy. As a BEERENAUSLESE, with a great amount of residual sugar, it is a unique and fascinating wine. The popularity of Spätburgunder wine in Germany is steadily increasing. Of the 4,486ha (11,085 acre) planted in Germany in Blauer Spätburgunder, 72% are in Baden where the vine benefits from the warm southerly climate.

Spätlese

Late-picked. Grapes intended for a Spätlese wine cannot be picked earlier than seven days after the start of the main harvest of the vine variety in question. Often the Spätlese harvest of an early-ripening vine, such as Müller-Thurgau, will have been gathered before the main harvest of the late-ripening Riesling or Trollinger has begun. By delaying picking, the grapes develop more sugar. The difference in MUST weight between a Spätlese and a QbA varies depending on vine variety and region, but it can be as much as the equivalent of 4.4% alcohol (the figure in Württemberg). No enrichment (ANREICHERUNG) is allowed.

Spiegelberg Rhh. w. ★★

Grosslage of more than 600ha (1,483 acre) covering some excellent individual sites on the RHEINTERRASSE at NIERSTEIN, incl. FINDLING, BILDSTOCK and PATERBERG. A few top-quality growers have done a great deal to build up the reputation of the v'yds and thus of the Rheinhessen as a whole.

Spielberg Rhpf. w. ★★★

Excellent Einzellage on the outskirts of BAD DÜRKHEIM making stylish, fruity Riesling wines. Grosslage: HOCHMESS. Growers: Bart, Bassermann-Jordan, Fitz-Ritter, Karst, Schaefer.

Spindler, Weingut Eugen Rhpf.

Widely respected family-owned estate of 13.5ha (33 acre), with cellars and administrative buildings on the s. edge of FORST. Holdings are at DEIDESHEIM (GRAINHÜBEL, LEINHÖHLE, KIESELBERG, HERRGOTTSACKER), RUPPERTSBERG (incl. REITERPFAD and LINSENBUSCH) and Forst itself (PECHSTEIN, UNGEHEUER and notably JESUITENGARTEN). Vines are 65% Riesling, 15% Müller-Thurgau, etc. The estate is known for its Riesling wines with restrained residual sugar, for which maturation in bottle over a number of years is important. Sales are mainly in Germany. Address: Weinstrasse 55, 6701 Forst.

Spritzig

Slightly sparkling. Term used to describe a wine that gives a gentle prickling sensation on the tongue produced by carbon dioxide. It can be found in M-S-R wine of all qualities up to and incl. AUSLESEN and adds to their freshness and charm. If an ordinary wine from elsewhere is *spritzig* it may well be the result of carbon dioxide being used as a part of cellar technique, rather than through the natural gas formed in fermentation. In Germany, whereas white and rosé wines are sometimes expected to be *spritzig*, red wine should have no noticeable carbon dioxide.

Staatl. Weinbauversuchsgut Lauda, Baden

6ha (15 acre) estate in the Badisches Frankenland, established in

1930, and owned by the State of Baden-Württemberg. Many vine varieties are grown, some on trial as part of research into resistance against frost. 35% of the wines are dry. Weissburgunder has much success, incl, a top award (DLG) winning Eiswein in 1984. 5,000 cases are sold mainly to the consumer in Germany. Address: Rebgutsstr. 80, 6970 Lauda-Königshofen.

Stahlig

Steely. Describes a wine in which the acidity is high and the flavour is very direct and clean. It is unlikely to be subtle and certainly not delicate. Wonderfully steely Riesling wines, esp. at top-quality QbA and KABINETT level from good estates, come from the Saar and from the R. Nahe nr. TRAISEN.

Stauch, Alfred & Hartmut Rhpf.

6.5ha (16 acre) estate with all its holdings at KALLSTADT, incl. part of STEINACKER, planted with 60% Riesling and 12% Gewürztraminer. Unusually, none of the wines is enriched, and elegance and fruit is aimed for in the vinification. Sales of the approximate annual production of 4,200 cases are to private customers and also through the estate's own wine bar. Address: Weinstrasse 130, 6701 Kallstadt.

Steeg Mrh. W. ★★

If Mittelrhein wines received the recognition the best of them deserve, Steeg, in a side valley of the Rhein gorge nr. BACHARACH, would be well known. The steep Riesling sites produce steely wines, with great possibilities for HALBTROCKEN (med-dry) wines, cheaper than an equivalent Rheingau wine by approx. DM 1.00 per bottle. Also excellent for sparkling wine in all but the best (i.e. warmest) years. Grosslage: Schloss Stahleck.

Steffensberg M-S-R W. ★★

Einzellage in a steep side valley of the Mosel at ENKIRCH producing firm, stylish Riesling wines. Grosslage: SCHWARZLAY.

Steil Rhg. r. W. ★★

Grosslage of about 140ha (346 acre) at ASSMANNSHAUSEN, between RÜDESHEIM and LORCH, planted in Spätburgunder and Riesling. The true-to-type red Spätburgunder wines are much respected locally. Expensive when drunk abroad.

Steillagen

Steep sites. The FLURBEREINIGUNG authorities define a steep site as having an inclination greater than 50%. Although running costs of such v'yds can be greater than those of v'yds on the level by as much as 300%, and the yield is always less, they do produce some of the best wines in Germany. To emphasize their origin, wines from steep sites are sometimes referred to as "Steillagenweine" but the term is not legally established.

Stein Franken W. ★★★

Most famous Einzellage in Franken, at WÜRZBURG. The steep slopes produce outstanding Riesling wines, powerful and with lasting flavour, as well as more gentle wines from Silvaner (see also STEINWEIN). Not in a Grosslage. Growers: Bürgerspital, Juliusspital, Würzburg Staatl. Hofkeller.

Steinacker Rhpf. W. (r.) ★★

Large, mainly sloping Einzellage at KALLSTADT, producing very good quality white wines from a variety of grapes and some less distinguished red wine from Portugieser. Grosslage: KOBNERT. Growers: Bonner, Kallstadt, Koehler-Ruprecht, J. Pfleger, Schuster, Stauch, Winzer.

Steinberg Rhg. W. ★★★

Single v'yd, its 32.1ha (79 acre) enclosed by a stone wall, nr. KLOSTER EBERBACH – Cistercian monks from Kloster Eberbach planted the first vines in the Steinberg in the 12th century. Today the v'yd is owned by the ELTVILLE STAATSWEINGUT. Vines are 95% Riesling and the wines have "size", breeding and finesse. They are sold simply under the name Steinberger – no village name.

Steiner'scher Keller Rhpf.

Wine merchants established in 1752 with a small v'yd holding at LANDAU in the Bereich SÜDLICHE WEINSTRASSE. The concentration is on dry wines with 250,000 cases being sold annually of the brand

"Raddegiggl" – a blend of Silvaner and Riesling. Address: 6740 Landau.

Steinmächer Rhg. w. ★★

Grosslage of some 600ha (1,483 acre) almost in the suburbs of WIESBADEN. The best-known wine village in the Grosslage is RAUENTHAL. Standard, good-quality wines that benefit from bottle age (esp. those made from Riesling) are sold under the Steinmächer name.

Steinwein

For at least 250 years, wine in BOCKSBEUTEL from WÜRZBURG in Franken was often sold simply as Steinwein. In this century the definition has become more precise, and since 1971 only wine from the STEIN Einzellage on the outskirts of Würzburg can bear the old name "Stein"

Stift

Religious foundation. A Stift must have religious connections whereas a STIFTUNG need not.

Stiftung

An endowed institution. Some of the finest wine-producing estates are endowed institutions, often with religious origins (e.g. the Stiftung Staatliches Friedrich-Wilhelm-Gymnasium in Trier). Many land owners hoped that by leaving their good farming land and their best v'yds to the church while in this world they would have an easier time in the next.

Stillwein

Wine with little or no carbon dioxide, in contrast to PERLWEIN or SCHAUMWEIN, is classified as Stillwein.

Strausswirtschaft

"Bush Inn." Those for whom vine-growing is their principal occupation are allowed for a period totalling not more than four months each year to sell their wine, accompanied by simple food, on their own premises. This ancient practice is advertised by a bush (Strauss) hung outside wherever the wine is being offered. Theoretically a good wine will sell without this publicity, for "a good wine needs no bush". Also known as BESENWIRTSCHAFT, where a "Besen" (broom) replaces the "Strauss", as "Heckenwirtschaft" ("Hecke" = hedge) in parts of Franken, and as "Buschenschank" in Austria and the Süd Tirol.

Strohwein

"Straw wine," made for centuries from grapes that had been dried on straw to concentrate their juice and increase the sugar content. Its production has been illegal in Germany since 1971. In style Strohwein was similar to a BEERENAUSLESE but even more of a rarity. Strohwein is still made outside Germany, and in particular in the Jura in France where it is known as *Vin de Paille*.

Strub, Weingut J. & H. A. Rhh.

Family-owned estate dating from 1864, with 17ha (42 acre) of

holdings at DIENHEIM and NIERSTEIN (HIPPING, ÖLBERG, ORBEL, PATERBERG and FINDLING). Vines are mainly Riesling, Silvaner and Müller-Thurgau (each 30%). A serious estate producing top-quality RHEINTERRASSE wine, traditional in style but now incl. some that are dry and medium-dry. Approx. annual production is 19,200 cases, sold in Germany and abroad. Address: Rheinstr. 42, 6505 Nierstein.

Stück

Wooden cask, twice as large as the more common HALBSTÜCK, used mainly for storage. See FASS.

Studert-Prüm, Stephan M-S-R

Estate of 6ha (15 acre), in the present family ownership since 1581, with holdings at WEHLEN (incl. SONNENUHR), GRAACH (HIMMELREICH, DOMPROBST) and BERNKASTEL (GRABEN) – all top-quality sites. Vines are 90% Riesling. The estate awards stars to its bottlings to differentiate between what it feels are the various qualities of AUSLESE wines: two stars equals fine Auslese, three stars equals finest Auslese. Annual production is 4,600 cases, sold in Germany and abroad. Address: Maximinhof, 5550 Bernkastel-Wehlen.

Stumpf

Blunt or dull. Describes a wine that has aged too quickly and has lost its character and life.

Stumpf-Fitz'sches Weingut

See Annaberg Stumpf-Fitz'sches Weingut

Stuttgart Würt. Pop. 590,000 r. w. ★→★★

Large industrial city and capital of the state of Baden-Württemberg, heavily damaged in World War II. Wooded hills and v'yds reach almost to the centre of the city, and Trollinger and sound Riesling wine is made. The Rotenberg Einzellage to the east of the city is a fine example of a modernized, reconstructed v'yd. Stuttgart is the site of the Intervitis viticultural and wine-related exhibition.

Stuttgart, Landeshauptstadt r. w. ★★

15.4ha (38 acre) estate of the city of Stuttgart, with vintage records dating from 1236. The v'yds are planted half in white vine varieties – incl. 4.2ha (10 acre) Riesling, and half in red – incl. 5.5ha (14 acre) Trollinger. 12,500 cases of dry and med-dry wine are produced annually and sold mainly locally. Address: Liegenschaftsamt, Abt. Weingut, Dorotheenstr. 2, 7000 Stuttgart 1.

Südliche Weinstrasse, Bereich Rhpf. w. (r.)

District covering the whole of the Rheinpfalz, known in the past for a high yield of undistinguished wine. The quality today is much better, although it cannot rival the best from the n. Bereich MITTELHAARDT/DEUTSCHE WEINSTRASSE.

Süffig

Tasty. Describes a light wine, probably of not very high quality, with balanced sweetness, pleasant to drink in large quantities. Just what a good glass of "HOCK" should be.

Südliche Bergstrasse/Kraichgau, Winzerkeller

The 4,300 members of this large cooperative cellar have 1,500ha (3,707 acre) of holdings in 57 villages n. and s. of HEIDELBERG. Vines are 42% Müller-Thurgau, 25% Riesling, 8% Ruländer, 9% Weissburgunder, etc. Approx. annual production is the equivalent of 1.2m. cases, typical of the Bereich Badische Bergstrasse-Kraichgau. 95% of the wines are dry or med-dry. No exports. Address: Bögnerweg 3, 6908 Wiesloch.

Sugaring

See Anreicherung

Süss

Sweet. EEC description, applicable to a STILLWEIN containing more than 45 g/l of residual sugar. In the case of good, estate-bottled wines, only Spätlesen and wines of a higher quality category are likely to be sweet.

Süssreserve

Sweet reserve: unfermented grape juice that is added to wine shortly before bottling to arrive at the required level of sweetness. It is widely used in most wines up to SPÄTLESE, to which a restrained addition of Süssreserve brings balance and charm. Complicated regulations govern the quality and geographical origin of a Süssreserve, but in principle both must be similar to that of the wine to which the Süssreserve is added. The use of Süssreserve has simplified the problems of bulk storage and has enabled sulphur-dioxide levels to be reduced. It has also made it possible to supply medium-sweet wines at the low price for which the consumer asks.

Sylvaner

See Silvaner Grüner

Tafelwein

Table wine. This term has been precisely defined by EEC regulations to describe the category below quality wine. It can only be produced from prescribed vines, growing within the EEC, and must reach certain analytical standards. DEUTSCHER TAFELWEIN is subject to additional national legislation. Strictly speaking, it is now incorrect to use the description table wine as a synonym for "dinner wine", or wine to accompany a meal.

Tafelwein, Deutscher (DTW)

See Deutscher Tafelwein

Tannin

See Gerbstoff

Tartaric acid

See Weinsäure

Tasting

"Probe." For details of wine tasting in Germany, see page 22.

Taunus

Mountain range, rising at its highest point to 880m (2,887 feet), defining the n. limits of the Rheingau and protecting the region from the worst extremes of the weather.

TBA, TbA

See Trockenbeerenauslese

Tesch, Weingut Erbhof Nahe

Family-owned estate est. in 1723, totally committed to quality-wine production. 38ha (94 acre) in LAUBENHEIM and LANGENLONS-HEIM are planted 75% in Riesling – a high proportion for the Nahe.

90% of the wines are dry or med-dry, and all are stored in vat with a minimum use of sulphur. Approx. annual production is 31,600 cases, sold in Germany. Address: Naheweinstr. 99, 6536 Langenlonsheim.

Teufelskeller Franken w. ★★→★★★

Well-known Einzellage on the slopes at RANDERSACKER overlooking the Main, planted mainly in Silvaner and Müller-Thurgau. Broad-flavoured wines, typical of the region. Grosslage: EWIG LEBEN. Growers: Bürgerspital, Gebhardt, Juliusspital, Randersacker eG, Schmitt, Würzburg Staatl. Hofkeller.

Thanisch, Weingut Wwe. Dr H, -Erben Müller-Burggraef M-S-R

Old-established estate – the Thanisch family has been associated with vine-growing in BERNKASTEL for many generations. The 13ha (32 acre) of holdings (62% Riesling) incl. part of the famous Bern-kasteler DOCTOR. Other sites are at BRAUNEBERG, GRAACH, WEHLEN and LIESER. The estate house, like that of the other major owner of the Doctor, Deinhard, is on the opposite side of the Mosel in the Kues portion of BERNKASTEL-KUES. The 1921 Bernkasteler Doctor

MOSEL · SAAR · RUWER

Berncasteler Doctor
1982er
Riesling Kabinett
QUALITÄTSWEIN MIT PRÄDIKAT 0,75 l e
A. P. Nr. 2 576 242-04-83

Wwe. Dr.H.THANISCH
Bernkastel-Kues

TROCKENBEERENAUSLESE, a great rarity, reached a sensational auction price in 1985 of DM 11,100. Sales of less exalted wine are in Germany and abroad. Address: Weingüterverwaltung Müller-Burggraef, 5586 Reil.

Thiergarten, Weingut
See Nell, Georg-Fritz von

Thüngersheim eG, Winzergenossenschaft Franken
Highly successful cooperative cellar that produces award-winning wines. The 365 members own 217ha (536 acre) of v'yds on the R. Main downstream from WÜRZBURG. Vat capacity of the cooperative is the equivalent of 650,000 cases. Exports account for 6% of sales. Address: Untere Haupstr. 272a, 8702 Thüngersheim.

Tillmanns Erben Weingut, H. Rhg.
Estate with 14.2ha (35 acre) of holdings at ERBACH (incl. MICHELMARK) and KIEDRICH (SANDGRUB). 91% Riesling, 5% Spätburgunder. The estate takes protection of the environment seriously: no herbicides are used in the v'yds and the wines are left to their own devices as far as the facts of wine-making and maturation will permit. The 500-year-old cask cellar provides a marvellous atmosphere for tastings. Approx. annual production is 8,300 cases, sold in Germany and abroad. Address: Haupstrasse 2, 6228 Eltville 2.

Tischwein
Literally, table wine. Not a legal definition but vulgarly used to describe a wine, probably not of high quality, that would accompany food well. See TAFELWEIN.

Ton
Has two quite separate meanings: it is a type of clay and also a characteristic style or accent. Thus wines from cellars that always follow one individual type of cellar procedure may be said to have a Betriebston, a sort of signature tune associated with the Betrieb or "works". A Kellerton usually indicates a slightly dirty "cellar flavour" in a wine.

Traben-Trarbach M-S-R Pop. 6,300 w. ★★
Health resort and tourist attraction divided by the R. Mosel, surrounded by the game-filled woods of the Hunsrück and the Eifel, and since the 16th century a centre for the wine trade. A number of wine export houses that incl. the name Languth in their title are based in the town. Their names are better known internationally than the wines from the local v'yds, many of which, nevertheless, are very steep and planted 100% in Riesling. Among the best sites is the Trabener Würzgarten, producing full-bodied, fruity wines, somewhat lower priced than those from the nearby villages of ERDEN or ÜRZIG. Grosslage: SCHWARZLAY.

Traisen Nahe w. ★★★→★★★★
Village close to BAD MÜNSTER AM STEIN-EBERNBURG with top-quality Riesling sites, incl. the BASTEI, by the Rotenfels cliff. The rhyolite rock is held to give the wine its particular background flavour, which combined with a firm, lively Riesling acidity is most attractive and positive. Grosslage: BURGWEG.

Traminer, Roter

Grape variety with red grapes that produce stylish, spicy white wine. Yield is low and the vine requires a first-class site. With the Gewürztraminer it is planted in 889ha (2,197 acre), mainly in the Rheinpfalz and Baden. Given the right weather conditions, estate bottlers will produce small quantities of single-vine wine from Traminer, regarded very much as a "speciality" by their customers. The Traminer seems to show unusually pronounced variations in character from one v'yd to another, making controlled improvement of the vine difficult on a national scale. A German Traminer wine does not have quite the pungency of a Traminer from Alsace. In the Bereich Ortenau the Traminer is known as Clevner. See also Gewürztraminer.

Trappenberg Rhpf. w. ★

Grosslage of more than 1,600ha (3,954 acre) in the s. Rheinpfalz. A high proportion of Müller-Thurgau is grown on the level sites, as well as Silvaner, Morio-Muskat and a variety of other new crossings. Some Riesling is grown in v'yds nr. the old cathedral city of Speyer. Wines sold under the Grosslage name Trappenberg are unlikely to be more than sound and agreeable.

Traube

Grape or bunch of grapes. Most German grapes are white, some are red and others, such as Ruländer and Traminer, lie in between. They are grown mainly for wine-making although varieties such as Gutedel, Portugieser, Müller-Thurgau, Huxelrebe, Bacchus and Ortega also serve as table grapes.

Treppchen M-S-R w. ★

Very much a steep Riesling Einzellage at ERDEN, recognized as one of the best Mosel sites. Produces top-quality, stylish wines. Grosslage: SCHWARZLAY. Growers: Bischöfliche Weingüter, Christoffel, Kesselstatt, Loosen-Erben, Mönchof, Nicolay, St Johannishof, Weins-Prüm.

Treppchen M-S-R w. ★★

Large, 250ha (618 acre) Einzellage at PIESPORT, on the right-hand bank of the Mosel, looking across the river and up to the famous GOLDTRÖPFCHEN site. Vines are mainly Müller-Thurgau and Riesling producing sound, good-quality wines, normally of no very great distinction. Grosslage: MICHELSBERG. Growers: Dünweg, Haag, Kesselstatt, Matheus-Lehnert, Reh (Marienhof).

Tresterwein

A rather unhealthy wine made by adding water to the pulp left behind when the grapes have been pressed. It cannot be sold commercially and is used mainly as HAUSTRUNK.

Trier M-S-R Pop. 99,000 w. ★★→★★★

Oldest city in West Germany, est. before the birth of Christ. In spite of considerable damage in World War II there are many old buildings, incl. the 2nd-century Roman gateway, the Porta Nigra, and the cathedral, part of which dates back to the 4th century. Trier has been involved with viticulture for centuries and there are more than 370ha (914 acre) of v'yds within the city boundaries. The Einzellage names are not widely known outside Germany but the city is the base for a number of important wine estates (Bischöfliche Weingüter, Friedrich-Wilhelm Gymnasium, Vereinigte Hospitien, etc.) with holdings in most of the best sites of the M-S-R. Trier is also the home of many wine-related institutions, and the birthplace of Karl Marx. Grosslage: Römerlay.

Trier, Verwaltung der Staatlichen Weinbaudomänen M-S-R

Fine 95.6ha (236 acre) estate, est. in 1896, owned by the state of RHEINLAND-PFALZ, planted with 88% Riesling. Like many state cellars it operates as a testing station for new vine varieties and viticultural methods. The fully modernized v'yds are controlled from four DOMÄNE with holdings at OCKFEN (incl. BOCKSTEIN and HERRENBERG), Avelsbach between Trier and the R. Ruwer, SERRIG on the Saar and at TRIER itself. The wines are light in alcohol, wonderfully refreshing and often slightly SPRITZIG. Approximate annual production is 56,500 cases, incl. the estate's own Riesling sparkling wine. Much is sold directly to the consumer in

Germany but exports are also important. Address: Deworastr. 1, 5500 Trier.

Trittenheim M-S-R w. **★★→★★★**
Small village nr. PIESPORT, set in a great half-circle of v'yds, already known for its wine in the 9th century. Said to be the site of the first planting of Riesling on the Mosel, in the 16th century. Today the v'yds lie on both banks of the river. Best known sites are APOTHEKE and ALTÄRCHEN. Grosslage: MICHELSBERG.

Trocken
Dry. A wine may be called Trocken if the residual sugar content is not greater than 4 g/l, or 9 g/l if the total acidity is less than the residual sugar content by no more than 2 g/l (e.g. residual sugar 8 g/l, total acidity not less than 6 g/l). A 10-year swing to production of dry wines in Germany seems to have slowed down in the mid 1980s. Today, about 14% of quality (QbA and QmP) wines produced in Rheinland-Pfalz are dry, 34% in Hessen and 24% in Baden-Württemberg and 45% in Bavaria (Franken). The export market is now beginning to show interest in dry Rhein wines of QbA or Spätlese quality.

Trockenbeerenauslese
An immensely rich wine with a minimum potential alcohol content of 21.5% (22.1% in certain districts of Baden), made from overripe grapes, usually heavily infected with *Botrytis cinerea* (EDELFÄULE). The most shrivelled and therefore the sweetest grapes are selected either at the moment of picking in the v'yd or in the press house. The MUST will not ferment easily and therefore, by law, the actual alcohol content need not be more than 5.5%, leaving the wine enormously sweet.

A Trockenbeerenauslese can only be harvested in fine vintages with good autumn weather. It is the ultimate in German winemaking and a high price has to be paid for it, often eight times greater than that for a "simple" AUSLESE. Production costs are also high and the yield is usually minute. It is not a commercial proposition but an act of faith.

Trollinger, Blauer
Red grape variety, usually known simply as Trollinger, planted in 2,196ha (5,427 acre) – all but 8ha of which are in Württemberg, where its popularity as a symbol of regional identity seems well established. Trollinger ripens late, even later than Riesling, prod. a light wine with much acidity, often vinified as SCHILLERWEIN. Yield is high (100-150 hl/ha), the wine pleasant but undistinguished.

Uelversheim Rhh. w. **★★→★★★**
Small village a few km. s. of OPPENHEIM. Its distinguished wines would be better known abroad if its name was more easily spoken. Grosslagen: KRÖTENBRUNNEN and GÜLDENMORGEN.

Ungeheuer Rhpf. w. **★★★**
Einzellage at FORST, S. of BAD DÜRKHEIM. All the v'yds at Forst are capable of producing excellent Riesling wines. Those from the Ungeheuer are powerful, full-flavoured and show earthy regional characteristics. Grosslage: MARIENGARTEN. Growers: Bassermann-Jordan, Buhl, Bürklin-Wolf, Forster Winzerverein, Kern, Mosbacher, Mossbacher-Hof Spindler, Wegeler-Deinhard, J. L. Wolf.

Ungstein Rhpf. w. **★★→★★★**
Village adjacent to BAD DÜRKHEIM producing excellent rich and fruity wine, possibly without the intensity of flavour of that from the finest Rheinpfalz villages. Grosslagen: HÖNIGSÄCKEL, HOCHMESS and KOBNERT.

Untergebiet
Sub-district. DEUTSCHER TAFELWEIN (DTW) may take its name from the four WEINBAUGEBIETE or their eight sub-districts (see pages 8-9). In some instances the Untergebiet name is better known than that of the Weinbaugebiet, so that whereas Deutscher Tafelwein Rhein-Mosel is not often met, DTW Rhein and DTW Mosel are relatively common.

Urban
Old Württemberg red vine variety, related to Trollinger, growing in 1.3ha (3 acre) at Weingut Graf Adelmann.

Ürzig M-S-R w. ★★→★★★

Village of half-timbered houses and old wine cellars. It lies at the foot of a sweep of steep v'yd on the opposite bank of the Mosel to ERDEN, a few km. upstream from TRABEN-TRABACH. The Ürziger WÜRZGARTEN is one of the best-known Einzellagen of the Bereich BERNKASTEL. Grosslage: SCHWARZLAY.

Valckenberg GmbH, P. J. Rhh.

200-year-old firm of wine merchants and v'yd owners, with the largest holding in the LIEBFRAUENSTIFT-KIRCHENSTÜCK Einzellage. As merchants, the best known brand is "Madonna" Liebfraumilch, exported all over the world. Annual turnover DM31.5m. (1985). Address: Valckenbergstr. und Weckerlingplatz, 6520 Wörms.

Varnhalt Baden w. (r.) ★★

Village in the Bereich ORTENAU, allowed to sell its quality wine in the BOCKSBEUTEL. High proportion of Riesling on steep sites, with flavour imparting porphyry rock in the soil. Grosslage: Schloss Rodeck.

Veldenz M-S-R w. ★★

Village in a pretty side valley of the Mosel nr. BERNKASTEL, looking across the river to the BRAUNEBERG v'yds. Produces pleasant, stylish Riesling wines. Grosslage: KURFÜRSTLAY.

Vereinigte Hospitien, Güterverwaltung M-S-R

Ancient charitable organization in TRIER, endowed over the centuries with v'yds, forestry and farming land. 55ha (136 acre) of v'yds incl. sole ownership of four sites: SCHLOSS SAARFELSER SCHLOSSBERG at SERRIG and Hölle at WILTINGEN on the Saar, Schubertslay at PIESPORT and Augenscheiner at Trier on the Mosel. The estate also has holdings at other sites at SERRIG, WILTINGEN (incl. BRAUNFELS, BRAUNE KUPP), KANZEM (ALTENBERG), Trier, PIESPORT (GOLDTRÖPFCHEN), GRAACH, ZELTINGEN-RACHTIG, BERNKASTEL,

WEHLEN and in the SCHARZHOFBERG. Vines are 90% Riesling, 4% Müller-Thurgau, 5% Kerner, etc. In the cellars under Trier, among the oldest in Germany, maturation is in oak and care is given to allow the wines to show the character of the vine variety and site. Annual prod. is 41,800 cases and sales are international. The Vereinigte Hospitien maintains a friendly contact with its opposite number in Beaune, the "Hôtel Dieu". Address: Krahnenufer 19, 5500 Trier.

Vereinigte Weingutsbesitzer Hallgarten eG Rhg.

Cooperative cellar dating from 1902. 95 members own 60ha (148 acre) of holdings (90% Riesling) at HALLGARTEN (incl SCHÖNHELL), OESTRICH (LENCHEN and DOOSBERG), HATTENHEIM and MITTELHEIM, producing the equivalent of 71,400 cases annually. The wines are full-bodied, positive in character, with good fruity acidity. Originally, only growers with more than 0.75ha (about 2 acre) of vines could join the cooperative, thus excluding the poorest. Address: Hallgartener Platz, 6227 Hallgarten.

Verschnitt

A blend of two or more wines or MUST, which should normally be better in quality than the individual parts from which the blend has been made. At its simplest, a soft Müller-Thurgau, for example, may be blended with a Riesling high in acidity to produce a better balanced wine with an enhanced commercial value. The laws that govern blending are complex and incl. geographical origin, vine variety, vintage and quality category.

Blending plays a vital role in the making of Champagne, Sherry, Port and often in red-wine production. In Germany its main purpose is to provide adequate quantities of one style of wine to meet the expectations of the consumer.

Versteigerung

Auction. A number of wine auctions are held in spring and autumn every year in different parts of the vine-growing area. It is usual for a group of growers to put up for sale parcels of wine in lots of not more than about 600 bottles, for which all bidding must be made through brokers. Before each lot is auctioned a tasting sample is poured for all those attending the auction. Among the most famous groups who auction their wines are the GROSSER RING, based at TRIER, and the Messe & Versteigerungsring of KLOSTER EBERBACH.

Versuchsanstalt

Experimental institute. The various Federal States own a number of viticultural institutes carrying out research and experimental work, e.g. the Staatsweingut der Landes-Lehr-und Versuchsanstalt Oppenheim, owned by the Federal State of Rheinland-Pfalz. See also LEHRANSTALT.

Verwalter, Verwaltung

Verwaltung, meaning administration, appears in titles of certain estates, e.g. the Verwaltung der Staatsweingüter Eltville. (The Schloss Reinhartshausen estate, on the other hand, actually uses the word "Administration" in its title.) The manager of an estate is known as the Verwalter.

Vier Jahreszeiten-Kloster Limburg, Winzergenossenschaft Rhpf.

Excellent cooperative cellar founded in 1900. Its 243 members own 322ha (796 acre) of holdings in the immediate vicinity of BAD DÜRK-HEIM. Vines are Riesling (30%), Müller-Thurgau (15%) and Portugieser (16%), producing all qualities of QmP up to a Huxelrebe TROCKENBEERENAUSLESE in 1983. Approx. annual production is equivalent to 416,700 cases, sold in Germany. Address: Limburgerstr. 8, 6702 Bad Dürkheim.

Villa Sachsen, Weingut Rhh.

22ha (54 acre) estate owned by the ST URSULA WEINGUT & WEIN-KELLEREI GmbH, producers of the Goldener Oktober range of quality wines. All the holdings are at BINGEN, incl. 12ha (30 acre) in

the well-known SCHARLACHBERG site. Vines are 50% Riesling, 9% Müller-Thurgau, 8% Kerner, etc. 23,000 cases of carefully vinified, elegant wines are produced annually, sold in Germany and abroad. 70% are dry or med-dry. Address: Mainzerstr. 184, 6530 Bingen.

Vintage

In German, JAHRGANG. For details of recent vintages in Germany, see pages 19-21.

Visiting vineyards and cellars

In German, Kellerbesichtigung. See pages 22-23.

Volkach Franken w. ★★

Small town 25km (16 miles) e. of WÜRZBURG, making wine from one large 150ha (371 acre) Einzellage, the Ratsherr. Principal vine varieties: Silvaner and Müller-Thurgau. Grosslage: Kirchberg.

Vollmer, Weingut Adam Rhg.

Long-established, family-owned estate with 4.5ha (11 acre) of holdings in GEISENHEIM (incl. ROTHENBERG, KLÄUSERWEG and MÄUERCHEN), planted 100% in Riesling. Annual prod. is 3,500 cases of typically spicy, elegant Rheingau wine, sold almost exclusively in Germany. Address: Winkelerstr. 93, 6222 Geisenheim.

Volxem, Weingut Bernd van M-S-R

Family-owned Saar estate dating from 1866 with 9.1ha (22 acre) at WILTINGEN (incl. BRAUNFELS, SCHLANGENGRABEN, GOTTESSFUSS and Schlossberg), OBEREMMEL (Rosenberg) and part of the famous SCHARZHOFBERG. Vines are Riesling (76%), Weissburgunder (10%) and Ruländer (5%), etc. The style of the wines stresses acidity and fruitiness, many are SPRITZIG, 30% dry and 10% med-dry. Approx. annual production is 9,200 cases, sold in Germany and abroad. Address: Dehenstr. 2, 5516 Wiltingen.

Vorlese

The picking of grapes in advance of the main harvest may be allowed as a result of poor weather conditions. The aim will be to rescue a damaged crop or to eliminate unsound grapes and thereby improve the general standard of the harvest.

Vulkanfelsen Baden r. w. ★★

Grosslage covering much of the KAISERSTUHL, the district in Baden with the warmest climate, well known for its red and white wines from Spätburgunder (alias Pinot Noir) and Ruländer (Pinot Gris). The white wines have a strong flavour that comes from the volcanic soil and are most often met as simple quality (QbA) wine.

Wachenheim Rhpf. w. (r.) ★★★

Village just s. of BAD DÜRKHEIM, with some of the best Einzellagen of the Bereich MITTELHAARDT/DEUTSCHE WEINSTRASSE. A top-quality Wachenheimer is fine, rich, fat and full-bodied in a good vintage. Riesling and other vine varieties grown. Grosslagen: SCHENKEN-BÖHL, SCHNEPFENFLUG AN DER WEINSTRASSE, MARIENGARTEN.

Wachtenburg-Luginsland eG, Winzergenossenschaft Rhpf.

Cooperative cellar with 320 members owning 330ha (815 acre) of holdings at Gönnheim and WACHENHEIM, incl. part of GERÜMPEL. As usual in the best part of the Bereich MITTELHAARDT/DEUTSCHE WEINSTRASSE, the proportion of Riesling grown is quite high (54%) for the Rheinpfalz, with Portugieser the next most widely grown vine (14%). Annual prod. is 446,400 cases, sold exclusively in Germany. Address: 6706 Wachenheim a.d. Weinstrasse.

Wagner, Weingut-Weinhaus Mrh.

7.5ha (19 acre) estate set in the idyllic and secluded Mühlental valley, five minutes' drive from the centre of KOBLENZ. The very steep v'yds are planted 50% in Riesling, 10% Müller-Thurgau plus a range of other varieties both old (incl. Ruländer, Gewürz-

traminer and Spätburgunder) and new. The estate is a member of the ERZEUGERGEMEINSCHAFT Deutsches Eck and sells most of its annual production of approx. 7,500 cases through its wine bar and wine garden. The concentration is on light, med-dry wines which win many regional and national prizes. Address: Mühlental 23, 5400 Koblenz-Ehrenbreitstein.

Wagner-Weritz, Weingut Rhg.

7.5ha (19 acre) estate, founded in 1878, with holdings in some of the best sites in ERBACH incl. MICHELMARK. SIEGELSBERG and Steinmorgen, which for Wagner-Weritz produces wines of great intensity of flavour. Other holdings are at HATTENHEIM and KIEDRICH (SANDGRUB). Vines are 85% Riesling, in line with the estate's aim to produce traditional Rheingauer wines. Approx. annual production is 6,600 cases, sold in Germany and abroad. Address: Eberbacherstr. 86-88, 6229 Erbach.

Waldrach M-S-R w. ★★

Village on the Ruwer upstream from KASEL, surrounded by hills. Its v'yds, planted with a high proportion of Riesling, incl. no absolutely top-flight sites but produce elegant, fresh wines that can step right out of their class in good years. Grosslage: RÖMERLAY.

Wallhausen Nahe w. ★★

Village with one of the largest areas under vine, 400ha (988 acre). A wide range of wine is produced, typical of the region, but usually not comparable to the finest. Grosslage: Pfarrgarten.

Walluf Rhg. w. ★★

Village nr. WIESBADEN, split into Oberwalluf and Niederwalluf by the little R. Walluf. Makes Riesling wine that is typical of the region and seldom found elsewhere. Grosslage: STEINMÄCHER.

Walporzheim Ahr. r. ★★

Small village, much visited by tourists, producing light, red wine from Spätburgunder that can usually only be sampled locally. Grosslage: Klosterberg.

Walthari

Process of winemaking, in particular, without the use of sulphur dioxide, developed by Werner Walter of EDENKOBEN. Its effectiveness is not yet universally accepted.

Wawern M-S-R w. ★★→★★★

Small Saar village overlooked by its hill, the HERRENBERG, from which almost the whole length of the Saar v'yd area can be seen. A high proportion of Riesling on steep sites guarantees outstanding wines in good years. If they lack the elegance and breeding of a fine wine from the neighbouring AYL, they make up for it by their sheer "zip" and life. Grosslage: SCHARZBERG.

Wegeler-Deinhard, Gutsverwaltung Bernkastel, M-S-R

Estate of 28ha (69 acre) dating from 1900 and owned by DEINHARD & CO in Koblenz, with holdings in KASEL, GRAACH, WEHLEN (SONNENUHR), BERNKASTEL (DOCTOR, GRABEN), etc. Vines are 91% Riesling, grown mainly on steep or very steep (more than 60% incline) sites. The grapes are pressed in Bernkastel-Kues and the MUST is vinified in Koblenz. The aim is fresh, balanced wines, true to the vine variety, with restrained amounts of residual sugar. Deinhard has an important holding in the Doctor, probably the finest site on the Mosel. Approx. annual production is 20,800 cases, 60% exported. Address: Martertal 2, 5550 Bernkastel-Kues.

(label:) MOSEL · SAAR · RUWER — 19 81 — Bernkasteler Doctor Riesling Spätlese — Qualitätswein mit Prädikat · A.P.Nr. — Erzeugerabfüllung Estate bottled Gutsverwaltung — *Deinhard* — Bernkastel-Kues-Koblenz — 750 ml — SHIPPED BY — PRODUCE OF GERMANY — 75 cl — REGISTERED TRADE MARK

Wegeler-Deinhard, Gutsverwaltung Deidesheim, Rhpf.

Estate acquired by DEINHARD & CO, Koblenz, in 1973, with 18ha (44 acre) in FORST (UNGEHEUER), DEIDESHEIM (HERRGOTTSACKER) and RUPPERTSBERG (LINSENBUSCH). Vines are 74% Riesling, 17% Müller-Thurgau. Approx. annual production is 13,300 cases. The wines, winners of many competitions, are sold all over the world. Freshness is more emphasized than in some Rheinpfalz wines. Experiments in maturation in new oak are under way. Address: Weinstrasse 10, 6705 Deidesheim.

Wegeler-Deinhard, Gutsverwaltung Oestrich, Rhg.

Important Rheingau estate, acquired in 1882 by Geheimrat Julius Wegeler, a partner in the Koblenz-based company of wine merchants, DEINHARD. The 55ha (136 acre) of holdings, planted 95% in Riesling, are at OESTRICH (incl. LENCHEN and DOOSBERG), HALLGARTEN (SCHÖNHELL), WINKEL (HASENSPRUNG, JESUITENGARTEN), JOHANNISBERG (HÖLLE), GEISENHEIM (ROTHENBERG, KLÄUSERWEG, etc.) and RÜDESHEIM (incl. BERG ROTTLAND, BERG SCHLOSSBERG, BERG ROSENECK) – all top-quality sites. The aim of the vinification is simply to translate the character and quality of the grape into the best possible Rheingau wine, with emphasis on maintaining the differences between the individual sites. Over 60% of the wines are dry or med-dry. Annual production is 37,500 cases. Sales are in Germany and abroad, esp. in the English-speaking countries. Address: Friedensplatz 9, 6227 Oestrich-Winkel.

Wehlen M-S-R w. ★★→★★★★

Pleasant village, backed by a hillside dotted with fruit trees, facing its most important sites across the Mosel. All are a little overshadowed by the worldwide reputation of the Wehlener SONNENUHR site that forms part of the continuous sweep of v'yd from BERKASTEL to ZELTINGEN-RACHTIG. Grosslage: MÜNZLAY.

Wehrheim, Weingut Eugen Rhh.

10.3ha (25 acre) estate owned by the Wehrheim family, involved in vine-growing since 1693. Holdings are all at NIERSTEIN in FINDLING, BILDSTOCK, PATERBERG, ORBEL and PETTENTHAL, planted 40% in Riesling, 21% Silvaner, 15% Müller-Thurgau, etc. The estate produces long-lasting, well differentiated wines of character. Annual production is 7,700 cases, sold in Germany and abroad. Address: Mühlgasse 30, 6505 Nierstein.

Weil, Weingut Dr R. Rhg.

Probably the best-known KIEDRICH estate, est. in 1867, with 17.8ha (44 acre) of holdings planted 92% in Riesling. Part of the estate house was built by John Sutton, the 19th-century Englishman who so marvellously restored the Kiedrich parish church. Dr Weil's

holdings in KIEDRICH incl. SANDGRUB and GRÄFENBERG, producing approx. 13,300 cases annually of carefully made, good-quality Riesling wine. The estate intends to increase the production of stylish Spätburgunder Weissherbst. 50% of sales are abroad. Address: Mühlberg 5, 6229 Kiedrich.

Weiler, Weingut Heinrich Mrh.

6.5ha (16 acre) estate owned by a family involved in vine-growing since 1607. Holdings are in steep, slaty sites at Oberwesel and Kaub, on either side of the Rhein, and incl. sole ownership of the 1.1ha (3 acre) Kauber Rossstein site. Vines are 57% Riesling, producing balanced, slightly earthy wine. Approx. annual production is 4,250 cases, sold in Germany and abroad, in cooperation with the ERZEUGERGEMEINSCHAFT im Tal der Loreley. Address: Main-zerstr. 2-3, 6532 Oberwesel.

Weinbau

Vine-growing. See pages 14-16.

Weinbaudomäne

See Domäne

Weinbaugebiete

The area from which a table wine is drawn. It is subdivided into UNTERGEBIETE and "Gebiete für LANDWEIN" – areas for country wine. There are no separate areas for making table wine and quality wine, as in France, and the name chosen to describe the wine will depend mainly on its quality. (See also pages 8-9.)

Weinberg

Vineyard.

Weinbrand

Brandy made from wine. Much sound brandy is produced in Germany, usually from imported wine, fortified up to 20% alcohol. It is unfortunately often served in restaurants and cafés in small glasses more suited to a mini-cocktail. Producers such as Asbach, Dujardin and Chantré are household names in Germany.

Weinbruderschaften

Wine brotherhoods. Societies whose main aim is to develop and encourage interest in wine in a spirit of altruism. Wine brother-hoods are found all over Germany and not solely in the wine-producing regions.

Weinessig

Wine vinegar, which in Germany may contain a certain amount of vinegar of non-vinous origin.

Weingarten

Term used in Württemberg for "vineyard", which in other regions is usually described as "Weinberg". There are also two wine-producing villages, in Baden and the Rheinpfalz, called Weingarten.

Weingärtnergenossenschaft

Name used in Württemberg for a WINZERGENOSSENSCHAFT.

Weingrosskellerei

Wholesale cellar that buys wine, much of it in bulk, from all over the world and supplies the wine trade, hotels and restaurants in Germany and abroad.

Weingut

Wine-producing estate. A term that can only appear on a wine label if the wine and SÜSSRESERVE have been made exclusively from grapes grown on the estate mentioned.

Weinhex M-S-R w. ★→★★

Grosslage of about 500ha (1,236 acre) on the Mosel upstream from KOBLENZ. Many of the individual sites are immensely steep and planted 100% in Riesling. The wines are steely and somewhat earthy compared to those from the well-known sites of the MITTELMOSEL. In this respect they resemble those of the neighbouring Mittelrhein.

Weinkellerei

Commercial wine cellar that buys grapes, MUST or wine but does not necessarily own v'yds. Often found in the form Weingut-Weinkellerei. This indicates that the company named owns v'yds from which it makes its own wine and also buys from other growers or merchants.

Weinlehrpfad

"Instructional wine path" through the v'yds, esp. in Baden but also at Schweigen and EDENKOBEN in the Rheinpfalz, WÜRZBURG in Franken and at WINNINGEN and REIL on the Mosel, etc. Notices alongside the paths give details about the sites, vine varieties and other relevant information. Such paths make it possible to com-bine study with a little exercise and often include a wine bar en route, offering a range of local wines.

Weinprobe

Wine tasting. See page 22.

Weinsäure

Tartaric or "wine acid", the acid that gives wine its backbone and grip. Unfortunately it can also appear in bottled wine as one of the causes of a white crystalline deposit (WEINSTEIN) that ideally should have been discarded while the wine was still in bulk. The deposit is harmless, natural, falls quickly to the lowest part of the bottle and is not evidence of a sickness, but its appearance in white wine often worries the consumer. (In red wine it is usually accepted as a natural result of ageing.) The likelihood of the formation of a "tartrate deposit", as it is commonly called, cannot always be both satisfactorily and totally eliminated, but objections to it are usually misplaced.

Weinsberg Würt. w. ★★

Town 7km (4 miles) e. of HEILBRONN, home of the important state viticultural institute (see next entry) where the Kerner vine was developed. Riesling and Trollinger produce wines typical of the region. Grosslagen: Staufenberg and Salzberg.

Weinsberg, Staatl. Lehr-und Versuchsanstalt für Wein & Obstbau Würt.

Oldest viticultural institute in Germany, est. by King Charles of Württemberg in 1868 to improve the economic position of viticulture. A large variety of vines is grown by the institute for experimental and also commercial purposes. (The Kerner, Heroldrebe and Helfensteiner grape varieties were developed at Weinsberg.) 53ha (131 acre) of holdings are all in the n. part of Württemberg nr. HEILBRONN. The aim is to produce fresh, stylish wines, models of what they should be. The reds benefit from a malo-lactic fermentation (see ÄPFELSÄURE).

Although the institute is the largest Weingut in Württemberg, its major contribution lies in the skill of the students it trains and the benefits that result from its experimental work. Address: Traubenplatz 5, 7102 Weinsberg.

Weinsiegel

See Siegel

Weins-Prüm Erben, Weingut Dr. M-S-R

4.5ha (11 acre) estate with small holdings in famous sites incl. WEHLENER SONNENUHR, GRAACHER DOMPROBST and HIMMELREICH, ÜRZIGER WÜRZGARTEN, ERDENER TREPPCHEN and PRÄLAT, ZELTINGER SONNENUHR, and on the Ruwer at WALDRACH, planted with 95% Riesling. 5,000 cases of fine, crisp, cask-matured wines are sold annually in Germany and abroad. Address: Uferallee 20, 5550 Bernkastel-Wehlen.

Weinstein

See Tartaric acid

Weinstrasse

Wine road, often met in France as *Route du Vin*. There are several Weinstrassen that follow a well-signposted, if rambling, course through the v'yds. The oldest (established in 1935) and best known is the Deutsche Weinstrasse that runs 80km (50 miles) through the Rheinpfalz and gives its name to the Bereich MITTELHAARDT/ DEUTSCHE WEINSTRASSE.

Weissburgunder

White grape variety, also known as Weisser Burgunder, and more widely outside Germany as Pinot Blanc. It is said to be the result of a mutation of Ruländer. There are 926ha (2,288 acre), mainly in Baden and Rheinpfalz, producing good-quality wine with less acidity than Silvaner and a NEUTRAL flavour. Its dry wine is increasingly popular. Only succeeds in Germany in a good site.

Weisser Elbling

See Elbling

Weisser Gutedel

See Gutedel

Weisser Riesling

See Riesling, Weisser

Weissherbst

Rosé QbA and QmP produced, with their SÜSSRESERVE, from a single grape variety in the regions of Ahr, Baden, Franken, Rheingau, Rheinhessen, Rheinpfalz and Württemberg. Originally Weissherbst was made from red grapes that had lost colour through *Botrytis cinerea* (EDELFÄULE). In Baden, Spätburgunder

Weissherbst is very popular for its full, fresh, gentle flavour and low tannin content.

Werner'sches Weingut, Domdechant Rhg.
Family estate est. in 1780, now into its seventh generation. The 12.3ha (30 acre) of holdings at HOCHHEIM, incl. DOMDECHANEY, KIRCHENSTÜCK and HÖLLE, are planted 96% in Riesling. Maturation in cask in the vaulted cellar reveals a traditional approach to wine-

making, balanced with sensible use of modern techniques. The result is racy, elegant, fruity wine with a touch of the soil in its flavour. Annual production is 8,300 cases. Sales are worldwide. Address: Rathausstr. 30, 6203 Hochheim.

Westhofen Rhh. w. (r.) ⋆⋆
Vine-growing village in the Bereich WONNEGAU with a reputation for good-quality wines. Not widely known outside Germany. Grosslage: Bergkloster.

Wiesbaden Rhg. Pop. 272,000 w. ⋆→⋆⋆
Capital of the State of Hessen, at the e. end of the Rheingau; a modern business city, centre of the German film industry and the home of the sparkling-wine producers HENKELL and SÖHNLEIN. In a region of much fine wine, the Wiesbaden wines are not well known. High proportion of Riesling grown.

Wilhelmshof, Weingut Rhpf.
9.5ha (23 acre) estate, planted with 30% Riesling, and 15% each of Müller-Thurgau, Spätburgunder and Kerner. 70% of the wines are dry or med-dry. Annual production: 6,400 cases, sold mainly to the consumer. Other activities incl. the development of v'yd machinery and the production of bottle fermented Sekt from the estate's own base wine. Address: Queichstr. 1, 6741 Siebeldingen.

Wiltingen M-S-R w. ⋆⋆→⋆⋆⋆⋆
Well-known Saar wine village, much damaged in the past by feuds between Luxembourg and the archbishops of nearby TRIER. A high proportion of Riesling is grown in sites on both sides of the river, producing wine of a quality and price similar to that of the best MITTELMOSEL villages such as BERNKASTEL and BRAUNEBERG. Grosslage: SCHARZBERG.

Wincheringen M-S-R w. ⋆
Village of the Bereich OBERMOSEL, becoming better known outside Germany, through the sales of its Elbling wine by the ZENTRALKELLEREI Mosel-Saar-Ruwer eG. Grosslage: Gipfel.

Wine Festivals
See Visiting the Vineyards, pages 22-23.

Wine Museums
See Visiting the Vineyards, pages 22-23.

Wingert
Rather a rustic word for a v'yd, found in a number of site names, e.g. Ürziger Goldwingert, Wachenheimer Königswingert, Piesporter Kreuzwingert.

Winkel Rhg. w. ⋆⋆→⋆⋆⋆⋆
Small village, close to the Rhein, known for Riesling wines of finesse, the best of which in a good vintage will develop over many

141

years in bottle. the straight Riesling flavour is powerful, without pronounced overtones from the soil. Wines from most of the leading, and many less-known, estates can be enjoyed in the Graues Haus (the oldest stone house in Germany) restaurant, owned by SCHLOSS VOLLRADS. Grosslagen: HÖNIGBERG and ERNTEBRINGER.

Winningen M-S-R w. ★★
Attractive riverside wine village, almost in the suburbs of KOBLENZ, much visited by tourists from Köln and the Ruhr district. Scene of Germany's oldest wine festival. The v'yds are excessively steep and planted mainly in Riesling. The wines, steely but possibly a little coarse compared to the best of the MITTELMOSEL, are well thought of in the district. Grosslage: WEINHEX.

Wintrich M-S-R w. ★★
Typical Mosel village, set back from the right-hand bank of the river, upstream from BRAUNEBERG. Some sites are planted 100% Riesling; others contain much Müller-Thurgau. Good wines, generally felt to be not quite among the finest of the river. Grosslage: KURFÜRSTLAY.

Winzenheim Nahe w. ★★
A part of Bad Kreuznach. Its best known Einzellage, Rosenheck, produces excellent Riesling wines from steep slopes. Grosslage: KRONENBERG.

Winzergenossenschaft
Cooperative cellar. The first cooperative cellar in Germany was est. in the Ahr valley in 1868 to improve the low income of its members. Today the aim remains similar, and the contribution made by the cooperatives to the economics of vine-growing can hardly be overestimated. Over three-quarters of the growers in Germany deliver their grapes, from approx. 38% of the total viticultural area, to cooperative cellars. 83% of the wine is sold in bottle; the rest is taken in bulk by the wine trade.

Although cooperatives can sell the wine from their members' grapes as estate bottled (ERZEUGERABFÜLLUNG), they are only involved in the wine-making and selling – not in the vine-growing. They have most support where growers' holdings are very small (e.g. Baden-Württemberg) but cooperatives in the M-S-R, Rheinhessen and Rheinpfalz have been the most active in the export markets.

The finest, most elegant German wines probably come from the well-known private or state-owned estates, but the well-equipped cooperatives have the reputation for producing sound, well-made wine, usually in considerable quantities. See also ZENTRALKELLEREI.

Winzersekt GmbH, Erzeugeremeinschaft
A producer's association (ERZEUGERGEMEINSCHAFT) with a membership of 350. 70 to 80% of the base wine supplied by the members is Riesling, (RIESLINGSEKT) usually from a named site. The association also offers a branded Sekt, "Burg Rheinstein". All the sparkling wines are fermented in bottle (FLASCHENGÄRUNG). Address: Michel-Mort-Str., 6555 Sprendlingen.

Winzerverein
Alternative name for WINZERGENOSSENSCHAFT (cooperative cellar).

Wirsching, Weingut Hans Franken
Estate est. by the Wirsching family in 1630, now run by the 14th generation, with 45ha (111 acre) of organically fed holdings at IPHOFEN (incl. KALB) and RÖDELSEE (part of the KÜCHENMEISTER). Vines incl. the traditional Franken Silvaner, Müller-Thurgau and Riesling, etc. The cellars date from the 17th century, but in 1970 a modern press house and machinery park were built outside Iphofen. Half the estate's concentrated, firm, lively wines are "FRÄNKISCH TROCKEN" Annual production varies enormously because of the local climate. Sales are in Germany and abroad. Address: Ludwigstr. 16, 8715 Iphofen.

Wisselbrunnen Rhg. w. ★★★→★★★★
Einzelage at HATTENHEIM producing good-quality, spicy Riesling wines. Grosslage: DEUTELSBERG. Growers: Knyphausen, Lang, Reinhartshausen, Ress, Tillmanns.

Wolf Erben, Weingut J. L. Rhpf.
18ha (44 acre) estate, owned by the present family for more than 80

years (the estate house, with an enclosed courtyard, was built in the Italian Renaissance style in 1840). Holdings (90% Riesling) are at WACHENHEIM (incl. GERÜMPEL and GOLDBÄCHEL), FORST (UNGE-HEUER, JESUITENGARTEN and PECHSTEIN) and DEIDESHEIM (HERRGOTT-SACKER and LEINHÖHLE). The wines are racy, elegant and range from dry to sweet. The estate started an adjacent wine merchants business ("Goldbächelkellerei") in the 1950s. Approx. annual production is 12,500 cases, sold in Germany and abroad. Address: Weinstrasse 1, 6706 Wachenheim.

Wolff Metternich'sches Weingut, Gräfl. Baden

One of the oldest estates in the region, with 36ha (89 acre) on steep granite slopes around DURBACH and some miles further south at Lahr. Sole ownership of Durbacher Schloss Grohl (5.5ha – 14 acre) and Schlossberg (16ha – 40 acre), and the Lahrer Herrentisch (6ha – 15 acre). The whole estate is planted with 30% Riesling, 21% Spätburgunder and 20% Müller-Thurgau. 12,500 cases of full-flavoured, spicy wines are produced annually and sold in Germany and abroad. Address: Grohl 117, 7601 Durbach.

Wonnegau, Bereich Rhh. w.

Covers the s. part of the Rheinhessen, the source of much good, unsophisticated rustic wine in which the taste of the soil is sometimes present. Not a name widely known on the international market – its appearance on a label is often simply a legal requirement rather than an aid to selling.

Worms Rhh. Pop. 73,500

Cathedral city that has suffered much from war damage in its long history. The v'yds of the LIEBFRAUENKIRCHE (Church of Our Lady) are known as the source of the original Liebfrau(en)milch. Many events connected with wine are held in the city and its environs, incl. the annual, oddly named "Backfischfest" (Fried-fish festival). Grosslage: LIEBFRAUENMORGEN

Württemberg w. r.

Wine region of 9,656ha (23,861 acre) spreading out on either side of the R. Neckar and its tributaries and incl. the smallest Bereich in Germany, the Bereich WÜRTTEMBERGISCHER BODENSEE. It is a region

of small v'yd holdings: more than half the growers own less than 0.25ha (0.62 acre). For most, vine-growing is a part-time occupation or hobby and more than 80% of the crop is delivered to co-operative cellars for processing. Half the region is planted in vines bearing red grapes, but 70% of the wine produced is white, mainly from Riesling, Müller-Thurgau and Kerner. Within the region, where nearly all the wine is drunk, the big demand is for the red wines made from Trollinger, Müllerrebe, Limberger, Portugieser and Spätburgunder. They are normally light in colour and tannin and often have varying amounts of residual sugar. The white wines are well up to standard for s. Germany and are generally cheaper than the red wines. Probably for present international taste, better value for money can be found in the regions further north. SCHILLERWEIN (a rosé wine) is a speciality of the region.

For the visitor to the region who is interested in architecture and historic buildings, and appreciates attractive, rural countryside, there is much to see.

Württembergischer Bodensee, Bereich Würt. r. w.

Smallest Bereich in Germany, with 8.8ha (22 acre) at Kressbronn/BODENSEE and in the Ravensburger Rauenegg – probably Germany's smallest Einzellage.

Württembergische Weingärtner-Zentral-Genossenschaft eG Würt

The central cellars of the cooperative movement in Württemberg supplied in part, or wholly, by 92 local cooperative cellars. 87% (17,000) of the region's growers are members of cooperative cellars, largely because their average size of holding (0.5ha or 1.24 acre) is too small for wine making to be economical on an individual basis. In recent years the harvest at the central cellars has varied from 65,000 hl in 1985 to 485,000 hl in 1982. The storage capacity of 970,000 hl has so far proved adequate for all occasions. The full range of Württemberg wine is produced. 75% is sold in the region, 24% elsewhere in Germany, and 1% is exported. Address: Raiffeisenstr. 2, 7141 Möglingen.

Würzburg Franken Pop. 128,000 w. ★★★

Fine university city and business centre, severely damaged in World War II. Fortunately many of the historic buildings survived or have been restored. The city contains a number of old cellars belonging to top-quality estates, incl. those of the BÜRGERSPITAL, the JULIUSSPITAL and the STAATLICHE HOFKELLER (see next entry). The v'yds in and around the city produce Franken wine of style, grip and positive flavour. They can be superb but are, regrettably, expensive. No Grosslagen.

Würzburg Staatlicher Hofkeller Franken

Estate founded in 1128, with many outstanding features but few more impressive than the magnificent vaulted cellar, filled wih impeccably maintained casks. If objective judgement can survive this underworld, so clearly dedicated to Bacchus, it may be able to remain sober when faced wih the Baroque splendour of the Prince-Bishops' "Residenz" above, with its magnificent Tiepolo ceiling.

Fortunately the wines measure up to the explosion of architectural beauty in which they are made. The substantial holdings cover 173ha (428 acre) at WÜRZBURG (STEIN and INNERE LEISTE), RANDERSACKER (incl. TEUFELSKELLER), Hörstein, Grossheubach, Kreuzwertheim, Handthal, Abtswind and Thüngersheim. Vines incl. Riesling (14%), Müller-Thurgau (22%), Silvaner (10%), Rieslaner (7%) and many other varieties. The variations on the Franken style from so many different vines and sites are fascinating, but all the wines are true to type and few are sweet. Approx. annual production is 83,300 cases, sold 98% in Germany. Address: Residenzplatz 3, 8700 Würzburg.

Würzgarten M-S-R w. ★★★

Steep Einzellage at ÜRZIG, 100% Riesling, producing some of the best wines on the river. The red sandstone, pushing in from the Eifel, adds spice (Würze) to the Mosel slate and flavour to the wine. Grosslage: SCHWARZLAY. Growers: Bischöfliche Weingüter, Christoffel, Loosen-Erben, Mönchof, Nicolay'sche Weinguts, Weins-Prüm.

ZBW

See Zentralkellerei Badischer Winzergenossenschaften

Zell M-S-R w. ★★

There are 23 towns called Zell in W. Germany, but little Zell an der Mosel, stretched out along the river, is known worldwide for its Grosslage SCHWARZE KATZ (Black Cat). Zell has a high proportion of Riesling in its steep v'yds and the wines are usually described as full, elegant and fruity.

Zell, Bereich M-S-R w.

Bereich that covers the v'yds downstream from Zell an der Mosel (see previous entry) to KOBLENZ identical to the Untermosel. The proportion of Riesling grown is high, many on their original root stocks, and the wines are generally very true to type, firm and positive in flavour, although the finesse of the best wines of the MITTELMOSEL is usually missing. Nearer Koblenz and the Rhein the wine takes on some of the Mittelrhein steeliness. Most of the exported wine comes from the Zeller SCHWARZE KATZ Grosslage.

Zeltingen-Rachtig M-S-R w. ★★★
Important village of old wine cellars, fine patrician houses and a long promenade by the Mosel. Its elegant wines, largely Riesling, are usually slightly cheaper than those of its neighbours WEHLEN and ÜRZIG. Grosslage: MÜNZLAY.

Zentralkellerei
Central cellars: the largest form of cooperative cellar, taking in the MUST or wine from smaller cooperatives (Winzergenossenschaften), as well as grapes from its own members. Six cellars function as Zentralkellereien: in Baden at Breisach, in the Rheinhessen at Gau-Bickelheim (also supplied by the Rheingau), in the M-S-R at Bernkastel-Kues, in the Nahe at Bad Kreuznach/Bretzenheim, in Württemberg at Möglingen and in Franken at Repperndorf. The wines of the first four are widely distributed on the export market.

Zentralkellerei Badischer Winzergenossenschaften eG (ZBW) Baden
Vast central cooperative cellar, founded in 1952, taking the crops from 25,000 growers in 4,500ha (11,120 acre) spread throughout Baden. Müller-Thurgau and Spätburgunder are the main grapes, with smaller quantities of Ruländer, Gutedel and Riesling. Wines of different origin are kept apart. Over 4m. cases of sound, good-quality wine is produced each year, sold mainly in Germany but a small amount abroad. Highly impressive large-scale wine-making. Address: Zum Kaiserstuhl 6, 7814 Breisach.

Zentralkellerei Mosel-Saar-Ruwer eG M-S-R
Rapidly growing cooperative cellar with 5,200-plus members, who deliver to it each year approx, 25% of the M-S-R grape harvest. Vines are 55% Riesling, 9% Elbling, 23% Müller-Thurgau. Pleasant wines, short on individuality. Annual production is equivalent to 3.6m. cases, 30% sold on the export market. Address: 5550 Bernkastel-Kues.

Zentralkellerei Rheinischer Winzergenossenschaft Rhh.
Central cooperative cellar with more than 6,000 members with holdings in the Rheingau as well as the Rheinhessen amounting to 3,000ha (7,413 acre) planted with a wide range of vine varieties. The Zentralkellerei has its own brand of LIEBFRAUMILCH ("Little Rhine Bear"), exported all over the world. Address: Wöllsteinerstr. 16, 6551 Gau-Bickelheim.

Zimmermann-Graeff GmbH & Co. KG M-S-R
Large firm of wine merchants established in 1886, with holdings at ZELL. Wine or grape must are bought in the main regions known on the export market. Annual turnover is 1.3m. cases sold in Germany and abroad. Address: Marientaler Au, 5583 Zell.

Zucker
Sugar.

Zuckerrest
See Restzucker

Zwierlein, Weingut Freiherr von Rhg.
Estate est. in 1794, planted 100% in Riesling, with 23.5ha (58 acre) of holdings at GEISENHEIM (incl. KLÄUSERWEG, MÄUERCHEN and ROTHENBERG) and in the Winkeler JESUITENGARTEN. The wines are made to last and are typical of the region and the vine. An analysis of each wine is available for customers, and the estate makes great efforts to recommend what food would best accompany its wine. Approx. annual production is 15,000 cases, sold in Germany and the USA. Address: Schloss Kosakenberg, Bahnstr. 1, 6222 Geisenheim.

German Wine in Figures

The German wine regions

The chart shows yield in hectolitres, vineyard area in hectares, the percentages of red and white grape varieties and leading varieties grown.

The ten-year average for 1976–85 is compared with the 1985 harvest.

Region		Yield Hl	Producing Area Ha	White %	Red %	Leading grapes%		1985 %	1964 %
						Bl. Spätburg.		37	23
	Decade	31,565				Portugieser		26	33
Ahr	1985	15,375	397	30	70	Riesling		15	23
						M.-Thurgau		37	25
						Bl. Spätburg.		22	20
Baden	Decade	1,216,481				Ruländer		12	13
	1985	686,452	14,851	77	23	Gutedel		8	15
						M.-Thurgau		49	32
Franken	Decade	314,330				Silvaner		20	55
	1985	61,530	4,672	97	3	Kerner		6	0
						Riesling		53	46
Hess.	Decade	27,735				M.-Thurgau		19	21
Bergstr.	1985	20,404	360	98	2	Ruländer		8	2
						Riesling		74	86
Mittel-	Decade	59,052				M.-Thurgau		11	8
rhein	1985	55,200	749	98	2	Kerner		6	0
Mosel-						Riesling		54	79
Saar-	Decade	1,256,022				M.-Thurgau		23	9
Ruwer	1985	1,104,485	11,623	100	0	Elbling		9	11
						M.-Thurgau		27	26
Nahe	Decade	361,320				Riesling		22	29
	1985	264,022	4,307	98	2	Silvaner		14	40
						Riesling		80	77
Rheingau	Decade	212,630				M.-Thurgau		6	12
	1985	176,952	2,742	94	6	Bl. Spätburg		5	2
						M.-Thurgau		24	33
						Silvaner		13	47
Rhein-	Decade	2,067,370				Scheurebe		10	1
hessen	1985	1,207,897	22,978	94	6	Bacchus		8	0
						Kerner		8	0
						M.-Thurgau		24	20
						Riesling		15	14
Rhein-	Decade	2,377,964				Kerner		11	0
pfalz	1985	1,507,064	20,766	89	11	Silvaner		9	40
						Portugieser		8	18
						Riesling		24	25
Württem-	Decade	891,492				Trollinger		23	28
berg	1985	303,013	9,575	49	51	Schwarzriesl.		13	5
						M.-Thurgau		25	21
						Riesling		20	26
National	Decade	8,815,961				Silvaner		8	28
total	1985	5,402,394	93,020	87	13	Kerner		7	6
						Bl. Spätburg.		5	3

Evolution of the vineyards

Vineyard area in hectares by wine region, 1950–85. The upper figure in each case is for vineyards yielding a crop, the lower for vineyards planted whether yielding or not.

Region	1950	1955	1960	1964	1970	1974	1978	1982	1983	1984	1985
Ahr	382	574	545	566 444	500 446	482 485	482 518	389 424	391 426	383 450	397 426
Baden	5,966	6,283	7,514	8,688 7,631	9,525 10,014	12,240 12,553	13,872 14,655	14,547 14,448	14,663 14,721	14,815 14,931	14,851 14,999
Franken	2,475	2,698	2,464	2,524 2,203	2,629 2,720	3,120 3,079	3,973 3,509	4,320 4,896	4,546 5,085	4,714 5,240	4,672 5,182
Hess, Bergstrasse	141	235	210	207 189	273 261	288 280	369 279	351 380	349 382	356 388	360 389
Mittelrhein	1,129	1,311	1,268	1,235 870	945 857	854 895	878 918	750 767	737 767	736 768	749 768
Mosel-Saar-Ruwer	7,265	7,967	8,797	9,605 9,835	10,714 10,962	11,525 11,499	12,053 11,879	11,517 12,456	11,768 12,658	11,719 12,747	11,623 12,799
Nahe	2,679	3,579	3,773	3,933 3,516	3,630 3,955	4,206 4,377	4,392 4,510	4,143 4,561	4,195 4,596	4,264 4,607	4,307 4,610
Rheingau	1,823	2,201	2,643	2,624 2,680	3,035 2,821	3,018 2,854	2,913 2,814	2,664 2,939	2,690 2,942	2,752 2,943	2,742 2,940
Rheinhessen	10,593	13,970	15,010	16,187 16,444	17,570 19,826	19,813 21,820	20,789 22,913	21,259 24,551	21,834 24,867	22,470 25,082	22,978 25,167
Rheinpfalz	10,608	14,127	15,326	16,394 17,066	18,621 18,676	20,217 21,338	21,187 21,552	20,047 22,359	20,104 22,618	20,537 22,853	20,766 22,869
Württemberg	6,418	7,016	6,630	6,660 5,844	6,258 6,834	7,264 7,840	8,009 8,124	9,035 9,100	9,095 9,324	9,449 9,600	9,575 9,656
National total	49,479	59,961	64,180	68,623 66,722	73,700 77,372	83,027 87,020	88,917 91,671	89,022 96,881	90,372 98,386	92,195 99,609	93,020 99,805

Trends in grape varieties

Variety	1964 ha	1972 ha	1977 ha	1981 ha	1985 ha	change 1981–85 %
White varieties in total	56,779	71,679	80,153	84,593	86,596	+2.4
Bacchus	2	257	1,642	3,174	3,573	+12.6
Burgunder, Weisser	465	748	824	872	926	+6.2
Elbling, Weisser	1,234	1,265	1,168	1,115	1,178	+5.7
Faberrebe	–	342	1,486	2,115	2,280	+7.8
Gutadel, Weisser	1,192	1,210	1,299	1,195	1,258	+5.3
Huxelrebe	56	393	1,057	1,606	1,758	+9.5
Kerner	5	780	3,374	5,784	6,960	+20.3
Morio-Muskat	1,052	2,381	2,821	2,975	2,641	–11.2
Müller-Thurgau	14,115	21,808	24,705	24,810	25,292	+1.9
Optima	–	61	402	514	499	–2.9
Ortega	–	74	718	1,170	1,208	+3.2
Riesling, Weisser	17,083	18,841	18,380	18,821	19,615	+4.2
Ruländer	1,283	2,929	3,322	3,379	3,123	–7.6
Scheurebe	342	1,722	2,941	4,083	4,385	+7.4
Silvaner, Grüner	18,781	16,739	12,684	9,184	8,050	–12.3
Traminer, Roter (Gewürztraminer)	435	770	915	937	889	–5.1
Other white varieties	734	1,359	2,415	2,859	2,961	+3.6

Variety	1964 ha	1972 ha	1977 ha	1981 ha	1985 ha	change 1981–85 %
Red varieties in total	9,906	11,348	10,970	11,016	13,119	+19.1
Burgunder, Blauer Spät-	1,839	2,944	3,287	3,753	4,486	+19.5
Dornfelder	–	–	41	208	620	+198.1
Lemberger, Blauer	365	406	406	413	542	+31.2
Müllerrebe	323	827	992	1,101	1,473	+33.8
Portugieser, Blauer	5,323	4,738	3,629	3,012	3,183	+5.7
Trollinger, Blauer	1,662	1,881	1,997	1,983	2,196	+10.7
Other red varieties	394	552	618	546	619	+13.4
Total Red and White	66,685	83,021	91,123	95,612	99,806	+4.4

ha = hectares

Year	Vineyard area ha	Crop hl	Average yield ha/hl	Quality rating	Average must weight °Oechsle*	Price DM/hl
1950	49,479	3,236,682	65.6	moderate		77
51	52,521	3,112,439	59.3	low to moderate		78
52	53,359	2,712,601	50.8	good		83
53	54,486	2,455,865	45.1	very good		114
54	58,942	3,097,721	52.6	low		105
55	59,961	2,404,941	40.1	moderate		106
56	59,695	928,671	15.6	good		211
57	58,743	2,263,826	38.5	moderate		127
58	59,135	4,796,542	81.1	moderate to good		82
59	60,995	4,302,661	70.5	very good		127
1960	64,180	7,427,347	115.8	moderate		53
61	66,265	3,574,479	53.9	good		105
62	67,137	3,927,919	58.5	good		121
63	68,354	6,034,147	88.3	moderate		87
64	68,623	7,185,349	104.7	good to very good		67
65	68,816	5,035,473	73.2	low		105
66	69,166	4,809,358	69.5	good		134
67	69,460	6,069,506	87.4	moderate		102
68	70,214	6,047,598	86.1	low		99
69	71,336	5,947,354	83.4	moderate		121
1970	73,700	9,889,019	134.2	moderate	66	78
71	75,514	6,027,328	79.8	very good	83	147
72	77,551	7,456,463	96.1	moderate to low	63	124
73	80,622	10,696,780	132.7	good	71	96
74	83,028	6,805,291	82.0	moderate	68	89
75	84,970	9,241,274	108.8	good to very good	75	125
76	86,296	8,658,762	100.3	very good	84	175
77	87,730	10,388,969	118.4	moderate to low	67	143
78	88,917	7,297,401	82.1	moderate	69	154
79	87,592	8,180,564	93.4	good	76	162
1980	89,485	4,634,960	51.8	moderate	71	197
81	89,007	7,159,176	80.4	good	74	195
82	89,022	15,402,949	173.0	moderate	70	124
83	90,372	13,040,937	144.3	good	75	83
84	92,195	7,993,489	86.7	moderate to low	63	155
85	93,020	5,402,394	58.1	good	76	226

Country	1985 Quantity hl	1985 Change 1984–5 %	1985 Worth DM	1984 Quantity hl	1984 Worth DM	1983 Quantity hl	1983 Worth DM
Great Britain	1,360,970	− 0.3	319	1,365,485	261	983,344	282
USA	506,291	−16.3	501	605,159	435	566,747	433
Netherlands	256,413	−16.0	290	305,312	261	274,501	274
Canada	153,482	−16.9	429	164,904	403	132,892	416
Denmark	114,519	−12.7	255	131,157	233	133,077	236
Sweden	84,822	−12.2	244	86,731	200	51,077	260
Japan	60,387	−18.0	523	73,626	471	66,648	466
Belgium & Lux	35,898	−30.2	331	51,423	268	48,442	291
Norway	29,365	+45.6	303	20,174	275	15,753	290
Australia	20,847	− 7.0	493	22,414	471	19,239	499
Ireland	19,022	−13.0	371	21,866	321	24,007	336
Brazil	11,778	+105.9	340	5,720	328	11,506	291
France	10,669	−11.8	340	12,094	249	12,572	260
Finland	9,823	+ 6.7	265	9,206	172	6,438	221
Switzerland	4,648	− 8.0	438	5,051	461	5,253	436
Iceland	4,278	+25.2	566	3,418	534	2,493	540
Hong Kong	2,971	+ 2.4	570	2,901	519	3,203	576
New Zealand	2,839	−51.6	568	5,863	521	4,354	558
Bahamas	2,830	+77.7	452	1,593	435	2,051	433
Mexico	2,294	+341.2	348	520	329	778	591
Other countries	32,882	−17.9	432	40,042	409	36,197	427
Total	2,727,028	− 7.1	360	2,934,659	313	2,404,984	333

Cooperatives

The German wine cooperative movement began with the establishment of the coop at Mayschoss in the Ahr in 1868. Today the cooperatives have around 70,000 members owning about a third of the German vineyard area. The coops thrive most conspicuously in Baden and Würtemberg where they are responsible for 80% of production.

Year	No. of coop	No. of members	Vineyard area in ha	Storage capacity in 1000 hl	Production in hl	Production in 1000 DM
1900	13	–	–	–	–	–
1938	490	28,748	–	–	–	–
1960/61	544	55,233	19,109	1,817	1,417,794	239,296
1970/71	497	60,827	31,769	4,602	1,750,000	487,000
1975/76	359	64,243	34,935	7,351	2,768,883	1,209,156
1980/81	348	67,691	31,889	9,246	3,094,740	1,272,041
1981/82	342	67,402	35,002	9,344	2,610,181	1,157,746
1982/83	327	69,346	36,567	10,267	2,795,059	1,136,956
1983/84	333	69,986	37,730	11,298	3,069,536	1,107,335
1984/85	329	70,155	37,730	11,522	3,602,203	1,270,503

Mosel-Saar-Ruwer

"Abteihof"
Beulwitz
Bischöfliche Weingüter
Christoffel
Drathen
Dünweg
Ehses-Berres
Ehses-Geller
Fischer, Dr
Friedrich-Wilhelm-Gymnasium
Fuchs
Gallais
Geltz
Haag
Haart
Hain
Heddesdorff
Hövel
Immich-Batterieberg
Kanzemer Berg
Karp-Schreiber
Karthäuserhof
Kees-Kieren
Kesselstatt
Knebel
Koch
Landenberg
Lauerburg
Lenz-Dahm
Licht-Bergweiler
Loosen
Löwensteinhof

BEREICH
BERNKASTEL

Piesport •

Mosel

Trittenheim •

Eitelsbach •

Trier • • Kasel

Konz •

BEREICH
SAAR-RUWER

• Wiltingen

• Ayl
Saarburg

BEREICH
OBERMOSEL

Mosel

Saar

12.8%

% of total
v'yd area

miles 0   5   10   15
km 0   10   20

BEREICH
MOSELTOR

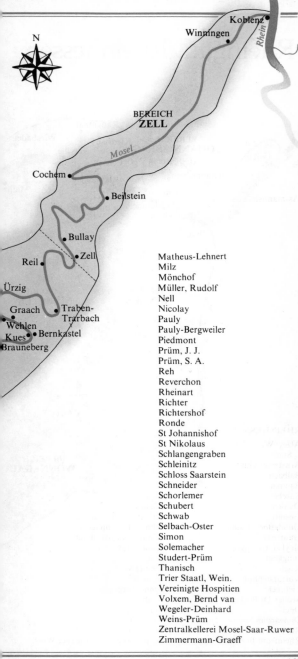

N

Koblenz

Winningen

Rhein

BEREICH
ZELL

Mosel

Cochem

Beilstein

Bullay

Reil

Zell

Ürzig

Graach

Traben-
Trarbach

Wehlen

Kues

Bernkastel

Brauneberg

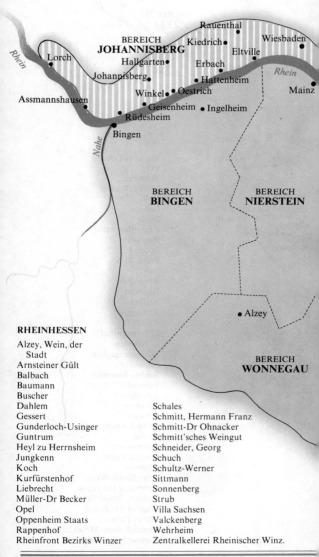

Rheingau, Rheinhessen

BEREICH
JOHANNISBERG

Rauenthal
Kiedrich
Wiesbaden
Lorch
Eltville
Hallgarten
Erbach
Johannisberg
Hattenheim
Winkel
Oestrich
Assmannshausen
Geisenheim
Ingelheim
Mainz
Rüdesheim

Rhein

Bingen

Nahe

BEREICH
BINGEN

BEREICH
NIERSTEIN

Alzey

BEREICH
WONNEGAU

RHEINHESSEN

Alzey, Wein, der
  Stadt
Arnsteiner Gült
Balbach
Baumann
Buscher
Dahlem
Gessert
Gunderloch-Usinger
Guntrum
Heyl zu Herrnsheim
Jungkenn
Koch
Kurfürstenhof
Liebrecht
Müller-Dr Becker
Opel
Oppenheim Staats
Rappenhof
Rheinfront Bezirks Winzer

Schales
Schmitt, Hermann Franz
Schmitt-Dr Ohnacker
Schmitt'sches Weingut
Schneider, Georg
Schuch
Schultz-Werner
Sittmann
Sonnenberg
Strub
Villa Sachsen
Valckenberg
Wehrheim
Zentralkellerei Rheinischer Winz.

RHEINGAU

Allendorf
Altenkirch
Arnet
Aschrott
Basting-Gimbel
Becker
Brentano
Breuer

Diefenhardt
Eltville, Ver. der Staats
Engelmann
Eser
Frankensteiner Hof
Frankfurt, Wein, der Stadt
Hallgarten Winzer
Hessisches Weingut
"Hof Sonneck"
Holschier
Hupfeld
"Johannisberger Rosenhof"
Johannishof
Jost
Kanitz
Knyphausen
Königin Victoria Berg
Lamm-Jung
Lang
Mumm
Nägler
Nikolai
Nonnenberg
Oetinger
Ress
Rheingau Gebiets, Winzer.
Richter-Boltendahl
Riedel
Schloss Groenesteyn
Schloss Johannisberg
Schloss Reinhartshausen
Schloss Schönborn
Schloss Vollrads
Schlotter
Schumann-Nägler
Simmern
Sohlbach
Sturm
Tillmanns
Vereinigte Weinguts Hallgarten
Vollmer
Wagner-Weritz
Wegeler-Deinhard
Weil
Werner
Zwierlein

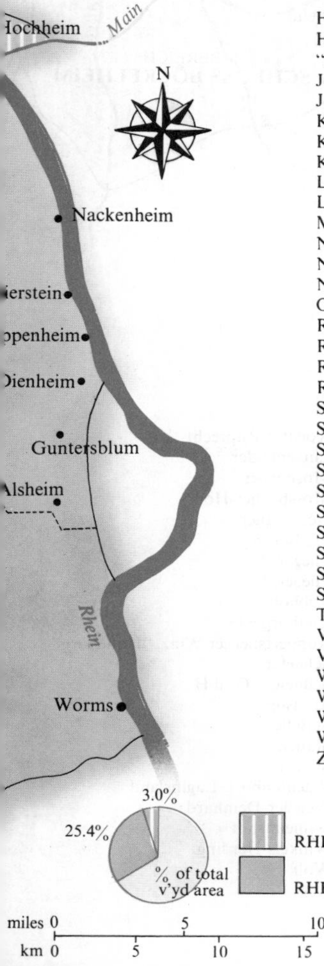

Hochheim — Main

N

Nackenheim

ierstein
ppenheim
Dienheim

Guntersblum

Alsheim

Rhein

Worms

3.0%

25.4%

% of total
v'yd area

▥ RHEINGAU

▨ RHEINHESSEN

miles 0 — 5 — 10
km 0 — 5 — 10 — 15

Nahe, Rheinpfalz

BEREICH
KREUZNACH

Bing

Dorsheim
Langenlonsheim

Rüdesheim
Traisen
Niederhausen
Schlossböckelheim
Norheim

Bad
Kreuzna

Meddersheim

BEREICH
SCHLOSS BÖCKELHEIM

Nahe

Alsenz

Glan

RHEINPFALZ

Annaberg Stumpf-Fitz'sches
Bart
Bassermann-Jordan
Bergdolt
Biffar
Bonnet
Buhl
Bürklin-Wolf
Christmann
Deidesheim Winzer
Deinhard, Dr
Deinhard Gutzverwaltung
Deutsches Weintor
Eberle
Fitz-Ritter
Forster-Winz
Friedelsheim Winzer
Hahnhof
Hammel
Hohenberg
Kallstadt Winzer
Karst
Kern

Koehler-Ruprecht
Lingenfelder
Mosbacher
Mossbacher-Hof
Neckerauer
Pfeffingen
Pfleger, J.
Pfleger, W.
Rebholz
Rietburg e.G.
Ruppertsberger Winz. "Hoheburg"
Schaefer
Schneider GmbH
Schuster
Spindler
Stauch
Steiner
Wachtenburg-Luginsland
Wegeler-Deinhard
Wilhelmshof
Winkels-Herding
Wolf

NAHE

Anheuser, August
Anheuser, Paul
Bad Kreuznach Staats
Crusius
Diel
Emrich-Schönleber
Finkenauer
Höfer

Nahewinzer eG
Niederhausen-Schlossböckelheim
  Staatl. Wein
Pallhuber
Plettenberg
Rheingrafenberg eG
Salm-Dalberg
Schlink-Herf-Gutleuthof
Schneider, Jacob
Schweinhardt
Tesch

Rhein

Worms ●

Bockenheim ●

Neuleiningen ●

**BEREICH
MITTELHAARDT/
DEUTSCHE
WEINSTRASSE**

N

● Kallstadt

● Bad Dürkheim
  ● Wachenheim
  ● Forst
  ● Deidesheim
  ● Ruppertsberg
● Neustadt

Speyer ●

● Maikammer
 ● Edenkoben
● Rhodt
  Schwegenheim ●

Siebeldingen
  ● ● Landau in
     der Pfalz
**BEREICH
SÜDLICHE
WEINSTRASSE**

▦ NAHE

▨ RHEINPFALZ

4.8%

23.1%

% of total
v'yd area

● Bad Bergzabern

miles 0   10
km 0   10   20

● Schweigen

Hessische Bergstrasse, Franken, Württemberg, Baden

HESSISCHE BERGSTRASSE

Bensheim, Weingut de Stadt
Bergstrasse, Staatsweingut
Berstrasser Gebiets Winzer.

FRANKEN

Bürgerspital
Castell
Franken eG, Gebeits.
Fürst
Gebherdt
Hohenlohe Langenburgsche
Juliusspital
Knoll & Reinhart
Löwenstein-Wertheim-Rosenberg
Popp
Randersacker eG
Schloss Saarleck
Schmitt
Thüngersheim eG
Wirsching
Würzburg Staatl. Hofkeller

WÜRTTEMBERG

Adelmann
Affaltrach
Ämälienhof
Bentzel-Sturmfeder
Haidle
Heilbronn-Erlenbach

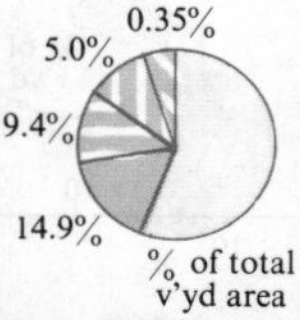

Main

Mainz
Darmstadt

BEREICH
UMSTADT

BEREICH
STARKENBURG

Seeheim
Alsbach
Bensheim
Heppenheim

Heidelberg

BEREICH
BADISCHE BERGSTRASSE
KRAICHGAU

Karlsruhe

Pforzheim

Rhein

Baden-Baden

BEREICH
ORTENAU

Durbach
Offenburg

BEREICH
BREISGAU

Neckar

BEREICH
KAISERSTUHL-
TUNIBERG

Breisach

Freiburg

BEREICH
MARKGRÄFLERLAND

Basel   Rhein

0.35%
5.0%
9.4%
14.9%
% of total
v'yd area

158

BEREICH
MAINDREIECK

Aschaffenburg

BEREICH
MAIN-
VIERECK

Main

Escherndorf • Volkach
Würzburg

N

Castell
Wertheim
Kitzingen • Iphofen

BEREICH
BADISCHES
FRANKENLAND

BEREICH
STEIGERWALD

Bad Mergentheim

Neckar

BEREICH
KOCHER-
JAGST-
TAUBER

BADEN

Bercher
Blankenhorn
Dörflinger
Frankenstein
Freiburg, Staatl. Wein.
Freiburg, Staatl. Wein.
  "Blankenhornsberg"
Gemmingen-Hornberg
Gleichenstein
Göler
Hoensbroech
Kaiserstühler Winzer
Laible
Männle, Heinrich
Meersburg, Staatsweingut
Neveu
Offenburg
Schloss Neuweier
Schloss Ortenberg
Schloss Staufenberg
Schlossgut Istein
"Schwarzer Adler"
Staatl. Weinbauversuchsgut
Winzerkeller Südliche Bergstrasse
Wolff Metternich
Zentralkellerei

• Heilbronn

BEREICH
WÜRTTEM-
BERGISCH
UNTERLAND

• Stuttgart

BEREICH
REMSTAL-
STUTTGART

Heinrich
Hofkammerkellerei Stuttgart
Hohenlohe Langenburgsche
Hohenlohe-Ohringen'sche
Neipperg
Sonnenhof
Weingärtner-Zentral-Genossenschaft
Weinsberg, Staatl.

	HESSISCHE BERGSTRASSE
	FRANKEN
	WÜRTTEMBERG
	BADEN

BEREICH
BODENSEE

BEREICH
WÜRTTEM-
BERGISCHER
BODENSEE

Meersburg
Konstanz •

BEREICH
BAYERISCHER
BODENSEE

miles 0   15   30
km 0   25   50

Bodensee

159

Ahr, Mittelrhein

Bonn

Königswinter

BEREICH
SIEBENGEBIRGE

Bad
Neuenahr-
Ahrweiler

Altenahr

BEREICH
**WALPORZHEIM
AHRTAL**

AHR

Marienthal, Staatl.
Weinbaudomäne
Mayschloss-Altenahr
Winzergenossensch.

Andernach

BEREICH
RHEINBURGENGAU

MITTELRHEIN

Jost
Perll
Wagner
Weiler

Koblenz

Braubach

Boppard

St Goar

Bacharach

BEREICH
BACHARACH

Lorch

Bingen

|||| AHR

▓ MITTELRHEIN

0.45%
0.8%
% of total
v'yd area

0 miles · 15
0 km · 25